ASYA

Michael Ignatieff was born in Canada in 1947. A former Fellow of Kings College Cambridge and a distinguished writer and broadcaster, he is the author of *A Just Measure of Pain*, *The Needs of Strangers* and *The Russian Album*. *Asya* is his first novel.

'Vivid and compelling . . . we fly over history on the magic carpet of Ignatieff's prose'
Independent On Sunday

'Wonderfully entertaining . . . moving . . . a dashing work emblematic of our hectic century'
New York Times

'A wonderfully enthralling first novel . . . unabashedly unpretentious . . . satisfyingly literate and informative . . . a reading feast'
Kirkus Reviews

'Swiftly paced . . . a multi-faceted finely crafted novel'
Chicago Tribune

'Consistently intriguing . . . both a love story and historical thriller'
Woman's Journal

D0552348

ASYA

Michael Ignatieff

ARROW BOOKS

Arrow Books Limited
20 Vauxhall Bridge Road, London SW1V 2SA

An imprint of the Random Century Group

London Melbourne Sydney Auckland
Johannesburg and agencies throughout
the world

First published in Great Britain by Chatto & Windus in 1991

Arrow edition 1992

1 3 5 7 9 10 8 6 4 2

© Michael Ignatieff 1991

The poems quoted on p.107 are from *Listen! Vladimir Mayakovsky:
Early Poems, 1913-1918,* translated by Maria Enzensberger, Redstone
Press 1987

Printed and bound in Great Britain by
Cox & Wyman Ltd, Reading, Berkshire

ISBN 0 09 997160 7

PART ONE

S HE PULLED ON her coat and boots, closed the pantry door and slipped away before anyone saw her disappear. Her breath streamed through her muffler and rose up into the birch branches above her head. The icicles on the eaves shed a steady stream of drops into the piled snowbanks on either side of the path; clumps of snow slid off the branches of the firs and subsided to the ground with a hiss; the uppermost branches of the birches sighed and cracked in the wind. She skipped down the hundred and twenty-six wooden steps to the boathouse singing to herself.

Inside the boathouse, slivers of winter light streamed through the gaps between the plank walls and sliced her body into planes of illumination and darkness. The racing sculls gleamed on the rafters above her head and the motor launch, suspended above its river berth by twin ropes, swayed slightly to and fro, making a dry, creaking sound.

She climbed down the boathouse ladder and tested the ice with her boot. Then she pushed open the great wooden doors and stepped out into the fierce light of the silver river. In the far distance, she could just make out the thin line of the opposite shore. Father had once crossed the river on snowshoes. She would too. She would astonish them all. She walked along, sucking her mitten.

She glanced back at the house, where she had left Lapin playing snakes and ladders with Nanny Saunders, but Marino had vanished in the mist. Whenever she stopped pushing her boots through the slushy ice, she could hear the river roaring beneath her feet. Soon the ice would begin to heave and crack, and the air would fill with a groaning sound as if the whole earth were in pain. Then the river would throw off its mantle and jagged chunks would begin to shift and then bob past the dock. She loved it when the frozen world began to move, when the torrent of life reclaimed the river for its own. Marino would awaken from its sleep. The boatman would sand Father's English scull, revarnish the hull of the motor launch and grease the oarlocks on the rowing boat. As soon as the ice was off the water, Father would dive naked from the boathouse and roar when he surfaced, throwing the hair out of his eyes.

She slopped through the slush, thinking of spring. By the time she reached the middle of the river, the mist had enveloped her. The boathouse behind her was gone, and the long, smudged line of her water-filled steps trailed away into nothingness. The pencil line of the opposite shore had disappeared. She stood still and listened. A faint sound. A scythe being drawn against a sharpening-stone. A blade being honed on something hard. She turned around, sucking her mitten, trying to figure out which direction the sound was coming from. Blades scything, blades hissing, coming closer. Where had she heard that sound before? Then she knew. It was a skater, out there in the mist, coming towards her. No one she knew. They were all inside. She could hear his breathing now, his body at full stretch, his blades slicing into the river's skin. She stood still, waiting for him, unafraid and alone. The veil of mist burst apart, the vast white figure hurtled past her and the ice beneath her feet gave way. She subsided into a dark hole of water, clutching at the jagged rim, while the river seized hold of her and tore her boots from her feet. The river roared in her ears and liquid warmth – like that of a nursery bath – rose through her body and she let herself be swept away.

Then faces were leaning over her, and hands were busy about her, rubbing her limbs frantically, wiping the tears from their faces with such a look of desolation that she wanted to ask what the matter was, but could not speak, only stare up at them from the warm watery place where she had gone. She was borne aloft and carried upwards, wrapped up tight, as if in swaddling. From where she lay in their arms, she stared up into the black, naked branches of trees lit by the pink sky of dusk. Beneath her and behind her she could hear the steady crunch of boots in the snow and a woman weeping. She could not move her head or see where she was being

4

taken, but she knew that she had reached the other side, the place where the spring came from, the place where the river wanted to take her.

She opened her eyes and saw that Praskoviya was bathing her face with a cloth. How much better it had been in the warm, watery place. How much better it had been out on the river. How beautiful their tears had seemed on the other side, when she could only lie there and watch them fall. How painful they were now, when you could reach up and wipe them from Praskoviya's face.

'My child! You have come back from the dead! The Lord be praised.'

Why was she talking of death? There was no death on the river, only warmth suffusing her body and the certainty of having seen a great vision.

'Whatever possessed you, my dearest?' Her mother's voice, close by, gentle, anguished.

Her eyes shut tight, Asya heard herself say in a shrill voice: 'I saw a skater. A great skater. Out there. On the ice.'

She looked up. They were all crowded around her bed: Father, Mother, her brother Lapin, Praskoviya, but she could tell from their faces that no one had seen what she had seen or heard what she had heard. All the remaining years of her life, she remembered that moment: when she discovered the abyss of unknowing that separated her from those she loved.

She looked about her. Where was Nanny Saunders?

Her father laid his hand upon hers.

'The groom is accompanying her to the station.'

'But why?'

'She has been dismissed for letting you out of her sight.'

All the way back to England? In the winter? She could imagine the black cabriolet trotting through the dark woods, Nanny Saunders with her boxes in the back seat.

'Don't cry, child, don't cry.'

But there was no stopping these tears, mixed with grief and rage. Much later, when she had learned what life was like, she remembered this as the moment when she discovered injustice, and the possibility that a father could be responsible for it.

'It was not Nanny's fault. You told me you crossed the river. It's not her fault! Call her back!'

Dr Feldman tried to force her head back onto the pillow. 'You mustn't, child, you mustn't . . .'

'I cannot call her back. My mind is made up,' said Father in that reasonable tone of voice that she knew issued from a will stronger than her own.

'But you told me you crossed the river on skates.'

'Did I, child?' His long face with its neatly trimmed beard, smelling of wintergreen, was close to hers. She could not bear to think that he had forgotten, that he took his words to her so lightly. She turned away from her father and began to cry.

It was a week before she was out of danger, and a month before she recovered the use of her legs. A new nanny, Mrs Moorehead, hateful and officious, was despatched from England to keep her under surveillance so that the dreadful, the longed-for adventure would never occur again. But Nanny Moorehead did not last. She saw to that.

She knew her adventure had set her apart. Everyone regarded her with awed puzzlement. Their neighbours, the Tatischevs and the Dolgoroukys, came racing up the drive in their sleighs to hear the story. The servants spread the word, so that next Sunday, outside the family chapel, the village women clustered around the master's daughter – only five years old, imagine! – who went out into the middle of the river alone. In the low bar at the nearby coaching inn, the Marino boatman, Anton Nicolaevitch, told every traveller how he had raced out onto the ice in his snowshoes and had slipped the rope around her waist just in time. Thus the tale spread through the district so that when Prince Vladimir Adamovitch Galitzine, marshal of nobility for the province, next went to Smolensk for a reception to welcome the new provincial governor, he introduced himself as the father of the little girl who had tried to cross the Vasousa ice.

She herself listened silently when the story was retold, feeling that it was being put to promiscuous use, to suit everyone's purposes but her own. Praskoviya used it to prove that you could never trust an English nanny, Anton Nicolaevitch to prove how

6

brave he had been, and her father to demonstrate that he had a wilful and intrepid daughter. As far as the little girl was concerned, these versions of her story missed the point. As she grew older, a faint memory became etched in the bright light of a shining vision. One night in the nursery, when she was eleven, she told her brother what she had really seen that winter afternoon on the ice.

'He was all in white, twice Father's size, and he was wearing one of those leather helmets like automobile drivers wear. There was an immense sound, filling the whole sky.'

Brother Lapin, who was lying on his stomach, studying the rotogravures in Larch's *Illustrated Mushrooms*, did not even bother to look up. 'So,' he said in his dry, precise voice, 'God is wearing skates?'

She reddened with shame and never spoke of what she had seen again. But she held on to that memory as tightly as a child will hold a marble in its fist. For it was the first lifting of the veil of infancy, the first moment she had any recollection of herself, of Marino, of her parents. Everything before, all the hazy film of earliest infancy, had been ripped from the camera, exposed to the white light of forgetting by that blinding walk across the ice. Having lost those earliest memories, she knew there was a dark place inside herself that would never see the light of her questioning mind. The shock of the river had frozen something inside her, and in the future that lay ahead of her there would be moments when her actions would issue from a dark and unknowable region of herself. That was the price she paid for crossing the river. What she won was fearlessness. Not for her a woman's life of aversion and withdrawal. In her case, the accident had conferred a dispensation. She knew that she had seen a vision, that she had been spared, and that henceforward she was free. All her life, people called her fearless, when in fact she felt fear just like them. What was different was that even when fear had her in its clasp, she knew that it would let her go, as the river had done. People who appear fearless often appear cold. When, in later life, people said she was cold, she never disagreed. For she knew, and some inner recess of her body never forgot, how cold the river torrent had been.

Her parents treated her with awe, as if she were a messenger

7

returned from some unvisitable country. The strange daring of their child, and her mysterious deliverance from fate, led them to search themselves – in vain – for some trace which might explain her nature. But – and she knew this about herself as soon as she became aware of the ancestral portraits on the walls of Marino – she did not descend from anyone in any obvious way. Her mother, an Ourousoff by birth, was shy, pious and practical, while she was exuberant, godless and unworldly. True, she had inherited her mother's tall, thin good looks. 'You look like a fine pair of Borzoi hounds,' Father used to say of them in his jocular manner, meaning that they were fine-boned and delicate of feature, with long, finely-tuned limbs. But there were other features that could not be traced to any pictures in the family album. She had curly black hair, pale white skin and lustrous black eyelashes. Her father said her most beautiful features were her firm, strong chin, indicating determination and character, her wide downy upper lip and her moth-grey eyes. But again, where did these features come from? 'If I were not perfectly sure to the contrary,' her father often said to himself, 'I would think she was not my child.'

She was delicate and gentle of aspect – the sort of girl you would expect to wear fine Brussels lace and help her mother arrange flowers – but her delicacy was deceptive. In temperament she was more nearly her father's child. She held the logs when he was working the cross-cut saw in the forest under the woodsman's eye. Her father taught her to fish with a pole cut from a riverbank willow and himself held the leading rope when she learned to ride the Arabian mare. Her proudest possession at the age of eight was not a doll or a fine pair of patent pumps, but a penknife from the French shop in Moscow. When Praskoviya bathed her in the nursery tub at night, she would point at the child's dirt-impacted knees and exclaim: 'You are a perfect savage. It is not ladylike to climb trees and dig in the gardens with the pantry servants.'

'I am not a lady,' she replied.

Again, in the mythology that she created for herself over the course of her life, she liked to believe – because her looks could not be traced to the imprisoning genealogical features of the family album – that she had been set free of family ties. When irremediable losses occurred, when everyone tried to console her, she insisted that she had never really possessed these things, or been possessed by them, in the first place.

She was born at Marino on the 19th of December 1899, old style, in the upstairs bedroom with the bullseye window. Praskoviya Ivanovna and the family physician, Dr Feldman, were in attendance, while the master paced the dancing gallery a floor below, smoking one Balkan Sobranie after another and reading, as his wife had instructed him, from the Lamentations of Jeremiah. She was dipped into the baptismal font at the family chapel at Marino and baptized Anastasia Vladimirovna. But the name was only used in front of visitors. 'My daughter Anastasia,' her father would say, his large hand resting on top of her head, and she would make the obligatory curtsey, feeling as if he were introducing not his own daughter but a complete stranger. Asya was her real name, the diminutive they all knew her by.

When she was eleven, a clever boy she met on the beach in Biarritz told her that the Western or Gregorian calendar was thirteen days ahead of the Julian. They both computed that she had been born on the 1st of January 1900. She ran back to the hotel and told everyone henceforward she wished to celebrate her birthday on that date. Alone of all the people she knew, she was born with the century, and having been spared at its beginning, she was convinced she would live to see its end. It took a long time, and many hard experiences, before she shed her childhood conviction that she was immortal.

Her closest companion was her brother, a straw-haired boy with a puzzled expression that accounted for his nickname. He had been christened Alexander, but was always known as Lapin. His mother pronounced the word in the French way, while his father pronounced it in the Russian manner, with the accent on the first syllable, and the hard rather than soft 'n' at the end. To English friends, Father explained that it was pronounced 'Lapin as in Mappin and Webb.'

Brothers and sisters were supposed to understand each other, she thought. But she never could understand Lapin. For he was maddeningly different. By day, in the classroom, his letters were

9

faint and precise, hers ink-spattered and thick. At night he folded his clothes on the nursery chair, while she left hers scattered about the floor. While she followed Father and the woodman into the forest clearing every morning, Lapin accompanied Mother to the greenhouses, holding a flowerpot to catch the dead leaves she clipped from the peach trees. When Asya and Lapin went mushroom hunting together under the deep shadows of the pines, he could spot their protruding forms when all she could see was a flat carpet of auburn pine needles. 'Ssssh!' he would say, eyes scouring the ground through his glasses. And she would follow behind.

'Why do I have to be quiet? I'm not frightening the mushrooms away.'

'Ssshhh. I can't concentrate.' His concentration was fierce and focused, bent over his stamp albums, over the Meccano set, while hers ranged restlessly over everything. Once, when he was poring over his stamp albums in the bright hard glow of the nursery lamp, she stood up and lifted off her nightgown and twirled around on tiptoes, quite naked, just behind him, but he did not notice. That night, when he was sound asleep, she pulled back his covers and saw, with amazement, that his penis was sticking up stoutly through the flies of his pyjamas, like an asparagus tip bursting through the soil of the kitchen garden. She touched it: a firm, springy shoot, a great mystery.

From the first flurries of autumn until the last blizzard of winter, they lived in Moscow behind the Kremlin on Nicolaevsky Street. Every spring, servants and piles of baggage would set off from Nicolaevsky Street to open up Marino for the summer season. The family followed later. It was a three-hour train journey due west from Moscow's Brest Station to the country stop a dozen miles from the estate.

The spring following Asya's accident, the coachman picked them up at the station and announced that, owing to the floods, he could only take them to the knoll at Putinka. At the crest of the hill, the estate road could be seen disappearing into the depths of a lake. Anton Nicolaevitch poled into view and manoeuvred a punt alongside. Father lifted Asya and Lapin from the carriage into

Anton Nicolaevitch's arms, and they all set off, poling silently through the fields, past marooned clumps of birch, past the greenhouses ringed with water, past the flooded English garden, the plaster nymphs in water up to their knees. When she saw her herb garden under water Mother burst into tears and Father promised that this year, without fail, he would build the flood dyke. Asya leaned over the prow of the punt, watching the gravel walkways and box hedges glide by beneath her, and felt she was not in a boat at all, but in the sky, planing over the garden like a bird.

When she was tucked up in the nursery, and her mother was kissing her goodnight, Asya said she wanted to arrive by boat every year, she never wanted the water to go down, she wanted to be marooned forever. She was disappointed when the river finally subsided, when the estate was no longer an island cut off from the world by the debris-strewn torrent. The floods of her childhood lodged in her mind a deep attraction for destruction, a fascination with the sweeping away of everything. She ran for a mile once just to see a peasant's thatch burn; she prayed for the river to burst her father's dykes.

In that spring of the floods, there were peasant insurrections, and some local estates were burned down. But Asya only learned of them in the history books long after; there were riots in the streets of Smolensk not thirty miles away, of which she heard not a word. Occasionally, her father would pause and frown over a headline in *Novoe Vremie* and would exclaim, in English, 'I'll be damned!' at which their mother would look up from the other end of the table and say reprovingly, 'Vladimir, *je t'en prie.*'

When the Russian Imperial Fleet sailed from its Baltic roadstead around the world to fight the Japanese, Mother began reading the papers to all of them at breakfast, her fingers smudged with newsprint. She had been a missionary in Japan in the 1890s and followed all the news of the war with equitable concern for the fate of both sides.

'The Japanese fleet has weighed anchor at Yokohama. Children, did I ever tell you about Yokohama?'

'What's Yokohama?' Lapin said, looking up from his toast.

'There was a trolley ride which took you right down along the quays, right past all the boats. A forest of masts. I rode in the back, holding onto my hat. I was the only white woman in sight. Some tea, dearest?' She held out her hand to take the cup from her husband. He had always thought he had rescued her from the lonely self-immolation of missionary work. Now it dawned on him that their marriage had ended the happiest years of her life.

The day room off Mother's bedroom was decorated with delicate brush paintings of Japanese monasteries and gardens consisting of a stone, a cropped tree, and concentric circles of white sand. Sometimes Asya's mother would put up her hair and don a kimono. The sight of her, seated in front of a mirror in the blue silk kimono with the small coiled pink dragons, her back turned, light falling on the nape of her neck, gave Asya a convulsive stirring of pleasure, as if she was being promised that her mother's beauty might one day be hers. On the night of the summer ball, she used to sit with her mother when she got dressed, of all her expressions loving most the guilty one that came over her when she allowed herself to be pretty.

At thirteen Asya was allowed at last to attend the summer ball. The Smolensk detachment of Father's old regiment sent a dozen young officers, and she danced with all of them. In her fawn muslin dress, her body just budding, she discovered from the flush of their faces, the sensation of their hands in the small of her back, the insistent pressure of their thighs against her hip, that she had become a creature men could desire. It was one of the most startling moments of her life. In turn they waltzed her from one end of the parquet to the other, and as she swept by in their arms, her head back, feeling the blood thudding in her neck, she caught sight of Lapin, in his first dinner jacket and tie, leaning against the window, alone behind all the watching couples, staring at her mournfully through his thick glasses.

By that time she had her own room with the bullseye window under the eaves, the very room in which she had been born. When she was alone she rose from her bed, let her nightgown fall, stood in front of the long mirror and turned slowly in the candlelit shadows. She cocked her head to one side, then to the other, looking at herself. Yes, it was all beginning. Already out there in the world was the man she would marry. Was he wearing a black hat? Was he carrying a rolled umbrella in the English style? Or was he an officer, with tight blue leggings with red piping up the side? Would his moustache rasp her cheek when he kissed her? Would his skin smell, as her father's did, of English talcum and lime? She stood naked before the mirror, trying to imagine who this stranger might be who would take her life in his hands.

Sitting beside her mother in the Japanese boudoir, she said once, 'When I meet the man I will marry, I will know immediately.'

'How will you know, child?'

'Here. Right here,' Asya said, tapping her breastbone through the high collar of her dress. She fingered the loop of pearls around her neck, as if each pearl was a moment of the future, seen, weighed and counted in advance.

Softly, her mother replied, 'It was not like that for me.'

Asya pressed the stopper of her mother's perfume bottle against her wrist.

'I will know,' she said, as the perfume filled the room with the scent of lilac.

Long afterwards, Asya had only to recall the smell of lilac and a fissure would open in the present and the light of this particular instant would stream through her mind: the look of tender distraction on her mother's face as she turned from her daughter and stared out through the window of the Japanese sitting room at the lawns of Marino.

At first none of them realized it, but Mother began to slip away from them, as if she, like her daughter, had decided to vanish down the path to the boathouse and step out alone on the silver river. What at first was no more than an ache, a certain stiffness when she stood up, became, as Dr Feldman put it, rubbing his hands and averting his gaze, 'something worse'.

Asya nursed her, cupping her head upright and holding the glass so that she could swallow the tablets, bathing her forehead, changing the dressing on the suppurating blossom on her breast. One night, when Asya was relighting the candle that glowed in

13

front of the icon of St Vladimir in her mother's room, she heard her mother say,

'I have not lived my life.'

'Mother, don't.'

'But you must *live* it, child. You *must*. No one must stop you.'

'Don't sit up like that, Mother. Don't tire yourself.'

'Don't let anything stop you. Not love, not your husband.'

'Yes, Mother.'

Her mother lay back, exhausted, pared away, with an imploring expression on her face as if uncertain that her child had really understood what she was trying, with her life draining out of her, to convey.

Then, at dawn one morning in the spring of 1914, Asya awoke from a brief doze at her mother's bedside and immediately saw that her mother's face was as empty, as deserted as the discarded nightgown on the chair. The last warmth had ebbed from the hand on the coverlet. It was now a sallow, clenched claw. Asya kissed it and began to shake. As clear and cold as a gust of winter air, it came to her that she had just been hurled through the black gates of life into adulthood.

They followed the coffin through the birch wood to the crypt, the priest and the icons, the servants and the villagers in one long straggling line, Father leaning on Lapin's arm, in black against the green leaves of early summer. At the end of the service they stood together and the sound of the Viechnaya Pamyat, the hymn of Eternal Memory, rose up into the trees. Until this moment, she had thought that her life stretched before her, like the river through the trees, broad and strong and endless, and now she knew that it did not, that time was not hers to use as she wished, that time was racing ahead of her own beating heart.

She took to wearing her mother's high-necked black dresses and went around, as she had done, with the keys to the pantry and the larder on a long blue ribbon around her waist. She sat with her father after lunch and read to him while he gazed at the ceiling and smoked a cigar. He so quickly became used to her as mistress of the house that both of them forgot that she was only fourteen.

One evening, several months later, he came up to her room under the eaves to kiss her goodnight. He rapped at the door, and when he entered he found her sitting on the chair in front of the mirror, with her curly black hair held up in a chignon with her mother's tortoiseshell comb. She was wearing her mother's silk kimono with the embroidered pink dragons.

'No!' he shouted and rushed out of the door, thundering down the stairs. The door of his bedroom slammed shut.

She pulled out her mother's tortoiseshell clasp, and then tore off the kimono as if it were on fire, flinging it in the corner. For a long time she stood in the near darkness, clutching herself, staring at the rumpled pile of blue silk on the floor, feeling shame flooding through her.

Next morning, at breakfast, while her father sat stiffly with his head bowed, she told the butler:

'Please lock the doors to the Japanese sitting room.'

They never ventured into it again. The room remained sealed, the curtains drawn, the dust drifting through the darkness and settling on the screens, the silk prints, the brocaded walls.

On the 1st of August 1914, she stood in the main entrance of Marino, with her arm around Lapin's shoulder, watching as Father's martial eye moved across the burnt faces of the peasant boys from his villages, their packs by their side. Suddenly he barked out: 'Marsh route!' and the still photograph dissolved into jerky cinema. The peasant boys turned and straggled off down the poplar alley, skipping to keep in step and filling the wood with the sound of their songs. Her father leaned against the doorway staring after the disappearing column.

After he had despatched his recruits, he stayed indoors in an old pair of slippers and a cardigan from Swan and Edgar, and played chess with Lapin or stared out of the conservatory window at the changing seasons, the war newspapers with their worsening news spread around his slippered feet. She went every day to the Smolensk Red Cross hospital to type letters for the illiterate convalescents. When she asked them what she should say about their wounds, they generally looked blankly at the little machine on her lap and said, 'As you think best, your highness.' On her return home she joined her father in the conservatory and told him how uncomplaining the soldiers were, how hopeless the look in their eyes. Father stroked her chin, rearranged stray hairs descending from her chignon and said she must never leave him. But she knew she must.

In June of 1916 she announced that she was going to enrol in the nurse's training course at the Anglo-Russian hospital in Petrograd and that she would stay with Uncle Dimitri Ourousoff at his apartment on the Fontanka. Father refused, saying she was too young. She stormed upstairs and locked herself in her room.

She found him in his dressing gown, on the hallway carpet, leaning against the wall next to her bedroom door. She got down on her knees. 'I am ashamed of myself,' he said, looking at the floor.

'Can I go?'

He stroked her hair, leaned his head forward on her shoulder and gave a resigned nod. 'If you take Praskoviya Ivanovna.'

The young lady and her nanny were the only people of quality travelling and had to enlist the stationmaster's help to clear them a path to their carriage, or to have the tea kettle for their samovar refilled at the buffets during the stops. They passed station platforms laid out with stretchers; piles of pine coffins on railway sidings; on all the roads, long lines of supply carts drawn by mangy horses; and on the loading docks of country sidings, sullen lines of teenagers, in their first beards, their necks bulging inside tight tunics, their service caps askew on their heads, none of them, she thought with a start of pity, any older than herself.

From the station, they took a *droshki* straight to the Dimitri Palace, headquarters of the hospital, the only building on the Nevsky Prospekt flying the Union Jack. When they were ushered into the office, Lady Muriel Paget gestured disdainfully.

'How old are you, m'dear?'

'Nineteen.'

Lady Muriel Paget looked quizzical.

'Experience?'

'I've rolled bandages in Smolensk hospital, typed letters for the soldiers . . .'

'Rolled bandages!' Lady Paget exclaimed.

'I have travelled five hundred miles. I will do anything.'

'Even lie about your age, it appears.' Lady Paget stared at Asya over her bifocals. 'Well, at least you're keen, which is more than I can say of some of your countrywomen,' she said. 'I make my round tomorrow morning at seven thirty sharp. Don't get in our way and we might be able to teach you something.'

Out in the hall, Asya squeezed Praskoviya's hand with excitement, but Praskoviya muttered, 'She saw straight through you, my child.'

'But I did it!'

All the way home to Uncle Dimitri and Aunt Olga's, with tears and remonstrations, Praskoviya Ivanovna begged Asya to reconsider.

'It is not a suitable activity for gentlefolk! If your mother were alive, she would forbid this!'

But Asya held onto a clear image of the glacial manner and the crisp white uniform of Lady Muriel Paget, and would not be dissuaded. She was there on the rounds next morning at seven thirty, and soon mastered the relative merits of Eusol and hypertonic saline solution in the cleansing of battlefield wounds. She watched, with her jaw clenched and her face drained of colour, as the ward sisters swabbed potassium permanganate on the gaping wounds, turning the livid flesh black.

Flesh laid bare, the body offering up its secrets to the skill of her hands: she had no horror of any of it. Confronted with wounds, she became clear, focused, rooted in the present. When she held hands that were shaking with fear, when she uncovered a sore and swabbed it down with solution, she lifted herself beyond the zone of danger and death. In her crisply starched uniform she strode between the beds ranged beneath the chandeliers, and when the eyes of the wounded soldiers were turned upon her she felt that she was no longer a girl of sixteen, but a woman at last. She hoped Lady Paget would invite her to join the mobile field hospital in eastern Poland. Then one September morning she received a telegram from Lapin telling her to return to Marino immediately.

Lapin met the carriage at the door. There was a new dusting of hair on his upper lip and all his clothes suddenly seemed too short. She kissed him three times and said he looked like a grasshopper in pants.

'What's wrong?'

'Go and see.'

She took the spiral staircase two at a time, still in her travelling coat. Father was lying propped up in bed, stretching out his hands to her.

'What is it?' she cried, taking his hand and kneeling by the bedside.

'Nothing, my dearest. Some angina, Dr Feldman says.' His voice was soft and blurred.

She soon had him up in a bath chair, wrapped in blankets, and wheeled him along the boxwood alleys. A week later, when they were in the greenhouses, palpating the fruit on the hothouse vines, he told her that he had decided to send Lapin to school in England a year early. The war was making it impossible for the Moscow gymnasium to prepare their boys adequately. The best mathematics teacher was somewhere in the Carpathians serving as a gunnery officer; the geography teacher was attached to the general staff at Mogilev in the cartography department; and all three foreign-language teachers had been killed on the Polish front in 1915.

Lapin was uncharacteristically excited. The express would get him to Petrograd overnight, where Uncle Dimitri and Aunt Olga would meet the train and help him to board the Baltic steamer. He would be met at Felixstowe by the housemaster who would accompany him on the journey to London. The journey would take a week, but there was no other way. The land route had been severed by the German army. They were camped within seventy-five kilometres of Petrograd itself.

The platform at Nicolaevsky Station was full of soldiers, and her father trained his experienced eye on the wary, restless recruits lounging about him.

'What a shambles!' he muttered.

The newspapers were censored, but stories filtered back from the front, telling of companies which had thrown down their weapons and melted away into the countryside. It was so obvious that they were sending Lapin to safety that nothing was said about when they would see each other again.

When the second bell sounded, Father shouted, 'Remember Aksyonov at the Azov Bank! Please give him my regards and do be careful with your allowance.'

As the train pulled away Lapin's last audible words were 'The Azov Bank! 36 Lombard Street EC1!'

That night in the Moscow house she wakened to the sound of groaning. When she reached his side, one of Father's hands gripped his chest, the other fumbled about on his night table, among the jars and glasses. She took him in her arms, put the pill on his tongue and felt him slip, wet and limp, into sleep. She knew now that she was trapped.

In the autumn of 1916 they closed up Marino for the season and went to live in the Moscow house, venturing out only for drives around the Kremlin in the cabriolet. There were marches in the streets, black and red flags dancing past their gates, but they closed their curtains and stayed inside. The Kremlin bells went silent. Within the dark brocaded walls of the house on Nicolaevsky Street, time was measured out in the pulse heard through the stethoscope, the arhythmic struggles of her father's heart.

One cold morning in March, the breakfast rolls were being served as usual on the silver salver. Her father pointed indignantly at the roll on his plate and looked imperiously at Vasya.

'A roll, your excellency,' said the butler.

'Don't be insolent, Vasya.'

'The flour is bad, your excellency. That is all there is to be had in the shops.'

With a look at once absent and wounded, Father tore a piece with his fingers and began to chew the bread of revolution.

'People's bread!' Asya heard Vasya muttering in the pantry, as he shone the knives and forks on his apron and dropped them back into the felt-lined compartments. 'White for the gentry, grey for everyone else. Now at least they know what it's like.'

He was too old and deaf to realize she was there, not ten feet away. Where had Vasya learned to mouth such platitudes? He had eaten white bread all his life.

Ever after she could see herself in that high-necked blouse of guipure lace, her hair up in a chignon, standing in the passageway, lit by a lozenge of blurred light from the skylight, watching Vasya shining the knives. The radiator hissed in the passage, the knives clattered into their felt-lined bins, and in her memory the passageway seemed to stretch and distend until she felt herself positioned not ten feet from Vasya, but on the other side of an uncrossable river.

They lived the first spring of the Revolution with the curtains drawn, Father in bed rereading his favourite comedies by Griboyedov and sipping bottled Narzan water, while she studied Gray's *Anatomy* and Burton's *Abdominal Injuries of Warfare*. Every morning she scurried out on foot in her plainest spring coat, hoping to escape the attention of the crowds who stood listening to the stump orators, and went to the telegraph office to send Lapin a message, but it was always shut. One morning in April she went out on the vast cobblestoned square in front of the Kremlin amid the demobilized soldiers in their grey and sand-brown greatcoats. She bent down among the horse dung and cigarette papers and out of curiosity picked up a few trampled revolutionary leaflets. When her father came down to breakfast, the leaflets were scattered about the white linen tablecloth of the breakfast table. As Vasya arranged the folds of his master's dressing gown around his legs, she waved one which read, 'Expropriate the bloodsuckers!' and burst out laughing.

Father snapped his napkin over his lap: 'You think it is all theatre, or some kind of entertainment. I assure you it is not.' He looked balefully at his grey-coloured roll and then at Vasya, who shrugged. 'I have decided on a cure. We are going south to the Caucasus spas.'

'What about Marino?'

Father shook his head. 'It is not safe. The Dolgoroukys were sacked. You didn't know? Well, that is how it is. God knows what has happened to Marino.'

Asya could see quite clearly the room with the bullseye window, the furniture in the salons covered in dust-cloths and the tiled Dutch stoves icy to the touch; the sealed Japanese room. All of it was waiting, and the dust was falling across pillars of light through cracks in the closed curtains.

'That is why you must put those disgusting leaflets away.'

She had not seen him so forceful in years.

'A cure?' she asked, handing the leaflets to Vasya who looked dubiously at them and marched them off to a bin in the kitchen. 'Father, there is a revolution going on outside.' She was incredulous.

'Precisely why I need a cure, dear child. Precisely why.'

EVERY AFTERNOON IN the summer of 1917 Father climbed into the trap and was driven down past the villas and sanatoriums, hotels and spas of Kislovodsk to pay a call on his old friend and regimental mess mate, Dimitri Isvolsky. Old man Isvolsky was a big, roomy gentleman with a large stomach, bisected by eighteen inches of buttoned flies. He wore suits of best English worsted stained with soup and cigarettes and a broad black-banded straw hat. His long, jowelled face gave him the appearance of a gundog. He sat on the veranda leaning back in his wicker chair, smoking his cigarettes down to the white holder, flicking ash off his waistcoat and listening keenly to Father, whose opinions he respected. Marooned together on the southern reaches of Russia, they spent their afternoons turning over the prospects of the army holding back the German advance and the provisional government stemming the general disintegration. Invariably, their conversations ended with one of them saying, 'It can't go on like this,' and the other sighing, 'But we must be cheerful. We must.' The sight of the two of them made Asya think of two children beside a sandcastle willing the tide to go out. She was surprised to feel so much older, so much more cynical than either of them.

'Why *must*?' Asya asked.

Isvolsky said gently, 'Times are bad enough. We must not make them worse with despair.'

There was a barrack-room bareness to Isvolsky's villa, the bitter smell of his cigarettes in all the rooms, piles of old newspapers on every flat surface and uncollected cups of tea teetering on the armrests of the sofas. Isvolsky was a widower who brought up his son Nicolai with the help of his old nanya. Asya asked him how he had lost his wife.

'Typhoid. In the municipal drinking water at Eupatoria.

Crimean resort town, do you know it? My son was two and a half years old. Typhoid in the municipal water supply,' he repeated with crisp contempt. 'Really, we are a lamentable country.'

Kislovodsk was four days by train south from Moscow and five from Petrograd, and to Asya it seemed as if the mountains which surrounded the town sealed them off from the old world entirely. But this was an illusion. In late October, Asya and her father were in the telegraph office sending Lapin a telegram when the manager pulled down the blinds and showed them a message just received from Petrograd, announcing that the provisional government had been overthrown.

'We must withdraw our savings,' Father said, but the manager pulled back the blinds on his window and pointed to the crowds forming around the already sealed doors of the Azov Bank. It was too late.

Several months went by in suspended animation. Then one night in March, Praskoviya Ivanovna was knitting by the fire in the parlour, Father was glancing over some pages of Lermontov on the sofa beside her and Asya was struggling to darn a sock when a motor car, its lights ablaze, lurched into the driveway and stopped. They were through the door before Asya had turned from the window, men with pistols, thundering upstairs to the bedrooms, coming through the back door herding the servants from the cookhouse. Praskoviya began to cry. The ball of wool rolled from her lap and unravelled on the carpet.

A boy in the salon doorway trained his pistol upon the three of them. His regimental tunic was stained, the epaulettes were ripped off, his face was fearful and insolent and the gun was too big for his hands. He waved his pistol: 'No! On your feet where I can see you.'

'My father is ill,' Asya said. 'We will sit down.' She pulled Father and Praskoviya down beside her on the sofa. The boy shouted and the safety catch of the gun made a small metallic click. She thought: now he will shoot. Now.

One second was followed by another, and then another. Her father's hand was clammy and cold in hers. Upstairs, drawers crashed onto the floor, knives sliced into mattresses and pillows, wood splintered and glass shattered, books tumbled from shelves.

'My father needs his medicine.'

'Don't move.'

'It is a green bottle upstairs in the medicine cabinet in the bathroom.'

'Don't move.'

Praskoviya tugged at her arm to be quiet. Asya shouted, 'Order someone to get it! Right now!'

A man in a black leather jacket with a sallow complexion put his head round the door. He paused, lit a cigarette, blew the smoke towards her and said amiably, 'If I hear another sound from you, I will have you taken into the garden and shot. Understand?'

They stared at each other in silence.

'Do you have a warrant?' she asked.

'Order of the Bolshevik Extraordinary Committee.'

'From where?'

'Kislovodsk Soviet. Now you know,' he said, grinding a cigarette into the carpet.

They left as suddenly as they had come, stamping out into the yard with pillowcases and sacks over their shoulders. Their car reversed and lurched off into the night. Everyone in the house stood where they were, while Asya raced up the stairs to the bathroom. Father's pills lay scattered across the floor. She gathered them up in the lap of her dress and ran downstairs. She put a pill on his tongue, and after Father had swallowed it, she held him tight.

'Where are the police? Why do they allow such outrages?' he whispered. All gone, she knew. And in their place? Just guns, boys with guns.

Next morning, there was a sheen of ice on the apple tree at her window. She traced her name in the hoarfrost and stood drawing the bright day into herself until she was ready to face the debris at her feet: ripped dresses, underwear strewn about, curtains slashed, jewellery box upended and chairs overturned.

Her father came and stood in the doorway of her room, in his nightshirt.

'I . . .' he said, 'I . . .' There was a puzzled, pleading expression on his face. He fell to his knees. She rushed forward to catch him.

'Praskoviya, help me!' she shouted.

His lips moved, as if he was trying to speak. Praskoviya held his hands and began saying her prayers.

'Be quiet!' Asya hissed.

She slapped his cheeks and pummelled his chest. His eyes remained rooted to a spot on the ceiling and his body began, ever so slowly, to slacken in her arms. He was still warm, his stubbly cheek was next to hers, and she breathed in the rich almond smell of his skin. She laid him gently upon the carpet and began to cry.

Before she knew what was happening, the servants were on their knees in the passageway saying their prayers. The shutters were drawn, and a candle was casting its light across the powdery mask of his face. She moved away and stood at the end of the room. In place of the body she had known, that stout torso rising from the Vasousa on summer mornings, there was a shrunken shape in a white nightshirt, two bare legs splayed out on the carpet. His flesh had sunk back against his skull and all the expressive mobility of his face had gone. From an arid place that had opened up inside her, a soundless voice cried: I am alone.

In a bitter March wind, the coachman, the yardman and the undertaker bore the pine box to the municipal cemetery. The gravediggers were still working and wet soil thudded down into the cramped space between heaved tombs and rusting crosses.

The undertaker, a ratlike man who rubbed his hands through his lank hair, whispered to her, 'No religious service. Can't be done. The town Soviet does not allow it.'

'Out of my sight!' she hissed, and he scuttled away.

While the servants wept, she held her head high and stared out above the miserable cemetery to the border of pines behind. Her voice, strong and uncracked, resonated through her whole body as she sang the Viechnaya Pamyat, the hymn of Eternal Memory.

Praskoviya and the servants left her and she threw herself down beside the sheer dark place where he lay. She ran her hands over the cold black earth as if she were caressing a sleeping face.

She heard footsteps behind her. Old man Isvolsky, hat in hand, came towards her, the gold band of his watch-chain bouncing on his waistcoat. 'My dear child,' he said, 'my dear child,' and took her hand and kissed it. 'I have just found out. How will you ever forgive me . . .' All her pent-up grief burst from her then and he went down upon his knees in the dirt and took her into his arms.

Back at the house, she dismissed the servants, giving the men her father's clothing, the women sufficient jewellery with which to pawn their way back to Moscow. She vainly telegraphed Lapin in London, Uncle Dimitri and Aunt Olga in Petrograd, and coldly endured Praskoviya's lamentations. Beneath the ice of her composure surged a river of sorrow, and she knew that if the ice were to crack, for even an instant, she would slip in and drown. At night, Praskoviya wept and pushed her food around on her plate and whispered, 'So it has come to this.'

'Shush. This is how it is.'

'When shall we ever return to Marino?'

'Never! Do you hear me, never!' Praskoviya had never seen her so cold with rage.

Asya went to see Isvolsky, to ask what she should do.

'We must escape, dearest.'

'But how?'

'The Black Sea ports. Novorrossisk, Eupatoria, Sevastopol. But you see, the lines are blocked. The White army is about sixty kilometres away, and the Reds won't let us get on the trains. We are trapped, dearest.'

His son, Nick, sat at his feet drawing a picture.

'What are you drawing?' Asya asked him.

In deep black crayon, the boy had drawn a stick man with a gun; in dark reds, a house; in blues, books and toys scattered about the lawn; in yellows, a boy with huge eyes. 'It is a search,' Nick said.

Isvolsky looked sadly at his son's drawing. 'Our turn is coming.'

When all her money was gone, when they had eaten the last of the mouldy lentils in the cookhouse and burned the last log in the stove, she and Praskoviya went to the municipal hospital. The head of surgery, unshaven in a blood-spattered gown, looked at her thin white hands and dainty ankles and the once fine pair of shoes and told her to follow him.

The corridors smelled of urine and were jammed with beds. In the wards, starving children stared up at her with huge, listless eyes.

'Scurvy,' the doctor said. 'Can you believe it, in Russia? Scurvy among children!'

'What can you do for them?'

'If we get them in time, we can feed them. We have found a few peasant farms, and they supply us. At a price.'

'Well?' he said, when they had returned to the entrance.

'I need to eat. Can you find work for my nanya?'

'In the laundry. Send her there.'

The lye burned Praskoviya's hands and she could barely manage the weight of the wet sheets in the tubs, but there was food – of a sort – in the hospital refectory, and the two of them met every lunchtime, bent over their tin bowls of gruel, like two prisoners serving a long sentence.

Three of the children in Asya's care died, and she wrapped them in winding sheets and laid them in tiny coffins. She tried to feel something for them, for their wasted tiny bodies, but she was inured to every sorrow.

She was tucking the children into bed one night when shots rang out in the courtyard. Men, with cartridge belts round their torn tunics and shapkas on their heads, ran through the corridors. One ran into her ward and pulled her down beside the window. He smelled of horses and dirt.

'Who's out there?' she called. A bullet whined past an open window. The children were moaning in their beds.

'Town guard. Red bastards!'

'Stop shooting!' she cried. 'There are children here!'

'Shut up! Keep their heads down!' he shouted, as the children wailed and crawled under their cots.

The Cossack yanked her to her feet and pulled her along the corridor and down the stairs. He dragged her out into the courtyard and forced her into the back of a haycart. Four other nurses and a doctor were already lying in the straw, covering their heads. The tailgate was slammed shut, a whip cracked, and they lurched forward out of the yard. Praskoviya ran after her, her face twisted with terror, as the cart hurtled away.

For an hour they rode on under the darkening sky. Then, just as suddenly, they jerked to a stop. They were ordered out and tottered to the ground. Asya found herself in some kind of encampment. Lights glimmered through tents, fires blazed, stacked rifles gave off shadows which vanished into the immense flatness of the plain at night.

They were shown into a mess tent, and were given food. They were bent over their mess tins gobbling down some kasha when the tent flaps flew back and a small, athletic figure with closely-cropped grey hair, a fleece jacket flung over his shoulders and a riding crop in his hand stood before them. He smiled grandly and announced:

'I am Shkouro. Captain Andrei Shkouro. Once in his imperial majesty's Chevalier Guards. Now commander of his majesty's southern irregulars, vested with the task of divesting the Bolsheviks of the town of Kislovodsk. We are short of trained medical staff. You will serve in the field hospital.' Then he bowed. 'We are well equipped. Good evening.' With a tap of his riding crop, he was gone.

Asya was led to the field hospital, three tents in a pine wood behind the camp. There were rows of wooden cots under swooping swathes of canvas. Spirit lamps hanging from the tent poles cast birdlike shadows over the moaning faces of the wounded. The air was rank with the smell of putrefaction. Through the dry, bare earth beneath her feet she could feel the crump of artillery explosions nearby.

A Red armoured train in Kislovodsk had scored a direct hit on two White batteries above the town. Two blood-spattered horsecarts piled with broken bodies arrived. The commander of one battery, a young lieutenant, was brought in with a shoulder wound. She accompanied his stretcher as the orderlies carried him from surgery. The lieutenant's left arm was spliced tight to his chest. His uniform, brown with dust, had been torn away at the shoulder. His bare white feet dangled off the stretcher; his auburn hair was matted with the imprint of his helmet. He was thin and muscular, and the gauze of his bandage glowed white against the tan of his skin. His cheekbones caught the light, while the sockets of his deep-set eyes lay in shadow. A blackened clot of blood gleamed in his left ear. The orderlies brought the stretcher up beside the cot, and as she put her arms around his chest to lift him onto the cot he winced, and his eyes met hers.

'Damn you!' he whispered.

'You have been lucky. Concussion. Perforated eardrum.'

'My shoulder, dammit,' he whispered.

She smiled.

'A shell fragment, neat muscular perforation, no wandering of the fragments down into the chest cavity. I am telling you, you are lucky.'

'How old are you?'

'Why? You don't think I know what I'm talking about?' She got up and went to get some gauze and some iodine.

'You were lucky.'

'My boys got me out of the ditch. Otherwise I'd be food for the crows by now.'

She cleaned the blood from his ear with a swab, sitting on the edge of the cot, holding his head still between thumb and forefinger. The iodine made him wince.

'What is your name?' she asked, to distract him.

'Gourevitch, Second Artillery.'

'Your real name,' she said softly, applying a gauze bandage to his ear. 'I'm not your commanding officer.'

'Sergei Apollonovitch.'

'Apollonovitch. Son of Apollo . . .'

'A drunken landowner from Volhynia.'

'Your father?'

He nodded.

When she had finished, he lay back on the pillow and stared at her. No man had ever looked at her like this before, with an unswerving gaze that made her feel as if her stained uniform, her torn woollen socks and spattered shoes, her hands smeared with his blood, her face wet with perspiration, were suddenly rimmed with light.

'And I am Asya,' she said, rising from the bed, leaving him to follow her with his eyes. She came back later and sat on the edge of his cot, watching his chest rise and fall, his eyelids flutter once or twice and his mouth form words she could not understand. Even in sleep, he seemed self-contained, compact and apart. She went back to her tent, curled up in a corner and fell asleep in her clothes.

The next day, he ordered her to get him up. She shook her head. 'You don't understand, do you?' he said, as he guided his damaged shoulder out of the covers. 'If I can't ride when they strike this camp, they'll leave me here.' He flung the covers back. 'Get me up.' He threw his good arm over her shoulder and she lifted him to his feet. 'Good. Now walk.'

They walked up and down the beaten grass path between the hospital tents and the main encampment. He leaned heavily against her at first. She smelled his sweat, felt the hard band of muscle around his waist.

'So we kidnapped you,' he said. 'Next time we'll take the town and drive them out, and you can go home.'

'Do you believe that?'

He gave her a fierce, bright smile. 'Who knows what the hell I believe.'

They struck camp suddenly three days later, when they came within range of a Red artillery train. Just as he had predicted, they left behind four men, too ill to move, with food and water and a red cross splashed on the tent.

'But we can't!' she pleaded.

'Oh, you are so sweet and well brought-up. This isn't the Anglo-Russian hospital.'

Asya helped to load him onto the fodder wagons. The whips snapped and they were off, his head on her knee, his good arm gripping his bound shoulder, his face grimacing at every jolt as the wagon bumped along the dusty road through the sharp cold night air. She didn't know where she was, she didn't know where she was going, and she didn't care.

That night, on the outskirts of their new encampment, they went for a walk together in a rock-strewn gully. They sat on a boulder in the dark, and she had her first cigarette, a puff or two from one of his. 'Who are you?' she asked.

'I told you. A landowner's son from Chelm in Volhynia.'

'Where is that?'

'A miserable place on the western border, full of Jews, Ukrainians and Poles. On the main street you're up to your axles in mud. And you?'

'It was called Marino. Smolensk gubernia.'

Massaging his shoulder, he said, 'There won't be anything left. Not if it's near Smolensk.' He looked back at the lamps glowing through the membrane of the tents and ground his cigarette out under his heel.

'And Chelm? What will be left of Chelm?'

'Nothing either.'

'Your father is a landowner,' she said. 'And your mother?'

'In Moscow. I don't see her. I live with my father. Or I used to. My father went to seed, slept with the wine merchant's wife, raised pigs and beetroot. And you?'

'My father is dead. My mother is dead. My brother is in England. My estate is burned to the ground.' She began to laugh, as if the absurdity of her complete dispossession had finally struck her, as if she could now be reconciled to the disappearance of everything – boathouse, gazebo, house, garden, gates, conservatory, gardeners, boatmen. When she stopped and wiped her eyes, she thought to herself, This laughter must be like dying: everything draining away, spilling into the dust and the tumult of laughter and tears echoing in your head. She looked at him and saw that her laughter had astonished him.

'Walk me back to bed,' he said, and caressed her chin with a soft and curious expression on his face.

In a driving rainstorm, two weeks later, Shkouro's cavalry swept down upon Kislovodsk and drove the Red detachment from the town. In the rainy bivouac where Shkouro's men were celebrating, Asya and Sergei lay side by side, watching the cigarette smoke curling upwards into the canvas.

'We're done for,' Sergei said.

'What do you mean? We've just taken the town.'

As if he had been thinking about it for a long time, he said, 'They have convictions, and we just have hatreds.'

'How do you know?'

31

'Because we take prisoners. I interrogate them.' He examined the glowing ember of his cigarette. 'And you, my little nurse, what about your convictions?'

'You patronize me.'

'No, I provoke you,' he said, and caressed her shoulder. 'So?'

She thought for a moment, then said: 'I want the old life back. I want the room with the bullseye window, the summer ball. I want to cross the frozen river and reach the other side. I want my father,' she broke off. 'You don't know what I'm talking about. It is hopeless, what I want.'

He passed her his cigarette. 'Hopeless. That makes two of us.'

The next morning, he accompanied her up the long winding road to what had been her father's villa. Shkouro's White guards were rounding up everyone who had served on the local Soviet and marching them off to prison, amid crowds who hissed and spat at them. Cossack guardsmen on horseback were prodding haltered prisoners from the Red militia through the streets. The light of revenge glowed in every eye.

As Sergei swung back the green gates at the end of the driveway, Asya bolted ahead and ran through the fruit trees towards the back of the house. Praskoviya just had time to rub her hands on her apron before being smothered in an embrace.

'My child!' she cried. 'I thought you were dead!'

Uncle Dimitri and Aunt Olga ran towards her from the back door. Sergei stood aside, watching them pat each other's cheeks in disbelief and joy. 'And you should have seen this child! Such a tigress!' Praskoviya wiped her tears away and gesticulated happily. '"Get his medicine! This instant!"'

'Enough, Praskoviya. I don't like to remember it.'

Olga took Asya in her arms. 'Your father . . .'

'They murdered him.'

'Indeed, child, indeed they did,' said Uncle Dimitri. 'There, there.'

Asya sobbed on Olga's shoulder and Sergei pulled on his cigarette.

Over lunch, Aunt Olga told Asya everything.

'In December, they came to the flat in Petrograd and quartered six people with us. Can you imagine? From the factory district. We were reduced to a single room.'

'By then the bank was nationalized. All foreign travel forbidden. I must have tried to bribe every fisherman and steamer captain on the Neva to take us to Riga. No good,' Dimitri said.

'And every night, searches, and by day these ridiculous guards with red armbands in the streets stopping you just because your coat looked better than theirs,' Olga said.

What an unlikely couple they were, and now, Asya thought with a rush of emotion, her only family: big bluff Dimitri, as forthright and practical as a peasant, and the only member of the family in commerce. He had been manager of the Petrograd branch of the Banque de Suez. Tiny Olga was a Siberian merchant's daughter by origin, her hair drawn straight back in braids and her Asiatic eyes tightened in a squint that drew parallel furrows down her forehead. A childless couple, their personalities were so intertwined they finished each other's sentences. 'I bribed a station-master and they let us travel south. Maybe we'll find the White army somewhere. Kislovodsk, I thought. Maybe we can catch up with Asya. Anything is better than waiting to be arrested. In your own house.'

'When did they get here, Praskoviya?'

'Three weeks ago, my child. We all thought you were dead!'

'Sergei saved me,' and Sergei grinned back at Praskoviya's jealous glare.

They spent the day together around the samovar in the bare and chilly parlour. Dimitri shared his last cigarettes with Sergei, Olga listened while Asya told her about her kidnapping. Praskoviya darned Dimitri's socks and clicked her false teeth with pleasure.

After dinner, Dimitri proposed that Sergei sleep in the empty cookhouse and despatched Praskoviya, muttering under her breath, to prepare his bed.

It was midnight before the house was finally quiet, before Asya was certain, from the deep snores from Praskoviya's room and the silence in Dimitri and Olga's, that she could slip away unnoticed. She wore her mother's last flannel nightgown. The night chilled her as she raced across the lawn, her feet stinging with the dew. As

33

soon as she had opened the cookhouse door, she heard a match being struck, and its wavering light guided her to his bed.

She let the nightgown slip to the floor, and then stood before him, so that he could see her, complete, in the golden glow of the kerosene lamp. His eyes mounted her body and their gazes met.

She shivered as he touched her, as she had shivered in the instant of her mother's death, uncontrollably, every fibre of her flesh tensed in self-defence. 'Are you afraid?' he asked, and she whispered – truthfully – that she was not.

'I just can't stop shaking.' The sheets held the heat of his body and she let him warm her gently.

'Your breasts are perfect,' he said drily. When she looked down at them, at the little ellipses with their raspberry nipples awaiting the touch of his hands, she began to laugh. He kissed them, making a ceremony of it, first one, then the other, and she watched him, feeling the echoes of a silent laughter rippling through her, a laughter akin to death, the laughter of abandonment.

She dreamed that night, as she had for months, of her father, this time coming soundlessly towards her in his white summer tunic, and when she awoke a stranger lay beside her with his mouth open, a fleck of saliva on his lip, his hand across her breast. Her cheeks were rasped and raw from the stubble on his chin, she was flooded with warmth, a burning in her own blood that pounded on and on, and she lay by his side and the kerosene lamp guttered and flared over the bare boards of the cookhouse wall.

When dawn lit the window, she moved his arm off her, stood up, slipped on her nightgown and blew out the lamp. Then she tiptoed out of the cookhouse door and sped across the wet grass in the faint light, feeling wetness drip from her as she ran.

At breakfast that morning with Dimitri, Olga and Praskoviya, Sergei sat down opposite her, meeting her glance with a curt nod. She realized, with a sudden sense of vertigo, that she had never deceived her family before. When Dimitri proposed that Sergei stay the following night in the cookhouse, Asya had to put her teacup down so they would not see her hands shaking with excitement.

She came to him every night of that week, when the house had settled into quietness, running across the grass, then feeling her way through the dark corridor to the room at the back, guided by a sliver of light under his door. He watched, amused, as she explored him. She ran her hands through the crisp golden hair on his chest, put her tongue to his nipples, to the drum of his stomach, to his sex. He threw back his head and shut his eyes. She would think wildly – I am doing this, I have this power.

On the fifth night, she sat on the edge of the bed as he lay naked and uncovered, with his arms behind his head, and said, 'I love you.'

He put his finger to her lips.

'You will wake the whole house.'

And then, with a fierceness which she had never known to be her own, she shouted out into the night: 'I love you!'

They were silent, waiting for the night to settle around the echoing tremor of her voice. Rain fingered the tin roof and a branch of the pear tree scraped the window. He lay in the shadows cast by the kerosene lamp and watched her.

'Come here,' he whispered.

She shook her head.

'Come here.'

'Not until you say it.' She crossed her arms.

He was upon her before she could move and they slithered off the bed and onto the floorboards, where suddenly she knew, as he flooded through her, moaning and grinding his teeth, that he had wanted to subdue her, but that it was she who had subdued him.

When she woke, his face was bathed in pale light from the window and she knew that it was morning and that she must hurry. She left him tangled in the sheets on the floorboards and dashed across the wet, icy lawn. At the veranda steps she looked up and saw the lace curtain in Dimitri and Olga's window quiver and fall back into place.

She was asleep in her bed in the house when Olga came in and sat down on the bed. As Asya emerged from her sleep, she was aware how strongly the ammonia smell of him was still upon her.

'Asya, dearest. Sergei is gone.'

'What! Where?'

35

'Mineralni Vodi. Shkouro is pulling out. We are being delivered over to the Reds.'

Olga pleaded with her. 'Don't follow him, dearest, please.'

Nothing they could say would make her stay another minute. She threw her things into a bag and ran off down the dusty white road to the station, Praskoviya pursuing her, pulling at her sleeve. She pushed Praskoviya away.

'No! This is the moment. Now! It has come.'

'What are you talking about, child? You are mad.'

There was no time to explain, there was nothing to be said. She left Praskoviya crumpled and dazed in the road, clutching her handkerchief to her face.

Dimitri ran after her. On the station platform at Kislovodsk, he pleaded with her one last time.

'In the name of your beloved father.'

'No.'

'Asya, you will be killed.'

She stared straight ahead, in a cocoon of conviction that shielded her from the people fighting to climb into the carriages beside her. She gripped the steel-girded lip of the window and would not look at him.

As the train pulled out towards Shkouro's lines and the diminishing figure of Dimitri was lost in the brawling crowd on the platform, she stood at the window and thought, mechanically: I am insane to be doing this: I have no idea where Seryozha might be, and the train is pulling me into the battle zone. But she was certain that the time had come which she had imagined so long before in her mother's Japanese sitting room, the moment when she must hurl herself at her fate.

One of Shkouro's men pulled her roughly into her seat.

'Away from the window, lady. There's going to be shooting.'

A journey that just a year before would have taken an hour now took most of a day, as the train crawled through a blasted landscape littered with dead and bloated animals, shattered and uprooted orchards and roofless villages.

'Mother of God,' one of the young soldiers said as he stared out of the window.

'That's civil war for you, boy,' said an older one, giving his cigarette paper a long, thoughtful lick.

When the train reached Mineralni Vodi station at sunset, gunfire shook the windows and everyone poured out onto the platform to take cover. Asya threw out her suitcase, jumped and fell hard on the platform, picked herself up and ran towards the buffet.

'Red armoured train up the line! Shelling the station!' someone yelled in her ear, and she dived to the floor and ended up under a table, still covered with a white cloth. Its knives and forks rattled under the bombardment. A young boy huddled beside her and grinned and winked after every explosion. Plaster dust rained down on them, and a shower of glass cascaded across the floor. In the long stillness that followed the last impact she felt a strange exaltation. At last real life – where everything might be risked – was finally beginning.

She got up, shook the glass out of her nurse's shawl and went out onto the platform. A White artillery train was slowly pulling out, gushing steam, and she walked along beside it until she was abreast of the engine. There, on the footplate, his face red with the glow from the open hearth of the boiler, stood Sergei, a revolver in his hand. She shouted, but her voice was drowned in a gush of steam and the grinding of the wheels. The locomotive bearing him away gathered speed, and she ran along the platform, pushing people aside, shouting his name, until the last red lamp on the last wagon had faded from sight.

Not knowing where she was going, she wandered wherever the frightened crowds took her, until at dusk she found herself in the vestibule of the town dispensary. 'I've come to help,' she said, and put down her suitcase.

They looked oddly at her and made her sit down. One of the nurses began pulling glass from Asya's hair and blotted a cut above her eye with tincture of iodine.

That night, lying on a cot on the dispensary floor, with the artillery barrage creeping closer and closer, and the cold floor shaking underfoot and the kerosene lamp trembling against its wallbracket, all she could do was to keep whispering, 'Oh my love, keep me from harm.'

Next day, when she went to the station to return to Kislovodsk, the crowds were so thick she couldn't even get into the station forecourt. The stationmaster climbed on a baggage wagon and shouted through a megaphone that the line to Kislovodsk was cut and the only way of escaping the Red advance was east to Ekaterinadar and Novorrossisk on the Black Sea coast.

She clawed her way onto a train that was heading east. She travelled for two days, exchanging her hat and gloves for food, sharing the corridors with crowds of frightened soldiers, too tired to harrass her. At every stop she jumped out of her carriage and searched the platforms, asking if anyone had heard where Shkouro's men were headed. She went from carriage to carriage through whole trainloads of White soldiers, asking a thousand dusty faces, over and over, 'Sergei Gourevitch, Second Artillery lieutenant in Shkouro's irregulars. Have you seen him?'

Everywhere she encountered the same nods, the same shrugs, the same looks of pity or derision.

In the White army headquarters of General Denikin's Southern Command in Ekaterinadar, the adjutant drew up a chair for her, pulled out a piece of expensive yellow vellum and poised his pen to take down her request. But he did not write anything. It was all too absurd.

'He is your husband?'

'My fiancé.'

'Last seen at Mineralni Vodi a week ago? With Shkouro's artillery train?'

She nodded.

'Princesse Galitzine, with the greatest respect . . .'

'So it is hopeless. You won't be able to find him?'

'Quite hopeless.' He leaned forward and whispered, 'Go to Novorossisk, any port on the Black Sea. Get on any boat you can. Get out of here. It's over. Forget him.'

The mocking voices of all these doubters pursued her as she took the train filled with stinking, exhausted soldiers from Ekaterinadar to Novorossisk. While everyone else slept, she pressed her face to the windowpane and realized that on their last night together she had not even kissed Sergei goodbye. She could not rid her mind of the image of him lying on the floorboards of the cookhouse, in a tangle of sheets, his chest bare, his skin warm with sleep, his mouth open, his eyes sealed beneath the curve of his lids.

When she reached the Black Sea coast, she took lodgings in a boarding house while waiting for a ship. Her deliverance came in the shape of the *Orient Star*, bound for Constantinople and Toulon. She boarded it late in the afternoon of the 17th of March 1919, having pawned her very last piece of family jewellery to pay for her passage.

The *Orient Star* had been used as a British troopship, and soldiers had carved their initials along the teak railings. 'A disgrace,' said Countess Rodischev, touching the railings with a disdainful fingernail.

'But it was a troopship at Gallipoli. What do you expect?' Asya said, suddenly furious that this old bat, with her lorgnette, could complain about the state of the ship that had come to her rescue.

'Oh,' said Countess Rodischev, moving off, in some dream world of her own, as if a million miles from the scene unfolding before them.

Sikh sepoys in dusty red turbans – muleteers with the evacuating British Expeditionary Force that had come to assist the Whites – were whacking their mules up the gangplank directly below her. The braying of these terrified beasts, teetering above the dark sliver of water between the flank of the ship and the dock, rose up to Asya now, and she watched their mangy backs filing past beneath her and disappearing into the hold. Beyond them on the quay she could see the queue at the passengers' gangway, the British officers in white, the Tommies with fixed bayonets, the line pushing, shoving, hands waving passports, money, jewellery, anything to bribe the officers. The officers were shouting in English, 'Back! Back! Only ticketed passengers! Only ticketed passengers!' The Tommies were pushing against the weight of the crowd with the butts of their rifles, and from the mass there rose the unspeakable wailing of children and the wheedling, fear-gripped voices of the adults. In the distance, up above the wide encircling bay ringed with villas, up above the grey, chaotic port, the White army was fighting to hold its own. The Red army had made ten kilometres that night. The exodus was turning into a rout. That morning, on her way to the boat, Asya had seen a platoon of men, their shoulderpatches ripped off, a bottle passing from throat to throat, surging around an officer on top of a bale at the quayside. His revolver was drawn. They were shouting, 'And what about us, your honour?' His gun was trained upon them, and there was no doubt about it, he was prepared to shoot.

Now the ship was only minutes away from departure. Sentries were already posted beside the sailors waiting to cast off the moorings. At every distant thump of the artillery batteries on the edge of town the crowd shuddered and pressed towards the gangway. Asya knew that her presence in safety far above the scene, dressed in white, was a torture to every soul below her, but she could not move. Her only thought was whether Praskoviya, Olga and Dimitri or Sergei would pick up the paperchase of messages she had left in every station buffet, in every army mess, in every boarding house along her route to the coast.

A man in Guards officer's uniform scampered up the gangway, carrying only a battered leather briefcase. When he reached the deck he took a cigar, lit it, and paced up and down, smoking lustily, occasionally glancing at the quayside scene as if it had been arranged as a spectacle for his enjoyment. She recognized him from the mineral-water baths in Kislovodsk. She could also recognize some Moscow neighbours, the four little Counts Trubetskoy, who marched up the gangplank in Eton collars and plus-fours with their English nanny chivvying them along, 'Do hurry up! Do hurry up!' as if they were not fleeing for their lives, but merely late for their lessons. She could see their father, the invalid Count Trubetskoy, biting the edges of his moustache while the sailors carried him up the gangplank.

She also saw Madame Apraxina, a professor's wife from Moscow, herding her three children up the teetering gangplank, her eyes fixed in mad determination on the deck. Her husband was calling: she did not once look back.

That night, when they were far away, and the Russian shore was no more than a smudge on the horizon, Asya found Madame Apraxina staring out at the *Orient Star*'s receding wake, a kerchief in her hand. Not the departure itself, not the widening stain of water between her and her native land, but the sight of utter desolation on Madame Apraxina's face finally broke the trance that had come over Asya since she had boarded the steamer alone that afternoon. It was as if, gazing out astern, Asya could suddenly see the cool white crypt where her mother lay in the church among the birches at Marino, as if she could see the cross on her father's grave, fresh among the jumbled stones of the municipal cemetery, as if she could see, distinct and ineffaceable, each one of her losses: Praskoviya, Olga and Dimitri, Isvolsky and his little boy. When she tried to think of Sergei, nothing at all came into her mind. She could only review the bleak facts: that she had not seen him for four months, that the pear tree grazed the window by their bed when they made love for the last time, and that she had been a fool to suppose she would ever see him again. Asya and Madame Apraxina stood on deck until the last crepuscular trace of the Russian shore had vanished. Then Madame Apraxina turned and said, 'But you will get a chill. And in your condition . . .' Until that moment, when the night wind flattened the long white dress against her body, no one had noticed that Asya was pregnant.

PART TWO

SOON AFTER THEIR arrival in France in 1919, Dimitri and Olga Ourousoff had rented a Provençal *mas*, with shiny dark-green shutters and seven dark red-tiled rooms, situated at the end of a cane-bordered track a dozen miles from the town of Saint Rémy de Provence. Inside, oil lamps burned beneath the icons, there were St Petersburg winter scenes on the walls, and a samovar steamed all day on the kitchen table. Olga lived there the year round, translating bank documents to make ends meet, while Dimitri laboured in the Paris headquarters of the Banque de Suez. Once a month he rejoined Olga, and often he took Asya with him.

Asya was brushing her hair at the window of the upstairs bedroom while two friends of hers, Botynsky and Razumkin, looked for her son in the courtyard. Niki had climbed into the mulberry tree in the centre of the courtyard and was concealed in the green canopy of leaves, while Razumkin and Botynsky wandered about, just beneath him, calling his name.

'Wretched boy. You are spoilt. And I don't care if you hear me say so,' Razumkin muttered and glared up at Asya, who looked down at him with sovereign amusement.

'I'm not going to waste the whole day,' he said, and tramped off into the kitchen. He returned with a hamper in one hand and two bottles of wine in the other, and put them in the boot of the rusty Renault that served the Ourousoffs for a car. Then he edged his plump body into the front seat and sat down with a sigh. The top of the car was down, and from Asya's vantage point at the windowsill she could see the oily coil of hair covering his bald spot.

Olga Ourousoff peered out of the gate of the courtyard in case Niki had hidden in the cane thickets, while Dimitri sat in a chair propped against the kitchen wall, sipping his coffee and reading *Le Provençal* for Saturday June 14, 1924. Beside him, with his long bare feet stretched out in a spear of sunlight, sat Lapin, over from Oxford. Side by side, they read the newspaper. Doumergue had fallen. Herriot was trying to form a government.

'No Russian news anywhere in this wretched paper,' Dimitri muttered. 'There could be famine and starvation . . .'

'Probably,' Lapin agreed.

'And exterminations.'

'Indeed.'

'And for all the French care it could be happening on another planet.'

Vladimir Isaacovitch Botynsky, a spider-thin gentleman in plus-fours with driving goggles perched on his forehead, circled beneath the mulberry tree, scratching his ear.

'Niki, don't be ridiculous. Where are you?'

Asya leaned out of the window and shouted, 'Jump!' And jump he did, right onto Botynsky's back. Botynsky let out a yelp, lurched around the courtyard with the boy clinging to him and collapsed backwards into the hammock.

'A direct hit! Bravo!' Asya clapped her hands and skipped downstairs, fastening her hair in a scarf.

'Lapin, Botynsky, Niki, come on!' she cried, and they disentangled themselves from the hammock and jumped into the car. The vehicle lurched out of the driveway, Botynsky hunched over the wheel with a deranged look of concentration in his eyes.

'Do you know how to drive this thing, Vladimir Isaacovitch?' Razumkin shouted.

'I am familiar with the theory of it,' said Botynsky, and he shifted gears, popped the clutch, and they were whiplashed forward. At each crossroad, Asya shouted directions into Botynsky's ear while bicyclists shook their fists in their wake.

'Like a racer, no?' Botynsky shouted gaily, tapping his leather helmet, his scarf flying back behind him.

'You are a menace!' she shouted. 'Come on, have you ever driven before?'

'Details, mere details!' Botynsky shouted back.

Botynsky was so tall and thin, and his arms hung so loosely about him, that when he sat in a chair, his knees tucked up under his chin, Asya said he looked like a praying mantis. Botynsky edited an émigré journal, *The Russian Voice*, and when Niki rummaged in his pockets he always found stubby bits of pencil, paperclips and gummy bottles of glue for sticking proof sheets together.

She knew he was entirely unsuitable: penniless, vague, frantically energetic, a typical Russian madcap. But he was also comfortingly persistent. He would climb the six flights of stairs to the small apartment where she and Niki lived on the Square des Batignolles, bringing her piroshkis still hot from the Russian bakery on the rue de Moscou, and saying: 'You must eat them this minute,' feeding them into her mouth and licking the pastry off his fingers. Very soon, he was a fixture in her life. When she returned from her shift at the clinic he was often waiting at the corner to escort her past the drunks in the square.

She broke his heart, but she couldn't help herself. He positively volunteered for punishment. She began leaving him with Niki while she slithered into her one decent black dress and skipped down the stairs to dine – with Razumkin one night, some former patient the next, some old relative the one after that, even Colonel Galitzine, her distant cousin, who had the disheartening habit of taking her hand between the brandy snifters and proposing marriage. He did this twice. She always said the same thing: 'I am not in love, and I know what love is, so thank you very much.'

Yes, she had once known what it was to be in love. By the light of the kerosene lamp in the cookhouse, she had been mad with love. She had relived every moment, walking up and down the deck of the *Orient Star* as it steamed through the Black Sea, struggling to hold in her mind the exact colour of his eyes – grey-green – the precise tone of his last words to her – 'Come here.'

During her first months in Paris, she had been like a nun wearing out the stones of her cloister, repeating over and over, 'I must stay true. He will return.' And then a man took her to dinner, and another man gave her flowers, and her son was born, and little by little, it seemed pointless to remain true to a phantom.

In time it was less a source of anguish and more a source of pride that with the young artillery officer she had known one week of perfection, and that from that week she had borne a son. Nothing like it would ever happen again.

'I've left perfection behind,' she said to Botynsky in a musing voice. 'And that is why I am happy.'

She sought out men who were avid only for the next moment, not for the marital everafter. There was that flaxen-haired banker from Berlin who brought her interesting editions from the émigré presses there, and who took her away for a weekend in a gold and blue bedroom in the Hotel Carlton at Vichy. They danced at night in the tree-circled ballroom outside, her fingers touching the wedding ring that he had had the good taste not to remove for the occasion. They had parted on the platform of the Gare de Lyon with the fraternal wave of partners in crime, knowing they would never see each other again. She returned home on the Metro, and came up the narrow, dark stairs on the Square des Batignolles, humming to herself. Waiting for her on the top step was Botynsky.

'I know I behave badly to you,' she said to him. 'But let us review the situation. I am twenty-two years of age, orphaned, exiled, penniless and unmarried. I have earned the right to be happy.'

Botynsky looked at his hands and said, 'You treat me like a eunuch.'

She opened her grey eyes wide.

'What an expression.' And then she said softly, 'You are free to go.'

'I know,' Botynsky said miserably.

Then there came the evening with Count Engalicheff. Botynsky was waiting up for her when she came up the stairs. She was so past caring what Botynsky might think that she hiked up her skirt, unfastened her stockings, rolled them down and sat dumbly in the kitchen, massaging her feet, while he looked away in embarrassment.

'What happened?'

'We went to the race meeting, he showed me his stable, we had dinner at the Closerie des Lilas.' She looked so weary Botynsky wanted to take her in his arms.

'Why do I tell you these things? Our relationship is unnatural.'

'Go on.'

'In the taxi he was familiar. I'm not exactly reserved, but I don't like being kissed unless I want to be kissed. Do you understand?'

Botynsky gave a commiserating sigh.

'So I tapped the glass and the cabbie stopped. In the middle of the Bois de Boulogne. Total darkness. I got out.'

Botynsky sighed again.

'And do you know what the wretched man said to me? "Women who say yes are remembered forever. Women who say no,"' and here she snapped her finger, '"are forgotten forever."'

'I don't believe it.'

'The very words. And he drives off, leaving me on the pavement. Can you imagine? I have spent an hour on the Metro. In my best dress.'

'It is people like him who made the Revolution necessary,' he said, and she began to laugh.

'You're angry. How touching.'

'He's completely wrong. Men are much more likely to remember women who say *no* than those who say *yes*. I should know.'

She kissed his forehead, went into her bedroom, closed the door and fell asleep fully clothed. When she awoke, she saw that before departing Botynsky had removed her dress and had lain her between the sheets.

Three weeks later, she left Niki behind with the Ourousoffs and led Botynsky to a stifling hotel bedroom in Aigues Mortes with stained paper on the walls. Lying beside him, she suddenly lost her nerve. She thought to herself: If only I were nineteen again. If only my body had no memory. If only I were just beginning.

'Take off your glasses, Botynsky,' she said to him. And Botynsky removed his glasses. Now he was naked, a stranger to her, with circles under his eyes where his pebble glasses hid his skin from the sun.

He gazed at her, awaiting her continued permission as his hands caressed her body. As she let him, she discovered that they were all wrong: Dimitri, Razumkin, all those who said Botynsky was just a joke. He knew what he was doing. He took her face in his hands, and she let herself go to him, naked, beaded in perspiration, tossing to and fro on the pillow. In a minute, her body had shed all its encumbrance of memory and was lost in the present.

When she woke, the room was cool and dark and he was still watching her. She had never seen so naked a look, so trusting a gaze in a man. One word from you, Botynsky, she thought, and I will be yours. But then he said, 'I can't see you without my glasses,' and before he could be stopped, he had pushed them over his ears, and those naked white circles were covered with the portholes of his wire rims. He smiled as if to say: There, now you see me as I am. Yet in reality he had just retreated behind his most effective disguise.

'Mami! Look, the beach!' Niki's voice shook her from her dreaming.

They were at La Tour des Sphinguettes already. The little black car was bumping along the breakwater leading to the lighthouse, the speargrass atop the dunes flailing to and fro in the wind. Botynsky drew up at the breakwater and they all piled out. The wind was blowing hard, and the sand hissed down the sloping shelf, biting at their ankles, making Niki yelp as he, Lapin and Botynsky ran ahead down the dunes. Asya walked behind, arm in arm with Razumkin.

It amused her to have both Razumkin and Botynsky together on this holiday: it was equal torture to them both. Both despised their roles as her humble servants. They openly grumbled about the way she had them wrapped around her little finger. But when she had proposed a week at the Ourousoffs, they helplessly agreed. 'We are her slaves,' Razumkin said, 'because each of us is ugly. She is beautiful, and we are bewitched. The whole thing is pitiful.'

She broke loose from Razumkin's arm and scampered down the sand dunes, a flurry of petticoats and a light print skirt, her curly black hair in a bright red scarf, her bare feet hardly seeming to touch the sand as she ran. The wind seemed to lift her and carry her scudding along the beach, free and far away. She crept up behind Botynsky and clapped her hands over his eyes, and when he lurched around she wrapped her arms around him and kissed him.

Razumkin turned and gazed furiously out to sea. To think he

had brought them together! The whole nauseating scene came back to him. His own flat in Neuilly: Botynsky in full cry, discoursing on Nekrasov and Belinsky and God knows who else, downing glass after glass of Razumkin's best Georgian reserve, while Asya watched him with the catlike concentration women always devote to their prey. What did she see in this absurd creature with his high collars, his suits two sizes too small, their pockets bulging with books and paste bottles and proofs, and those fishlike eyes behind his glasses? A penniless dreamer, when he, Razumkin, wore the best cream linen, had a beautiful flat with a view of the Bois de Boulogne, spoke as many languages as Botynsky and loved her just as dearly. No comparison, and yet he knew, with wretched certainty, that Botynsky had found his way to her bed.

Razumkin cursed the sand seeping into his heavy black shoes, and the weight of the picnic basket, and the wind which lifted his hat and sent it bowling along the beach. He followed her, his great black shoes obliterating her delicate footprints.

'You pity me, that is why you have me around,' he had once said to her.

'Don't be ridiculous,' she had replied. 'I have you around because you are loyal.'

When she had come to his doctor's office for the first time, she sat on the edge of the examination table, demurely covering herself, like the Meissen figurine of the shepherdess on his mother's mantelpiece in Neuilly, small, delicate, white as porcelain, her nipples tiny and erect, the rectangular lozenges of her kneecaps stretching the skin, her tiny feet, with their high arches, just touching.

As she lay back on the couch and let him palpate the tightly stretched dome of her stomach, he asked her: 'Is your husband pleased?' She was, after all, no more than nineteen.

'I have no husband.'

'I'm sorry.'

She sat up and smiled, covering herself with the sheet.

And then her story tumbled out. How she had buried her parents, how she had left Praskoviya Ivanovna behind in a dusty street in Kislovodsk, how she had searched in vain for the father of her child, though, she added with disarming candour, she had known him for only thirty-one days and had slept with him exactly five times.

'You are fortunate to be so fertile,' he said, and she smiled and looked down at the splendour and fullness of her body. For anyone else her age, pregnancy would have been a disaster. For this friendless, exiled girl, giving birth to a fatherless child seemed to be a cause of blind, if radiant, excitement. She did not seem helpless in exile. She was like a kitten, too young to know fear, tossed from a window and landing on its feet in the Paris streets. Then and there, Razumkin felt himself being dragged down by the sickening undertow of love.

When she told him she had trained at the Anglo-Russian hospital, he said he might be able to find her a place at the Maison Velpeau, a private clinic run by his friend Antonov.

'Chock-a-block with indigent Russians. Just the place for you,' he said. When she asked him whether he had trained in the Petersburg or Moscow faculties, he pointed to his diplomas on the wall, from the École de Médecine in Paris, class of 1917. She squinted up at them in a shortsighted way he found adorable. Feeling ridiculous, he blurted out that he had been born in Paris and that he lived with his mother in a flat in Neuilly. Half of his class in surgery had been killed or wounded between the Somme and Verdun. He had been turned down for service: too fat, too asthmatic. He looked down at his stomach as if to say: You see, and she had laughed and begun to put on her clothes.

Antonov took her on immediately and she worked every morning until her ninth month. She walked the old counts and countesses up and down the long corridors and listened to the ceaseless tide of their bitterness and grief. Exile. Dispossession. Frankly, she was sick of hearing about it. 'It is not their ailments that kill them. It is their nostalgia,' she said to Razumkin.

'Why doesn't it kill you?'

'Because I am going to have a child,' she said.

The birth was difficult. He did not enjoy seeing her under the anaesthetic: stripped of the apparent invulnerability of youth, slack-jawed, babbling and drained of colour. When they had cleaned up the little thing and lain it in her arms, Asya burst into tears. She kept crying and saying he was exactly like Seryozha, which Razumkin knew was quite absurd, as the thing looked the way newborns always did: crumpled, wet and purple.

'Yes, dearest,' Olga said. 'Look at the colour of his hair.' Apparently the child did have his father's auburn hair.

'Now I need my Praskoviya,' Asya said, looking down helplessly at the creature Razumkin placed in her arms.

Olga moved into the Square des Batignolles for the first months to help Asya learn motherhood, and afterwards, until Botynsky had shown up, there was a succession of nursemaids whose wages consumed Asya's meagre earnings from the clinic. Razumkin offered to help, but she refused.

One night, several years later, Asya had called him, begging him to come as quickly as he could. Clad only in his dressing gown and slippers, he flagged down a taxi and raced across Paris. He was shocked to see how she lived, so mean, so poor, so uncomplaining, the boy beside her in her own bed, white, feverish and frightened. She was not one to make a fuss for nothing, and this was serious, meningitis. Razumkin rushed them both to the American hospital, where he spent a week with a happy, tight feeling in his chest knowing that she needed him. When the little boy finally toddled unaided out of the front door, she turned in the hospital lobby, and in front of two of his colleagues kissed him fervently on the lips. It had been then that he had finally dared to ask her out, dared to pay some of her expenses.

He took her to dinner at Chez Georges on the rue Mazarine because he thought she would enjoy the way the sweating old Ukrainian cook leaned out through the hatch for a smoke and proffered a greasy hand to his clients. Asya seemed just as much at ease in the bohemian smoke of Chez Georges as she was at the grand annual ball of the Russian Red Cross Society. He, Razumkin, never felt at ease anywhere. At the Red Cross ball, highlight of the émigré calendar, he trailed behind her, sweating in his frock coat, bowing uneasily when she introduced him grandly as 'my doctor'. Then, the very next day, she would say, 'I hate all those people, don't you?' and command him to take them to the swimming pool at the Molitor. She seemed to specialize in scenes that embarrassed him. She knew full well that he would never expose his great stomach and veined legs to the insufferable demigods lounging around the pool. So he sat up in the spectators' gallery, unhappily watching her emerge from the women's changing rooms in her black woollen bathing costume, so tight against those adorable breasts. She would leap in feet first, to the surprise of the fashionable ladies at the poolside who kept their hair dry. She surfaced and swam to and fro with crisp, mannish strokes, while her child toddled up and down on the lip of the pool keeping pace with her. Razumkin would sit above her in the balcony, watching the muscles churning between her shoulder-blades and the water curving against her open mouth as she turned for air, and feel a nauseated longing to be some other person than Ilya Ilyonovitch Razumkin.

And now, as he settled himself in the sand of La Tour des Sphinguettes and buried the white wine within reach of a tidal eddy to keep it cool, he realized that he had become ridiculous, the impotent and disappointed 'admirer', the 'family friend'. He looked up: she was still running up the beach, her summer dress blowing against her legs.

She obviously thought, he mused bitterly, that he was sexless. She would have been more than surprised to see what he became at Madame Dany's on a Friday night. There he was received with honour, there he was a king. In the upstairs bedrooms, reclining beside the full-length mirrors with Regine, he could even look at himself, at his great heap of flesh, and feel tremors of pleasure at the sight. Regine did not mock him, she did not regard him with Asya's irony. Regine, bless her, did not know what irony was. She did what she was told. A good girl.

Then, when Regine dressed him again, buttoned him up, straightened his hat and sent him out into the street, Razumkin felt the greatest pleasure of all: to saunter down the rue de Rennes through the crowds coming out of the Montparnasse cinemas, savouring the enjoyment of a double life.

Nothing was such a good protection against the indifference and sarcasm of other people as a double life. When he thought about it, that was why he had begun the after-hours business. Very lucrative, but very illegal. Worth your licence if you were caught, a possible prosecution for manslaughter and a heady slide into public disgrace. But that was the attraction of it all. At first it was that girl from Madame Dany's. He couldn't even remember her name. And then the word began to spread, and he found he could pick and choose, and they paid cash, ridiculous sums, to be rid of their mistakes. It was gruesome work, but he learned to discard the sentimental side of himself. He liked the money, but it was not just the money, not just the need – the frightened people at his mercy, begging him to save their marriages, their reputations, their health. No, what he discovered with real surprise was that he loved having a secret. No one but his clients and his assistant knew. Until five p.m. he was a respected professional with a shiny brass plate above the buzzer, a good address in Neuilly. After five p.m. there would be a furtive knock, and another life would begin. He found it irresistible to have a secret – because he was ugly, because no woman would love him, because Asya thought he was above reproach.

He squinted into the sun, and there she was, far away up the beach, her dress tucked into her stockings, wading in the waves up to her calves, her hands in her pockets, doubtless singing to herself as she always did when she was happy.

Closer, half-lost in the glare of the light off the waves, Lapin and Botynsky were building a sandcastle around Niki who sat in the centre, cross-legged, like a household Buddha.

Razumkin busied himself building a windbreak with the umbrella and Asya's beach towels. He nestled behind it and cut himself a slice of sausage with his penknife. Asya came up beside him, dropped down on her knees and began untying the laces on his big black brogues.

'Whoever heard of wearing shoes on the beach! You look perfectly ridiculous!'

He let her roll his linen trousers up to his calves and tottered gamely after her when she went to inspect the sandcastle. He cupped his hands around her match as she lit a cigarette and knelt beside the castle, inspecting the shells that Niki had laid on the inside, the water lapping at her feet, wetting the hem of her dress.

'Tide's coming in,' she said.

When Botynsky poked his glasses up the rim of his nose and observed the turrets sliding into the waves, she burst out laughing.

'Disaster! How delicious,' she said.

Niki said, 'Let's swim!' and Asya lifted him to his feet. She looked around her. Lapin, Botynsky and Razumkin all shook their heads.

'What miserable specimens! Not even you, Lapin?'

'Not even me.'

There was not a figure in sight, just their car on top of the breakwater, and the long sweep of the waves disappearing into the white glare. She lifted her dress over her head, stepped out of her underwear and, clapping her hands, ran with her son into the waves. The three men – Lapin, Razumkin and Botynsky – sat by the castle with their trouser legs rolled up, sharing a cigarette, watching Niki leaping and shrieking and the waves slapping and splashing Asya's naked body.

'You are *such* cowards!' she cried, as the waves burst against her back and Niki scampered about her.

When they came running out, Botynsky had her towelled beach robe ready and Razumkin handed her a glass of white wine. Her nipples were puckered and her skin was scoured pink from the beating of the sea. Curls of her wet black hair adhered to the nape of her neck and runnels of water slithered between her shoulder-blades. Razumkin was seized by the keenest desire to lick her all over.

She opened up her robe and Niki crept in, while Botynsky and Lapin rubbed them both down, getting down on their knees to reach their calves and ankles. Then Asya and Niki waddled together inside her robe back to the shelter of the lean-to, where they flopped down and Razumkin served them lunch from the hamper.

Niki's head lay in her lap and he quickly fell asleep. She looked down at him, and as she gently stroked his ears the men saw the smile fade from her face. She was thinking: My love has lost its map. Sergei's image was now as hazy to her as the curve of the beach in the flat glare of the sun, and her boy had become a shadow exiled from the source of its shape.

They were all silent, listening to the sand driving up against the windbreak. They sipped their wine, watching each other's faces in the vivid beach light, watching the boy sinking down into the fathomless depths of sleep. She looked out to sea and pulled her robe about her, and said she had not gone swimming naked since before the war.

'Where?' Botynsky asked, taking a sip of wine.

'With Lapin and Father. From the boathouse. At Marino. Remember, Lapin?'

'Of course,' Lapin said. 'Who ever forgets such things?'

It was the first time in Razumkin or Botynsky's company that she had been even briefly overtaken by reverie. She was immune to the émigré's disease. Indeed, hers was the opposite syndrome: often Razumkin could see, just beneath her breathless energy, her gaiety and good humour, the strain of her headlong flight into the future.

'It's over. Well and truly over,' she said, looking tenderly at Lapin.

Lapin nodded. '*È finita la commedia.*'

'Oh, Lapin, why do we live apart? Why you in London, and me in Paris? Why this ridiculous Oxford? There are so few of us left. We must stick together.'

'This ridiculous Oxford? The best time of my life, Asenka, and in two months I start with Barclays. I'm dug in. Too late, I'm afraid.'

'Too late? I hate the thought of you becoming an Englishman. I hate it.'

'But I'm not! Never!' But by then she had gone for him, tickling him under his ribs where she knew he was helpless, rolling him over onto the sand while he pleaded for mercy and Botynsky and Razumkin looked on, eating their sandwiches.

They went for a walk along the curving beach, in single file, bending and picking up shells which they passed along to each other and dropped into Niki's bucket. The light turned purplish grey, the wind began to blow cold off the sea, and they headed back to the car, Asya leading the way, Lapin carrying Niki piggyback, Botynsky carrying the hamper, Razumkin bringing up the rear, the laces of his black shoes knotted around his neck.

When they were back in the car, and had put up the black canvas top, Asya gazed into the rearview mirror and put on her lipstick.

'That was the happiest day since . . .'

'Since Russia,' Lapin said.

She stared back at the sea. 'Yes.'

They drove Lapin back to the Ourousoffs to finish his holiday in Olga's care, and Dimitri drove them all to Avignon station to catch the midnight train. Asya ladled the little boy into the lower berth, vaulted into the upper one and blew a kiss to Dimitri on the platform. Then she leaned over and kissed Botynsky and Razumkin.

'Goodnight, my suitors, goodnight!'

When the train was at full speed and Botynsky could tell from Razumkin's snoring that he was sound asleep, he reached over and took Asya's hand, but she too was asleep, and so he lay alone, looking at her face in the nightlight's glow. His thoughts drifted from her to train journeys of his vanished boyhood, from Kiev to Vienna, to Trieste, how after going to sleep in the filmy white of the Austrian Alps he would wake and see at last from his window the bright blue of the Adriatic lapping at the track's edge. He lay there, weighing the composition of his sadness, wondering how much was exile and how much was knowing that the woman whispering in her sleep across from him would never love him as he loved her.

Promptly at seven on Sunday morning the Paris–Lyon–Méditerranée pulled into the Gare de Lyon. They stepped down onto the platform, Asya leading the way, Botynsky and Niki hand in hand, and Razumkin bringing up the rear, walking grandly beside the porter he had engaged to carry the cases. The papersellers were just rolling up the blinds of their kiosks, and in the cafés opposite the station the chairs were still piled high on the tables. It was Asya's favourite time in the city, when everything was quiet and deserted, when the ice-trucks were making their rounds and the gutters gurgled with water. The taxi took them past the booksellers setting out their wares on the quais in the gauzy light reflected off the river, then up the avenue Marceau, around the Arc de Triomphe, along the avenue Wagram, to boulevard Pereire, skirting the high wall of the goods yard and then stopping in the squalid square.

'I can never understand why you live here,' Razumkin said as they stepped out onto the pavement. Even on a Sunday morning the goods trains were shunting in the yards and grit-laden black smoke was rising from their funnels.

'Since you insist on being grand this morning, and making fun of the Square des Batignolles, Ilya Ilyonovitch, you can pay for our breakfast as well as the taxi.'

Razumkin produced a large banknote, which Asya handed over to Botynsky with instructions to run down with Niki to the rue de Moscou for blini, serniki, sour cream and black bread.

'And vodka,' Razumkin added, loading himself up with their suitcases.

He didn't care what she thought, the place was beneath her. Railwaymen between shifts lounging about in the garden, smoking and telling dirty stories, this dark, winding stairwell, with beggarly Russians behind every door, cabbage cooking on every stove and frightful characters in their underwear lined up in the morning for the toilet at the end of the hall. She had to be rescued from here.

'I am not in need of rescue, Ilya Ilyonovitch,' she said, climbing the stairs ahead of him. 'I am within walking distance of the church, the bakery and the Tivoli baths. Niki and I walk in the parc Monceau when we are feeling rich, and when we are feeling poor we play in the cemetery.'

'More of your bravado, my dearest,' he said, pausing at the top of the stairs, out of breath, while she fished around in her bag for the keys.

Over her shoulder she said, 'The trouble with you, Ilya Ilyonovitch, is that you have never lost anything in your life. You are needlessly attached to *things*.'

When she dined in his flat she ran her fingers over the knickknacks, the little figurines, the bibelots, the antimacassars on the backs of the chairs, and teased him that he had the tastes of an old lady.

'I am willing to help you, that's all, and you, with your insane pride, are always refusing.'

She swung the door open, gestured him in and said, closing the door behind her, 'I'm happy for you to buy me my train ticket, pay for my taxis and even buy us breakfast, but I'm not about to become a kept woman.'

'Whoever suggested such a thing?'

She lit a cigarette, eyed him with amusement, and then went into the kitchen to light the kettle for tea.

Razumkin settled down in a kitchen chair and watched her briskly wiping down the linoleum on the kitchen table, pulling down her tea-tin and setting out her cracked cups. From where he sat he could see into every room in the apartment: the bathroom with her stockings and a pair of Niki's underclothes hanging up to dry over the bath, the double bed where she and the child slept, a heap of bedcovers visible through the open door, and the salon with its dismal view onto the shunting yards. She bustled by him, plumping up the pillows on the sofa, pulling out two chairs in preparation for breakfast. There were a few Russian books on the tables, several snapshots of Niki, gawky and thin, shielding his eyes from the sun, and one picture, Razumkin noticed crossly, of Botynsky, in a phoney pose of wisdom and maturity, with his hand on an issue of *The Russian Voice* and a trail of smoke rising from his cigarette. No ancestral pictures, no silver, none of the antique odds and ends that gave émigré apartments their particular atmosphere of claustrophobia and closure.

No photograph of the mysterious Sergei. For all Razumkin knew, he might as well be a figment of Asya's imagination.

'What do I need a photograph for?' she replied when he asked her, and as always he was left to wonder whether this was more of her bravado.

Bravado or not, she did seem immune to émigré sorrow. Razumkin had seen his share of that, climbing the stairs of tenements like this to put his stethoscope to the rachitic lungs of some hermit wasting away in the magpie nests of exile, amid piles of old newspapers, half-eaten meals, dust-laden books and a few yellowed spoons. How he hated the Russian milieu! When he made his annual visit to the rue d'Aru for the Easter service he always recoiled from the embraces, the gossip, the feeling that everyone was preserved in an aspic of genteel decrepitude. He knew what it was that he couldn't stand about Russian exiles: it was their failure. He wanted to keep himself as far away from failure as possible.

'There!' Asya exclaimed, and patted down the bright red tablecloth under the pot of flowering geraniums that she had brought in from the rusted wrought-iron balcony overlooking the square. Yes, she was astonishing. The depressing salon had been made to look almost cheerful. Perhaps she *was* happy here. But he thought, as he watched her eyes glancing happily around a room which felt like a prison to him, that he never quite knew what was bluff, what was true about her. His love for Asya, he realized, was tinged with pity for the sheer energy that went into her self-delusion.

They were alone in the salon. She went over to the window and looked down into the street to see if she could spy Niki and Botynsky running back from the bakery. Razumkin knew what would happen were he to seize this moment, come up behind her, run his hands through her hair and kiss her windburned neck. It had happened before.

She would not stop him. She would let herself be kissed. He could still remember the faint fragrance of her neck and cheek. But afterwards, when she pulled away, there was an absolutely insupportable look of amusement on her face. He reddened to think of it.

'Are you sulking, Ilya?' she asked, turning around.

'It's nothing, dearest,' and he forced his face into a bright beam of a smile. What point was there in candour, in letting her know the portion of hatred that was mixed in with his love?

Then Botynsky and Niki clattered up the stairs, laden with breakfast, both of them shouting, 'Quick! They're hot!' Asya expertly emptied the hot piroshkis onto plates and bore them to the low table. As they gobbled them down, the men toasted everything in sight.

'To France!'

'To Asya!'

'To Niki!'

'To vodka!'

After draining his glass, Botynsky stared gloomily into the bottom of it, as if puzzled to find it empty again. Razumkin simply glowed redder and redder, like a corpulent Slavic Buddha.

'Are they drunk?' Niki wanted to know.

'They certainly are,' Asya replied.

Soon Razumkin had stretched out on the sofa while Botynsky lay on the floor, massaged his chest and sighed. The table was covered with pastry crumbs, and Niki's face was decorated with sour cream. Asya proposed the order of activities for the rest of the day.

'First, the Tivoli baths!'

'Whatever for?' Razumkin wanted to know.

'So we can sweat some of your weight away.'

'Impossible.'

'And so I can get the beach sand out of me,' Asya said, munching on a piroshki.

'And so I can beat you!' Niki chimed in.

'So you can beat me. He is merciless with the birch leaves,' Asya said, caressing Niki's ear between finger and thumb. Every Sunday they bought birch branches from an old Ukrainian outside the baths and Niki applied them to Asya's back while she shivered with pleasure.

'And then our devotions.'

'Oh, no!' Botynsky and Razumkin groaned in unison.

'I won't have my child grow up a heathen. Praskoviya, wherever she is, would pursue me like a Fury if I did. First our devotions at the rue d'Aru, followed by lunch at the Ville de Petrograd.'

'You are bribing me with my own money,' Razumkin said.

'Exactly,' said Asya, clapping her hands, as she always did when she was happy. 'Now give me a minute, gentlemen, and I will make myself presentable.'

They heard a faint rapping at the door.

'Niki, go and see,' said Asya from the bedroom.

'Who is it?' she called from behind the door.

Niki had opened the door. A man stood in the hallway. He was carrying a small cardboard suitcase, tied together with rope. There was a misshapen military cap on his head, and his trenchcoat was frayed at the cuffs and stained in several places. Niki wiped the sour cream off his face and looked down at the stranger's mud-spattered hobnail boots.

'I don't know, Mami,' Niki said over his shoulder.

'Botynsky, find out who it is,' Asya shouted, and Botynsky rose to his feet, wiping his mouth on a serviette, and peered around the salon door at the stranger in the hallway.

'Who is it?' Asya called again. The man in the hallway said nothing.

'A visitor, Asya,' Botynsky said.

She was coming out of the bedroom door, reaching behind to zip up the skirt she was going to wear to church, when she stopped halfway into the hall. They all saw her go completely still for a moment and then raise one hand to her face.

'Niki,' she said in a faint voice. 'It is Sergei. Your father has come home.'

Botynsky stood holding an empty vodka bottle. Razumkin rose from the sofa and straightened his waistcoat. Niki turned halfway around and gave his mother a frightened look. Asya remained quite still, in her stockinged feet, staring at Sergei, returned from the dead.

Razumkin was the first to move. 'I think we should be going, Vladimir Isaacovitch,' he said, and Botynsky nodded.

As they slipped by Sergei, Asya said, in a weak voice, 'My friends,' and Sergei nodded.

'Come in,' she whispered. He crossed the threshold and dropped down to the boy's level.

He looked at Niki, then up at Asya.

She gave the faintest of nods. 'Your son.'

Sergei's hand was a fraction of an inch from the boy's face when Niki ducked, dodged past him and ran down the stairs.

'Botynsky! Wait!' the boy cried.

Asya ran after him. 'Niki, please! Come back!'

Botynsky appeared on the landing below, holding the boy in his arms.

'Oh God! What do we do?' she cried.

'We are going to the baths,' Razumkin said decisively. With that the two men and the boy resumed their descent. The porte-cochère clanged shut and their footsteps faded into the street. She turned, and there Sergei was, leaning against the doorframe, his eyes shut. She said, 'I'm sorry,' and touched his stubbly cheek. He drew her to him as she buried her face in his filthy trenchcoat.

Her sobs shook loose the scaffolding of everything solid and certain that she had managed to build inside her in her six years alone. This stranger, into whose coat she poured her tears, this man whose face, whose smell, whose hands, she hardly recognized, stroked her hair with a gesture at once patient and infinitely tired.

It was a long time before she could get out a single word.

'How?'

She looked into his face and saw with a shock how much older, how much more lined and thin he was. He smiled faintly and said, 'Make me some tea.'

His boots thudded against the linoleum floor of the kitchen. He sat down on the little chair. She eased the coat off his back. Underneath, he was wearing a sort of blue serge boilersuit, faded from many washings, stitched and restitched at the cuffs.

'From prison?' she asked, running her hand along the shabby sleeve, and he nodded.

She put the tea in front of him, and he poured one, two, then three full spoons of sugar into it, stirred it and drank it down in feverish gulps during which he ceased to be aware of her presence at all.

'Where have you come from?'

'I walked from the Gare de l'Est.'

'When?'

'Last Thursday. I slept in the garden,' and he pointed down into the square.

'We were at the Ourousoffs in Saint Rémy. How did you find us?'

'*Je cherche une dame Russe*,' he said. '*Je cherche une dame Russe*. Everyone kept saying, "*Allez à Clichy, ils sont tous là bas*."' He shrugged his shoulders. 'I didn't know where that was. So I walked.'

'And who told you to look for me here?'

'The baker on the rue de Moscou. I begged a roll.' He rubbed his face. 'I have a son?'

She nodded.

'Give me a cigarette.' She lit two and put one of them between his lips. He pulled the smoke deep into his lungs, shut his eyes and breathed it out in a high stream. His fingernails were black with dirt, and the once white hands, lightly dusted with auburn hair, were thick and calloused. He removed his beret, and she saw that his hair was thinner, high on his forehead, matted and dirty.

'How long have you been travelling?' She caressed the sleeve of his jacket.

'What day is it today?'

'Sunday, June the fifteenth.'

'I was in a Stolypin wagon right up to the border. I couldn't see anything. They took the handcuffs off, pointed to a train, and I got in.'

She had once seen such a wagon on a railway siding sometime before the war, with black-grilled compartments, and spectral convict faces behind bars. So: the Soviets still called them Stolypins.

'You're so pale,' she said.

'Moscow, Minsk, Brest, Warsaw, Berlin, Paris. I begged on every station platform.'

'So white.' She touched his face.

'I haven't seen the sun in two years. The sun never shines on the Solevetsky Islands.'

She knew there was a monastery up there, north of Leningrad, north of Lake Ladoga. They had imprisoned him in the Polar darkness.

'I've been doing my religious penance.' And she tried to imagine the cells and the buckets of swill, the bare, frozen floors.

She said, 'Come,' and he got up slowly, tottering slightly. She stood in front of him and undressed him, dropping the boilersuit at his feet, making him lift his arms so that she could remove the filthy

65

vest. She ran her hand over the squarish blur of tissue on his left shoulder, where the wound had been. He smiled faintly, and she got down, pulled off his massive boots, and slipped off his underwear. He stepped out of them as if asleep, and she helped to lower him into the bath. She soaped his back and shoulders, dipped his head and washed his hair, and then scrubbed his hands and feet. She saw his erection grow and decline, and he saw it too and smiled, as if it was all happening to someone else.

She turned, and there they were in the hall, Botynsky and Niki, staring through the half-open door. Botynsky gave the boy a push forward and then withdrew down the stairs.

Niki half-sheltered behind Asya and looked at the expanse of the man in the tub. 'What's your name?' Sergei asked, searching the little boy's face as if for proof, in his auburn hair, grey eyes and slight body, that he was his own.

'Niki,' said the little boy from behind his mother's back. Suddenly he bent forward, kissed his father's hand and darted from the room.

'Be gentle with him. He has had a terrible shock. So have I.' She looked about her at his clothes on the floor. 'We shall have to burn these.'

'Keep them. I want to remember,' he said. So she picked them up and put them on a hanger in her closet, then rummaged around to find some clothes for him to put on.

She came back with some underwear and socks.

'Whose are these?'

She took a deep breath. 'You see how it is.' She didn't know how to go on. 'I thought you were dead,' and she leaned against him for a moment. 'They are Botynsky's. I let him stay sometimes.'

'Sometimes?'

'Sometimes.' And then she covered her face and began to cry.

He caught one of her tears on the tip of his finger and licked it.

'Don't worry,' he said.

Over lunch around the kitchen table, Niki kept close to his mother, but never took his eyes off the stranger who was wearing Botynsky's loosely-fitting shirt and trousers. After lunch, she lay Sergei between the sheets and shut the door.

When she was sure that he was safely asleep, she and Niki tiptoed down the stairs and then ran the five blocks through the vacant Sunday streets to the apartment above the rue de Petrograd where, with tears of alarm and joy, she asked Botynsky what she was to do. He told her to sit down, prepared a space on his workdesk where Niki could play with his glue and his scissors, and after disappearing behind the blue curtain that concealed his stand-up pantry, returned with two small cups of coffee and sat beside her on the bed.

She remembered how they had collapsed backwards onto this bed in each other's arms and how, with a dust-filled rumble, the shelf above their heads had tilted forward, and books and papers had cascaded over them. They had rolled onto the floor, their bodies smeared with dust, and had made love among the scattered volumes of a complete edition of Turgenev.

Her skin, Botynsky thought, was the colour of smoke. A creature of autumn, the season when they burn the leaves. The magenta lipstick. She had once placed the perfect mark of her lips, like a passport stamp, on the opened palm of his hand. And her red nails, the long, thin fingers, the network of blue veins beneath the smoky skin, those hands and arms holding him tight. He would never get over it, how, miraculously, she had once wanted him.

'He is so changed,' she said. 'What do I do, Botynsky?'

He pulled his knees up to his chin.

'You marry him right away.'

As if there was nothing else that could be said. Not knowing what to reply, she sipped her coffee and they both looked at Niki, in a circle of light from Botynsky's desk lamp, cutting out the figure of a rabbit.

'Come out for a walk with us,' she said, wanting him to know that some things would never change, but he shook his head and looked at her through the portholes of his glasses, like a traveller taking his last leave of his native land.

After wandering about the parc Monceau, she fed Niki and put him to bed on the sofa of the sitting room, and stood in the doorway of her bedroom watching Sergei sleep. She kept absolutely still, trying to make the moment of peace endure, to slow the beating of her heart to the measured rise and fall of his chest.

She knew Botynsky so much better than this sleeping figure. She knew that Botynsky would give his life for her and for Niki. She knew all of this, and none of it mattered any more. When Sergei woke, she fed him soup, spoonful by spoonful.

The day drained from the windows, and they were soon just two faces lit by the bedside lamp, sharing cigarettes, talking in low voices so that their child would not wake. He had been with Shkouro, he said, then with the White forces under Wrangel and Denikin; had been captured in Piatigorsk, escaped, and ended up behind the earthworks at Perekop in the autumn of 1920, at the White army's last stand on the Crimea.

'Why didn't you escape?' she asked. Paris was full of taxi drivers who said they had been at Perekop.

'Disgust,' he said. 'I couldn't be bothered. You should have seen the rout when the Reds broke through. Gun-carriages being cut from their harnesses and run down the cliffs into the sea, men swimming for the boats, clubbing each other to get on the ladders of the British and French boats.'

He hadn't run, he hadn't joined in the rout. He had dismissed the three men left in the battery, watched them vault over the dugout and disappear down the hillside to the water. And he had sat beside the gun, feeling it cool, waiting for the Reds to come swarming over the earthworks. He wasn't moving. His war was over.

'You told me once, "They have convictions, we only have hatreds,"' she said. He nodded.

'They had hatreds too. Battlefield executions, men dragged down muddy lanes behind horses, prisoners beaten and made to run the gauntlet.' He lay back and smoked calmly, seeing it all again.

'Why did they imprison you?'

'Because I escaped from internment in the Crimea. I was recalcitrant, as my father would have said. So they put me in a railway wagon and I ended up, more dead than alive, in Solevetsky.'

She listened to his calm and precise voice, and felt all her love return. But she knew that years now divided them and could never be made up.

'Strange. The first Red officer to interrogate me after Perekop was Oniuskevitch. We were at the same staff college in '16. Don't you see?'

She nodded, but no, she did not see.

'Half of the officer corps went to the Reds. Half to the Whites. Brother fighting brother. It suddenly seemed pointless.'

His voice was slurred with fatigue. 'Tell me everything,' he said.

'I couldn't,' she said quietly.

'Well, then, tell me something.'

She told him how she had searched the troop trains in Ekaterinadar and the quays of Novorossisk for a sign of him. She told him how the *Orient Star* had sailed to Constantinople, how she had looked for him there, how she had reached Toulon, how she had survived in Paris, working in Antonov's clinic, and how her new 'family' as she called it, Botynsky and Razumkin, Olga and Dimitri, had taken shape around her.

'I never thought I would see you again,' she said.

He stroked the tip of her chin and looked so wise, so tender, that she began to cry.

'I gave up,' she whispered. 'I just gave up.'

'It's only human,' he said, and rocked her back and forth in his arms.

'How did you know I was here?' she asked.

'I thought: Paris or London. If Dimitri survived, then Paris. If Lapin survived, then London. I thought: I will try one, then I will try the other.'

She hugged him. He hadn't given up. It was a miracle.

When their stories were done, he kissed her and unbuttoned her blouse, parting its folds and caressing her breasts, drawing the memory of them and their reality together in his hands. She lay back on the bed and he slipped off her skirt and her underwear and then sat down beside her, surveying her body with a look of distant affection in his eyes.

'You're shivering,' he said.

'Like the very first time,' she said, her eyes full.

He nodded. It was then that his finger made contact with the little ridge of flesh girdling the top of her delta of black hair. It was then that he saw her Caesarean scar, saw what the birth of their child had cost her. It was then that he began, without a sound, with his eyes open, to cry.

EVERY NIGHT WHEN she came home from the clinic she would find him reading the newspaper under the light of the kitchen table, the frayed red dictionary beside him. Often she went to bed alone, with him still in the kitchen next door, muttering to himself, working the wrinkles out of his pronunciation. His French was soon as smooth as a freshly laundered tablecloth.

At dinner he ate everything she put before him, methodically wiping his plate clean. Within a month the hollows under his cheeks had gone and his gaunt frame began to fill out. He did his exercises every morning, staring at himself in the mirror as if he were banishing a ghost from his mind.

One evening she came home and he was waiting for her wearing charcoal-grey flannel trousers with baggy pleats, a light-brown herringbone jacket, and an open white shirt. His hair was slicked down and he was smoking a cigarette in a holder.

'Razumkin took me to his outfitter.'

She sat on his knee.

'Shall I wear this to our wedding?' he asked.

She straightened his collar, trying not to let him know how shocked she was. Who was he? she thought wildly. What has he become?

'Do you want to get married or not?'

She kissed his neck, laid her head on his shoulder.

She knew, without having to ask, that Sergei would never agree to a church wedding. He would have thought it sentimental. She knew this just as clearly as she knew that he would never consent to their having another child.

At the Mairie de Clichy, the municipal official in charge of marriages asked the bride and groom who the little boy was.

'Our son,' said Sergei with an equable smile.

The official scurried through the formalities in a monotone. Asya held on to Niki's hand, and Lapin, Dimitri and Olga, Botynsky and Razumkin grouped themselves in an arc behind her. Sergei stood at her side in a tailored charcoal-grey pinstripe suit, with a look of calm detachment on his face, throughout the absurd little ceremony. Next to the dusty tricolour there was a blank space on the wall where the picture of the president of France should have been. As the formalities were intoned, her mind wandered. Why had the picture disappeared, she wondered. Millerand, Doumergue, Herriot: she couldn't even remember who the president was supposed to be. In another life she would have been married in the chapel at Marino. Father would have been at her side. She would have been wearing her mother's wedding gown, not this plain black dress. All this had vanished, like the picture on the wall, leaving behind a smudged space in her memory.

When Seryozha took Asya in his arms and kissed her, Niki looked up at her with a puzzled expression, as if the incantations of the mayor's clerk had cast a spell upon her. Asya got down on her knees, took his face in her hands and said, 'I'm still here. Nothing has changed.' But she knew this was not true.

Afterwards, Razumkin bundled them into several taxis and took them to the best Russian restaurant in Paris, Le Caneton, rue de la Bourse.

'But you shouldn't!' Asya cried.

'But I have,' said Razumkin, as he escorted her to a table by the window, set with flowers and shining silverware. There was caviar and salmon, Georgian white wine and sturgeon laid upon fresh dill.

They toasted each other, Botynsky made a noble and comic speech about the end of his hopes and the dawn of hers, which made Asya cry, and they all fed Niki scraps with their fingers. To everyone's surprise, Lapin rose and made a toast to the groom.

'He had vanished. Gone. Quite disappeared. Into the Polar night of the Solevetsky Islands. And now, like the hero of a fairy tale, he has returned!' said Lapin with an uncharacteristic flourish of his glass. 'To his resurrection! To their happiness!'

Dimitri said he had never seen Lapin so animated. It couldn't just be the champagne. 'He must have a woman somewhere,' he whispered.

Olga told him to hush, but everyone heard, and Asya said, 'So, Lapin, is there a woman? Tell us!' and by Lapin's blushes she concluded there was indeed. 'Her name?' Silence. 'Come on. Her name.'

'Sally. She works in the bank.'

Asya tickled Lapin under the ribs. 'Come on. What colour hair?'

'None of your business. She is blonde.'

'Come on.'

'None of your business. She is tall and she is a colonel's daughter, and that is all I am ever going to tell you.'

'How scrawny you are. Is she going to feed you up?'

'Asya, stop it!'

Sergei sat at the end of the table, watching Asya and Lapin with his princely gaze.

Then Asya left Lapin alone and stood up.

'To Ilya Ilyonovitch, who made this day possible,' and she leaned over and bestowed a kiss on Razumkin's large, damp forehead. As she touched her glass against his, the plain gold band on her finger, the happiness in her eyes, and her carmine lips made Razumkin ache with desire.

At the end of the meal, when everyone was gazing at the wreckage of the feast, a man Sergei's age, dressed with punctilious formality in a wing collar and black suit, approached from another table. He bowed and clicked his heels and addressed Sergei in Russian:

'Do I have the honour to be speaking to Artillery Captain Gourevitch?'

'You have that honour,' said Sergei drily.

'I believe we saw service together in the Crimea.'

'Your memory is better than mine.'

'You were taken prisoner?'

'I was.'

'And you were released?'

'As you see.'

'General Kutiepov would welcome the opportunity to hear about your experiences in person.'

'I cannot give him that satisfaction.'

'May I ask why?'

'I have no desire to join a political organization.'

'I see.'

The man bowed and rejoined a table of young men. Sergei returned their stares with his narrow gaze.

'What a ridiculous man. Who is this Kutiepov?' Asya whispered.

Botynsky was staring moodily out at the cloche hats and trilbies, berets and kepis, bobbing past above the lace curtains of the restaurant window. 'Association of Tsarist Veterans.'

'And who are they?'

'The most reactionary and unreconciled émigré group of all.'

'Quite right,' Razumkin added, piling franc notes onto the silver salver. 'Stay out of politics.'

They lurched home in a cab, Asya's head lolling against Botynsky's shoulder, Niki on Sergei's lap, Lapin and Razumkin singing the regimental march of Petersburg's Chevalier Guards.

'Quiet, you two!' Asya cried. 'Tell me about Kutiepov.'

In a low murmur, Botynsky began telling her some long story about Count Guchkov's circle in Berlin, about Baron Wrangel's group in Prague, about Kutiepov's attempt to assemble all the veterans of the Tsar's army in Paris. All Asya could gather was that these groups were bent on the restoration of the old regime and were smuggling in weapons and agents through the Polish and Finnish frontiers.

'With no discernible result?' she asked.

Botynsky nodded gloomily. 'Futile Bourbons, the lot of them. Learn nothing, forget nothing. I want constitutions, laws, English institutions for Russia, and they want the knout, the whip, the reintroduction of serfdom, God knows what horrors. Hopeless.'

'You are very innocent, dearest. Why is all this news to you?' Sergei said, stroking her earlobe.

She shrugged. 'When I came to Paris, I was pregnant. I had nothing but my suitcase, and I thought: Well, that is finished. And so when I went out to dinner with Russians and they invited me to come to join some circle, the thought of it made me want to lie down and never wake up again. So I thought, right, I want to go dancing or swimming or horseracing.'

'But they killed Father,' Lapin suddenly interjected.

'They? The Bolsheviks. Yes, they did,' she said. 'And nothing we do can ever bring him back.' She lay her head against Sergei's shoulder and watched the voluptuous façades of the city at night slithering by the windows of the taxi.

After the others had sung them up the dark stairwell and Niki had been put to bed, Sergei and Asya were alone at last. She undid his studs and slipped off his suit, and he peeled off her sheer black dress and carried her into the bathroom. He turned on the taps, and when the bath was full he laid her in the water and climbed in opposite. They sat facing each other in the tub, legs entwined. Her temples were pounding, the champagne surging through her like an electric current.

'Man and wife,' he said, lying back, his hands caressing the insides of her thighs. His eyes were shut. His nipples, ringed with hair, were lapped by the water. Above his auburn head, the copper sunflower of the shower. Behind her back, the taps. My wedding night, she thought.

As quick as a cat, she turned on the cold tap, and water cascaded down onto his face. He roared, rose from the bath, picked her up, and carried her down the dark hallway to the bedroom. He pitched her onto the bed and they writhed and grappled, biting and laughing on the wet sheets.

With her head over the edge of the bed, the tidal rush of his breathing in her ear, her body wet and burning, the slim equine strength of his thighs between hers and blood surging through every fibre, she cascaded downwards into sleep.

When she awoke a sliver of light was bisecting the darkness. In the column of light through the half-open door into the hallway stood Niki, looking at them both. His bare feet were standing in the puddles left from their passage from the bathroom, his lips were parted, his eyes wide, his left hand a tight fist against his pyjama leg.

She shut her eyes and heard him running back to his bed. She moved Sergei aside, put on a dressing gown and hurried down the hall after him.

'Are you all right?' she whispered, kneeling beside his bed.

'What were you doing?'

'He loves me . . .'

'What were you doing?'

'. . . And I love him.'

'Why was there water in the hall?'

She caressed his face. 'None of your business. Move over.'

She soothed him with a story, willed his eyelids to grow heavy, to close. When he slipped away, she lay there beside him in the dark, wondering what a child could understand and what a child could lose in such a moment, standing in that half-opened door into the dark.

Next morning, when Sergei found them asleep side by side, he bent over and kissed her awake. 'So, I have been abandoned.'

Niki turned over, muttering in his sleep.

'He discovered us last night,' she whispered. 'He wanted to know what we were doing.'

Sergei kissed her on the lips. 'That's what we were doing.' But she looked so unhappy that he sat down on the bed and caressed her cheek.

She helped Niki to dress, gathered up his satchel and walked him to his school. At the school gate, Niki turned.

'Is Sergei going to live with us forever?'

He looked so bewildered that she got down on her knees and smoothed the hair off his forehead. 'He is your father.'

'Will Botynsky still be coming to our house?'

'Of course.'

He walked slowly away from her into the schoolyard, the satchel on his back, alone with all of the opaque adult world to understand.

After work at the clinic, Asya took Niki home, and when he was safely asleep she dashed off, as she always did on Tuesdays, to Botynsky's for tea.

'Off to your lover already?' Sergei looked amused.

'I am faithful to my customs.'

Botynsky placed the sugarlump, as he always did, on the teaspoon, dipped it in the glass of tea, and then spooned it into her mouth. She swallowed and smiled at him. She had shared every part of Niki's growing up with Botynsky. Now something had happened that she could not report. So she sipped her tea, fingered a book on top of the teetering pile by her chair.

'What am I going to do with all these men? Niki, Sergei, you.'

Botynsky sipped his tea.

'He could at least be jealous. I find it infuriating that he is not jealous.'

'Why should Sergei be jealous?'

'He should pay me the compliment of jealousy. At the very least.'

She changed the subject and got him to talk about the latest thing, a new volume from Khodasevitch, and the first Soviet export edition of Mayakovsky's poems. She wanted her visit to mean that all this should continue. She wanted Botynsky to understand that she still kept faith with her former life. When she rose to leave, she planted a kiss on his forehead and gave him a teasing little wave as she tripped down the stairs to return home. She knew, not altogether disagreeably, that it was torture for Botynsky to see another man making her as happy as this.

Next morning as she went out to work, Sergei put on the suit he had been married in, and when she asked him why, he smiled, putting his finger to his lips. 'A secret.'

All day long in the clinic, while she took temperatures, checked blood pressures and plotted the lines on fever charts, she wondered what he was up to. When she came home that night, there were flowers in a vase on the worn linoleum of the kitchen table, and he handed her a glass of wine.

'I have a job.'

He was going into the import–export business with a friend of a friend, a man named Andronnikov who had two rooms and a phone in Passy and who specialized in importing Baltic timber from Latvia, via Hamburg and Le Havre.

'Who told you about this Andronnikov?'

'A man I met inside.' He paused, and she could feel the shutters ringing down to close her off from this part of his life.

'What man?'

He kissed her on the nose.

'I am going to rescue you from the clinic.'

'I don't need rescuing.' She began to take off her coat.

'Keep it on. We're going out.'

'I'm still in my uniform.'

He pressed up close. 'I can't resist women in uniform.'

She put her finger to his lips.

'What about Niki?'

'Take a look.'

When she opened the door of the salon, there was Botynsky, with Niki beside him on the sofa. They were reading a story. Botynsky made a forlorn wave. She blew him a kiss.

As they were going downstairs she said, 'We are torturing Botynsky.'

'He is a willing victim.'

'No one is forever.'

Sergei took her to the Bataclan. She didn't ask where the money came from, but let herself go, and they danced and drank cheap champagne. Sergei had never seen anyone do the Charleston before. His eyes followed a girl in a short skirt which wiggled so lewdly when she kicked her legs that he laughed out loud.

Up on the stage were twenty American girls wearing ostrich feathers, bathed in pink light, their breasts sparkling with sequins, their nipples painted with bright silver stars, their thighs wrapped in fishnet, their legs tapering into high heels. They danced and winked and sang a song. Asya cuffed Sergei. 'Look at you, mooning over these beauties!'

He turned, with a look of foolish happiness in his face. 'I dreamed about this in the Solevetsky. Exactly this. What are they singing?'

His head was cocked to one side, with a comical look of strained attention on his face that reminded her of the dog on the records listening to his master's voice through the amplification horn. He was still deaf in one ear: the shattered eardrum she had cleaned that first afternoon in Shkouro's hospital tent had not healed.

'It's in English, and it's too stupid,' she said.

'Tell me.'

'No, too stupid.' But he insisted. She had to shout: '"When they ask us are we Français, we say *qu'est-ce que vous pensez? Voilà les Nonstop, voilà les Nonstop Nudes!*" It says in the programme they're all nice girls from New York.'

Everyone was applauding as the girls can-canned off the stage, faces frozen in an identical rictus, high heels clattering on the boards, ostrich feathers waving on their backsides.

'Wonderful! A prisoner's dream! Nonstop Nudes! I love this place! This is Western civilization!' His face was lit up with love and champagne. He had only been out of prison a month or so and here he was in a nightclub in Paris, looking as if he had never been anywhere else.

'I am joining all of this,' he said, with an expansive wave over the men in dinner jackets at the next tables, and the women in boas and expensive perms and the cigarette girls in their tight pink-sequined tutus wending their way between the tables. 'We buy Russian timber and copper and furs, and we sell them machine parts and grain. Can't lose. I had years in the darkness of Solevetsky to figure it out.'

'You frighten me,' she said softly, but the band struck up some New Orleans jazz, and he didn't hear.

'And now with NEP . . .' he said, dropping a note in the tray the cigarette girl carried about her neck, and picking up a pack.

'What is NEP?' she asked, draining her champagne and looking about her. The dancers whirled so close to their table that the women's dresses swished against her legs.

A look of exasperation crossed his face and he enunciated each word against the jazz thundering around them: 'New Economic Policy.'

She caressed his cheek. 'Now, darling, NEP is there, I am here. Why should I know?'

'Because,' he said, rising and taking her hand and leading her onto the dance floor, 'because I am going to be an NEP man.' He encircled her in his arms and they were off.

'An NEP man in Paris,' she said, brushing his ear with her lips. 'You are deaf in the other ear, aren't you? I can tell.'

'Sssh. Our secret.'

'Do you remember how I looked after you? In Shkouro's tent?'

'And I quivered like a dog.'

'Like a dog,' and she wrapped her hands around the small of his back and let him take her where he wanted.

Every morning at seven o'clock he went out to Andronnikov's rooms in Passy and worked there until after dark.

'Who is this Andronnikov?' she asked.

'An utterly uninteresting man who happens to run a timber business.'

'You are so secretive.'

'Not at all. No secrets. The timber business is nothing but boredom, which I should spare you.'

'I want to meet Andronnikov. I imagine a sort of gnome, with a sour expression, dirty fingernails and cigarette ash on his lapels, always muttering into the phone in bad German.'

'Wonderful! Wait until I tell Andronnikov,' Sergei laughed.

But she never did meet Andronnikov.

At first it was Baltic timber, shipped from Riga to Le Havre. Then he went into grain.

'Why do you want to know?'

'I want to know everything about you.'

'All right. Andronnikov buys on the Chicago Grain Mart. I sell it to the starving Russians.'

Then, emptying a wastebasket in the salon, she found a business card with the words 'Jack Cummings, Toronto Office, Massey Harris Ferguson'.

'Who is Jack Cummings?' she asked him that night as they were eating together, Niki on her knee pinching the fried potatoes from her plate.

Sergei popped a sliver of potato into his son's mouth. 'Your mother is spying on me.'

'Who is spying? What is a woman to do? You tell me nothing.'
She handed him Jack Cummings' card.

'I see,' he said, and a flash of annoyance crossed his face. Then he announced, 'Let us go away for the weekend. I want to show you something.'

Jack Cummings himself was on the quay at Le Havre to meet them. Sergei lifted Asya and Niki up the gangplank of the Canadian freighter and Cummings led them to the open hatch.

Sergei pointed down. 'The mystery explained. Look.'

Tractor after tractor, fifty of them in neat rows. 'Massey Harris Ferguson' on the bright-red engine cowlings. Niki was enchanted. 'Can I drive one?'

'Sure,' said Jack Cummings, and they clambered down the hatch ladder into the hold and lifted Niki into the seat of one of the tractors.

'For the north Caucasus collective farms.'

'For Stavropol? For Kislovodsk?' Asya smiled at him, and Sergei nodded. She had seen those villages from the train once, in the late summer of '17, their orchards heavy with fruit and the whitewashed walls blazing like snow in the sunlight, and then only a summer later – their summer – devastated by civil war. Now Sergei's tractors would plough up the abandoned soil. The orchards would bear fruit again. She squeezed his hand.

'Your husband is one hell of a smart businessman,' Jack Cummings said. Sergei, impeccable in rue Saint Honoré tailoring, made a bow to the rumpled Canadian in a raincoat.

That night, at the Deauville casino where Sergei took Asya to celebrate, he told her he was going to buy out Andronnikov.

'Where will you get the money?'

'From the tractors. Three per cent on fifty tractors.' He smiled and lit a small cigar. 'The details are tedious.'

'I love you.'

'I mention money, and you say you love me.'

'I don't give a damn about the money.'

He laughed. 'Neither do I.'

That deal was the beginning of the Eastern Trading Company.

'An unimpeachably boring and respectable name, don't you think?' Sergei said when he consulted her about it.

'Doing exciting and unrespectable things, I hope.'

'Exactly.'

Soon he was travelling abroad; his overnight case was plastered with stickers from the Rome Hotel in Riga, the Adlon on the Unter den Linden in Berlin, the Imperial in Bucharest, and Niki had a collection of hotel soap and notepaper brought back by his father from each trip.

The making of the company came in 1927 with imports of Baku oil. A Franco-Armenian oilman called Dujmeijan did the direct dealings with the Soviets, leaving Seryozha to arrange the French side of the sale. That much she understood.

'I don't want you dealing with the Soviet Trade Commission.'

'Why not?' he asked.

'Botynsky says it's a nest of spies.'

'Botynsky,' Sergei mused. 'What do poets know about spies?'

'Don't be condescending.'

'What are you worried about? That the Soviets will kidnap me?'

'Don't joke. What do I do if you get into trouble?'

'What trouble?'

'You have no documents. Neither do I. Just the Nansen passports for stateless people. What happens if you get arrested on one of your trips?'

'By whom, dearest?'

'I don't know. You never tell me anything.'

'The secret,' he said, stroking her nose, 'is that business is a bore. You are so much more interesting.'

She was unmoved. 'No direct contacts with the Soviets. It frightens me. Promise.'

'They never see me. I'm in the wings. It's Dujmeijan who is on stage.' Dujmeijan would smile and reach over and light her cigarette. Then the two men would bend quite close together, Dujmeijan's dark Assyrian face and Seryozha's auburn angular one nearly touching, whispering to each other.

'It's a game,' he said when they were in the taxi on the way home.

'Looks serious to me.'

'Just a game.'

'Where is all this money coming from?'

'Five per cent at each end of the deal. Five per cent of sixty-five hundred barrels of Baku oil buys a considerable amount of silk underwear,' he said, running his hand up the curved warmth of her upper thigh. Gently, she stopped him.

'Why don't I ever get my way with you?' he said softly.

'You don't do badly. What you mean is: you get your way with everything else, why not with me?'

'Some resistance . . . a refusal somewhere. Interesting,' he stroked her lips with his fingers.

'All this because I refuse to let you . . . in plain sight of the taxi driver?'

He laughed again. 'Look at your chin. Stubborn. Wonderful sight, your chin.'

When they drew up in front of the Square des Batignolles he paid the driver, and as they mounted the long, dark, winding stairway, filled with the smell of disinfectant and cabbage, he said, 'I have found us a new apartment.'

She looked at him. 'You are determined to play the magician.'

'Aren't you pleased?'

'Of course. How could I ever be nostalgic about this place. But . . .'

'But what?'

'It is a *fait accompli*. Why can't I decide where I want to live? You are hopeless,' and she pushed him aside and opened the door on the grey apartment where she had once been mistress of her own life.

The new apartment comprised seven rooms with shiny parquet floors on the rue de Solferino, around the corner from the Gare d'Orléans. From their bedroom window she could see the barges on the Seine and the little footbridge leading to the École des Beaux Arts. Niki had his own room, decorated with pictures of steam engines. There were rooms for a nanny and a chamber-maid and a spare room which Asya kept in readiness for Lapin's visits from London.

83

Sergei said it was ridiculous for her to continue working when she didn't have to.

She conferred with Razumkin.

'But I enjoy nursing.'

'Look at you, dearest. This fur wrap, these little red leather shoes on your delightful feet. And this dress,' he stroked the purple silk appreciatively. 'What is someone like you doing with bedpans and sick old Russians?'

'I like my sick old Russians.'

'Leave them to me. You have better things to do.'

'Such as?'

'Your son. Your husband. "The coming man." They all say it.'

'Who is *they*?'

Razumkin smiled. 'The whole community is divided between jealousy and approval.'

'Mostly jealousy.'

'Some. Look, he needs you. You know how Russians are. They say: "But he is married to Princesse Galitzine. So he must be suitable."'

'So I make him suitable?'

'You do.'

The truth was, she sometimes wondered whether he was suitable herself. Occasionally he went too far. On one of his trips to Le Havre, to supervise the unloading of a shipment from Leningrad, he brought a crate back with him. He jemmied it open in their living room, threw aside the woodchip packing and pulled out a dinner plate with a crest on it, showing her the Imperial factory's mark on the back. Then, after rummaging down at the very bottom, he came up with a small, chipped icon of Saint Sergius. 'My patron saint,' he said, and handed it to her. 'For you.'

She burst into tears and turned away from him. 'You are robbing churches. Put it away!'

He put everything back in the crate, while she watched, sobbing, from the couch. He said, with steely calm, 'Great houses are being vandalized. For all you know, Marino has been looted or burned.'

'Stop it this instant!' she cried.

'Churches are being demolished or turned into carpenters'

shops. Treasures are going into state guests houses or being melted down to add to the gold reserve, and you are sitting in Paris, crying your eyes out. Why? At least these treasures have found a safe home.'

'Not in my house!' she shouted.

'Well then, somewhere else.' And he disposed of the whole consignment to an antique dealer in New York. At five per cent.

If, as Razumkin had said, it was she who made him suitable in the eyes of the community, the effect of her good name was beginning to wear thin. She knew Kutiepov's people whispered against him. Every time she went in to the Russian cathedral on the rue d'Aru silence would descend around her.

'So what?' she could hear him saying. So what? He defied every single claim from the past. He was the only free man she had ever known.

He made Asya feel as if their ascent from the Square des Batignolles and the smell of émigré poverty – that compound of cabbage, black bread and paraffin stoves – was in the natural order of things. He acted as if it was the least they could expect. After all, he said, they had both been born in houses with servants and parquet floors.

'Were you?' she asked. 'You tell me so little.'

'Father's estate? I shall tell you. The floors squeaked just like this, and an old peasant called Tolya would put felt pads on his shoes, and after laying down the wax he would spend the whole day skating around the house on them, grumbling and skating, until they were buffed into a hard, bright shine. I followed him from room to room. "Out of my way, savage,"' Sergei laughed. 'Then my father took up with the wine merchant's wife, and my mother moved out and went to live in Moscow, and nobody gave a damn about the floors after that. So, my dearest, I am now returning to the floors of my childhood, and so are you.' And he put out his arms and danced her across the salon.

'What became of your mother?' she asked him as they swooped around the parquet.

'Dead. All dead. Tolya. Mother. Clean sweep. Famine of '20. I

85

searched for her when I came out. Not a trace. So you see, I am quite free.'

'You are,' she said, nestling against his shoulder.

'We are coming home. To what we deserve,' he said, as he swung her gently to and fro on the shining parquet floors.

She wasn't so sure. Sometimes she would return after an evening out, throw her wrap on the sofa and catch a glimpse of herself in the hall mirror, and think: I am twenty-six and he is twenty-nine. How are such things possible?

In the spring of 1927 they left Niki with Botynsky and the nanny and went down to Nice by train to take delivery of a Hispano-Suiza 50 horsepower open-topped roadster, shipped from Genoa. They went to watch Suzanne Lenglen play Helen Wills for the French championships and then stayed overnight at the Grand Hôtel Cimiez. On Sunday morning they went to the church on the rue Longchamps where Asya's parents had been married. She went in and lit a candle to the icon of Saint Vladimir. It was dark and damp inside, and the old women – the church mice, her father used to call them – were huddled in the candlelit recesses, watching her with black eyes. She wanted to stay longer, to remain within the candle's glow, but Seryozha was outside, pacing up and down in his driving leathers.

The journey to Saint Rémy took them the whole day. Sunk deep behind the windscreen with her feet resting against the great transmission hump of this huge beast, she watched Sergei drive, goggles down, his gloves gripping the wheel, his lips slightly pursed in concentration. She watched him as if he were a man she had just met.

As night fell, they stopped for petrol. Asya suddenly said, 'I ran my father's house. I brought up a child alone. And now I am a spectator of my own life. You have taken it over. It is a disaster.'

He laughed. 'What are you talking about? I can't persuade you to do a thing. Give up the old Russians, I keep telling you. Put away your uniform. Nothing. Zero. You are incorrigible. Unbudgeable.'

She laughed, lit cigarettes for both of them, passed his to him and watched its tip furiously burning as the car roared away into the funnel of the darkness. But as the cigarette burned down to ash and the night rushed overhead, she could see that she had surrendered her life to him and did not know how to get it back.

An hour later, the car was creeping down the rusty track to the Ourousoffs, the ragged cane so overgrown it clattered against the fenders. Olga was at the gate in her red kaftan and black apron, with a bundle of firewood under her arm like a peasant woman, shielding her eyes from the headlights.

'My God!' Olga cried when they drew to a halt beside her. 'Such a car! I thought: The police!'

Sergei led the way inside with a crate of oysters and a magnum of champagne under his arm. Dimitri helped them off with their leathers, but when Olga thought no one was watching she gave the driving gloves Sergei had tossed onto the hallway table a covert sniff.

Olga just didn't like him. There was nothing Asya could do about it. All Olga would ever say was, 'It is none of my business, darling. He is the father of your child, but . . .'

'But what, Olga?'

'He is so . . .' and she would puff furiously on one of the cigarettes that had darkened her teeth and yellowed her fingers. 'So un-cosy.'

'So un-what?'

'So hard, dearest. Any other woman but you would be crushed by him.'

Dimitri was in the low-ceilinged kitchen with the smoke-blackened beams, and as Asya kissed him she picked a thread of bramble from the back of his black woollen sweater.

'Still battling the jungle, dear man,' she said, and he bared his arms to show her the bramble scratches. On his monthly long weekends down from Paris he disappeared into the acre of wood behind the house, returning in the dark for some of Olga's mushroom soup, oblivious of the leaves lodged in his hair, the brambles snagging his overalls.

Seryozha said, 'Dimitri, why don't you give up? It is futile. The very epitome of Russian futility.'

Asya, who was laying the table, turned and gave her husband a poke in the chest. 'Wretch, you should give him some help.'

'If I give in, the wood will become a jungle,' shrugged Dimitri.

'So what?' Seryozha said, to tease him. So what? was his favourite expression, his invariable retort to one of Botynsky's woolly expatiations on the future of the Soviet Revolution, or Razumkin's gloomy theories of human depravity, or Dimitri's grim industry.

'Stop this "So what?" business,' Asya said. 'I can't stand it. People will begin to hate you.'

'So what?' he replied with a grin, and she pummelled his chest in mock exasperation.

Dimitri said, 'A wood is beautiful, a jungle is not.' And to settle the matter, Olga pointed to the festoons of dried mushrooms hanging from the beams of the kitchen.

'If Dimitri doesn't keep the paths clear, I won't be able to make my mushroom soup.'

'Your soup is so delicious, I surrender,' Sergei said, pouring them both a glass of champagne. 'To your health!'

Olga and Dimitri gave Asya the impression of being one person reproduced in a male and female version. Even when she heard them arguing with each other – 'Why did you leave the cream out? You're not in Tambov, you idiot, this is Provence, it will curdle' – it was as if she was eavesdropping on a single soul muttering out loud to itself.

Dimitri, formerly so cheerful and unafraid, was now a quieter, grimmer man.

'Monsieur Ourousoff, you *were* our Petersburg manager. You were indeed,' the French bank president had said when Dimitri arrived in Paris. 'But now, Petersburg no longer exists.'

'You should have slammed the door on him! After everything you had done for that wretched bank,' Asya had cried.

'We are not in a position to make romantic gestures,' Dimitri had said, looking down at his hands.

Dimitri had started again at the bottom. He counted cancelled cheques with clerks half his age; he put on his rubber thimble and sat on the cashier's stool, counting out other people's cash through the tills. Inch by inch, he climbed his way back. After eight long years, he was made deputy manager of the Eastern European division. He would muse bitterly, 'They expect all Russians to give up.'

'They haven't reckoned on the Ourousoffs,' Asya would say to cheer him up, but some days she could not lift his mood. A melancholy bafflement at the hardness of life ran like a subterranean river in the temperament of all Ourousoffs. When Dimitri looked out of the window at the wind driving through the cane, Asya would think of her mother staring out at the river from the conservatory window, rotating her wedding ring over and over on her finger. It was a look Asya both loved and feared, as if that bafflement were in her nature too, as if one day she too would be disarmed by the harshness of fate. What had her mother said that night as she lay dying? 'I have not lived my life.'

No, Asya thought. Not me. I *will* live my life.

Seryozha shucked the oysters, splintering the rims of the shells with his knife, while Asya diced the lemons and licked the juice off her fingers.

'Why *do* you disapprove of me, Uncle Dimitri?' Seryozha asked with the equanimity which infuriated those who did not like him.

Dimitri smiled in an embarrassed way.

'Because it has happened so quickly, is that it? Perhaps you think I am what the English call a bounder?'

Dimitri shook his head, smiling shyly.

'Well then, because I am trading with the infamous Bolsheviks?'

Dimitri nodded. 'The infamous Bolsheviks.'

'But so are you, Dimitri.'

Dimitri shrugged. 'My bank is. Who isn't nowadays?'

'My point exactly.'

'I will be fired if I don't. But you,' Dimitri said softly and in good humour, 'would trade with the very devil.'

Sergei went on shucking the oysters. After a silence, he suddenly said, 'We were on a siding somewhere in the autumn of '19, chained to the grille in our Stolypin wagons, being transferred north from Krasnodar to Lefortovo prison near Moscow, as it turned out. The bridge had been blown out up the line by bandits.

Anyway, through the bars we could see it was famine country, somewhere near Ekaterinburg, fields devastated as far as the eye could see – flat, flat, not an ear of corn. They took us out and made us dig pits by the side of the track. All day and the next until the men were falling over and the guards had to get them up on their feet with rifle butts. Then the freight cars began rolling up, and they ordered us in with pitchforks and told us to fill the pits.'

They listened, quite still. His voice was soft.

'The freight cars were filled with bodies. Whole families. Naked or in rags. Starved to death. Little bundles of bones. Pushed into the pits by men with pitchforks. Falling like dolls. I did that with these hands,' and he held out his hands, wet with the oysters, little crumbs of shell on his fingertips.

No one said a word.

'And then we threw powder of lime on them and covered them up. Three of us fell dead from exhaustion and hunger and they made us push them into the pit as well. Then they loaded us back into the Stolypins and we rode north.'

Asya got up and went and stood in the open doorway, looking out at the chill courtyard. The moon was up and cast sharp-fingered light through the mulberry tree onto the luminous flagstones. She lit a cigarette to stop herself shivering.

When she returned, Dimitri was saying, 'And that is why you've just shipped twenty-six boxcars of grain through the Vienna-Kiev line.'

Sergei shook his head. 'I leave the charitable work to Herbert Hoover.'

'Of course, everything at five per cent. But still, help the regime, you help the people.'

Sergei shook his head again. 'That was not the point of my sentimental little story. War communism was a disaster. The country was in ruins. When I looked through the bars of the Stolypin wagon at those empty fields, I realized that anyone exporting them grain on five per cent commission would have to be very stupid not to make a great deal of money.' He blew smoke up into the blackened beams. He resumed shucking oysters, and passed one on the tip of his knife to Asya. She shook her head.

She was too close to him, too deeply bound to find the exact words for what she felt. She had only to look at the way he inserted the knife, rotated it between the clenched shells, pried them back, shucking the shell into the wicker basket at his feet and sucking his fingers to taste the juice, to know that she loved him. Every gesture was neat, economical, perfect of its kind.

'The Banque de Suez is financing an asbestos operation in Voronezh. The whole operation is run by foreigners, Swiss foremen, German engineers, an American manager, complete with Taylor methods,' Dimitri said. 'Have you thought of running a concession there?'

'Would *you* want to manage Russian labour? You remember what it was like, Dimitri.'

'Put them on piecework.'

Sergei shook his head. 'I'd have to be there. Manage on site. The police might object. Though that could be fixed.'

Dimitri raised an eyebrow.

'Of course. Everything can be fixed. For how much longer, I'm not sure. But right now, yes. But that's not the problem. My problem is over there,' and he raised a glass in Asya's direction.

'I must remain in the wings. She insists.'

'I lost him once. Why should I lose him again?' she said.

There was a pause, and then Sergei turned to Olga. 'I hear you have a problem.' Olga cast a look of embarrassed reproach at Asya.

'Tell me,' Sergei went on.

'Our lease on this place runs out in three months. They want us out.' Olga looked so bereft that Asya put her arm around her and rocked her back and forth.

'How much will it take?' Sergei asked, looking about the low, blackened kitchen. 'To buy him out?'

Dimitri opened his palms outwards. 'More than I have, Sergei Apollonovitch.'

'Leave it to me,' Sergei said.

When Olga had stoked up the fire in their bedroom and had withdrawn, blowing Asya a kiss and keeping her eyes comically averted from Sergei and his bare chest above the sheet, Asya whispered, 'Do we have the money?'

'It can be found.'

She nestled against his shoulder, her ear against the little square scar. He ran his fingers through her smoke-scented hair and they watched the shadows from the fire leaping and dying against the bedroom wall.

After a while, she whispered, 'You never told me about burying those bodies in the limepit.'

'Live skeletons pushing dead skeletons into a ditch.' He laughed softly in the darkness. 'I thought, if I ever get out of this alive, I will never be afraid of anything in my life. I will make my own rules.'

She pulled him close, pressed her body against him, so that he would be sure of her, so that he would feel the full force of the new life that was his after that moment on the railway siding when he had stared into his own grave.

'They broke me. They did. I am not proud of it.'

She was not sure she had heard. He spoke so softly.

'Darkness, beatings, the cold, the work. In the end, they won.'

'It's over. Here,' she said. 'I am warm. I can make you better.'

'It's never over.' He smiled and stroked her body, and then said, 'I am what they did to me.'

'I love you,' she whispered.

'I am what they did,' he repeated.

The next day they drove into Saint Rémy, and while she sat in Le Relais des Alpilles, warming herself with a Calvados and watching the farmers whacking *belote* cards down at the next table, Sergei went to the notary who handled the Ourousoffs' lease. When he came back an hour later, he was smiling. 'It is arranged.'

'What? A new lease?'

'I've bought it. It's yours.'

Dimitri was ashamed. 'No, Sergei Apollonovitch, impossible.'

'Not impossible at all.'

'But I can't accept . . .'

Sergei clapped him gently on both shoulders.

'Dimitri, you cared for Asya and Niki when I was in prison. My turn.'

For the next five years, Asya and Niki spent every family summer at the Ourousoffs'. Seryozha joined them for ten days and would focus entirely on Niki. Asya had only to look at the photographs that Olga took, and meticulously dated, to bring back every scene:

1927. Up and down the dusty track, Niki on the wobbling bicycle, Sergei running beside it. 'That's it! Keep straight!'

1928. At La Tour des Sphinguettes, in the waves, Niki on his father's shoulders shrieking: 'No! Too cold! Stop!' and Sergei laughing, his muscular body gleaming in the sunlight.

1929. Niki and Sergei seated cross-legged on the carpet in the sitting room playing drafts in their bathing suits, identical solemn expressions, the same tawny skin and auburn hair.

1930. By the carp pool in the Ourousoffs' garden, Seryozha teaching Niki the names of the insects they caught and released; baiting a worm on a hook and some fishing line for Niki to catch the old carp that cruised through the lime-green shadows.

One summer morning in 1931, Sergei stood up and announced: 'This place needs a swimming pool.' And, incredibly, that very week the hole was dug behind Dimitri's wood, in a sunlit hollow backing onto a maize field. To all of them, to Olga, Dimitri, and above all to Niki, Sergei was the miracle maker.

On the days when they hiked together in the Alpilles, Sergei told them about the times he used to hunt with his father in the brackish marshes of his estate, and Asya felt herself reaching out to a tousle-haired boy, hands smeared with blood, searching for the fluttering and shot-riddled birds in the long grass.

She would sit under the mulberry tree watching the light fade against the flanks of the Alpilles, and she would hear the sound of Niki's voice, reading Chekhov to his father in the hammock. And she would remember how Sergei used to carry the boy up to bed, his dust-powdered feet bouncing gently against his father's trouser legs. It seemed incredible that Niki was now thirteen.

Yet even in the most time-suspended moments of family life, even when they were just playing cards together at the dining-room table, Asya could hear the beat of Sergei's will, relentlessly counting off the seconds. It was as if he could not bear the formless character of family life, as if he was only truly happy when time was short, when there were only seconds left, when some opportunity had to be seized. She once implored him, 'Why can't you just *live*? Why can't you just *be*?'

He seemed genuinely puzzled, and was unexpectedly gentle when he answered, 'I have to leave that to you. You know how.' It was as if, for one instant, he was begging her to teach him. But she never could.

For just as suddenly as he descended on them, just as completely as he had taken up Niki and turned the searchlight of his attention upon him, Sergei would be gone again, to Milan for a meeting with the Italian buyer of his Romanian rapeseed, to Zurich for a meeting with his banker, to Riga or Stettin or Danzig for a purchase of Baltic lumber.

'Where does he go?' Niki asked.

'I never know,' Asya replied.

'Why don't you know?'

'Because,' she answered, 'he is a law unto himself.'

When Sergei was away on his travels, she and Niki resumed life as it had been before his return. He no longer slept in her bed at night, but Botynsky came over in the evening and helped him with his schoolwork, and read him stories from Vladimir Dahl's anthology so that Niki would learn his Russian from the purest sources. One weekend in 1933, Lapin came over from London, and they all went for a drive in Razumkin's grand black Citroën. They were returning to Paris in the dusk when they came around the corner of a deserted country road and Asya saw a pair of stone gateposts topped with a pair of lions, and behind them a long cathedral nave of poplars.

'Stop!' she cried, and they all tumbled out and followed her as she strode off through the gateposts. Niki caught up with her.

'Where are we?'

'It's just like Marino.'

Lapin nodded. 'Yes, the gateposts.'

'But Mother.' Niki didn't understand.

She took his hand and said, 'Come,' and they ran together up the darkening avenue of poplars.

This was how it would be, she explained to him. Only the stone lions would have remained on their pedestals, chipped, over-grown, guarding the entrance to a garden that no longer existed, a path to the big house, remaining only in the memory of old and frightened peasants thereabouts who would not speak to anyone of a life they had once observed through the fence. As they walked between the poplars together, with Lapin, Botynsky and Razum-kin following behind, she told Niki of the great peach-coloured house, the room with the bullseye window under the eaves where she had been born, the garden laid in box hedge and the greenhouses warm and verdant amidst the hard white snow. She had never told him this before. They came to a clearing at the end of the poplar alley, and his mother threw back her head and began to laugh.

'Look!' she cried.

There were three suburban villas in pink stucco, side by side. Three walled gardens, with dogs on chains ranging behind them, lighted lamps behind metal shutters, and three sets of lives inside drawing in from the chill of dusk. Once there must have been a great house here, must have been a grand destination for the poplar alley, and a reason for the stone lions and the gateposts. But not a stone remained.

Asya cried, 'This was what the Revolution was for! Don't you see? The château was burned and put to the sack, all for this. Three villas! In pink stucco!'

None of them ever forgot the strange exhilaration that grip-ped her. It was as if she was dancing on the ashes of her memor-ies, rejoicing in her refusal to surrender to the pathos of all her losses.

On the way home in the car, Niki asked her, 'How many rooms were there?'

'One hundred and fourteen. Lapin and I counted them.'

'And how many servants?'

'I told you. We had forty butlers. Forty butlers, and forty pairs of white gloves to go with them,' and she laughed and lit a cigarette. But no, he really meant it. How many? And so she began to count: Nanny Saunders, and Praskoviya Ivanovna, and Anton

Nicolaevitch, and the pantrymaid, what was her name? and soon she lost track.

'Why don't you have any pictures?' Niki asked.

And she put her arm around him in the darkness of the car, as the lights of Paris splashed by the window. 'Because I don't need any.'

'Tell me,' he said, and she told him about the summer ball and about the time she took the young lieutenant from the Smolensk garrison into the greenhouses alone and how Praskoviya had discovered them sitting together on the garden bench beneath the peach tree, and had shooed him away. 'Well, I mean, it was almost dark, and we were holding hands, but I was hardly in any danger,' Asya said.

'On the contrary. It was the lieutenant who was in danger,' Razumkin said from the front seat.

Niki wanted to know what had happened to Marino.

Lapin said, 'Burnt. To cinders.' There was a hurt in his voice that made them all go silent. He reached into his pocket and pulled out a small envelope.

'I'm sorry, Asya dearest. I am a coward. I have had this in my pocket all weekend and I didn't dare show you.'

It was a letter, mailed from Berlin, stamped and counterstamped by sorting offices right across Europe. Addressed to Alexander Galitzine, Saint Paul's School, London, in an uncertain Russian hand. 'The school forwarded it to the bank.'

The note was in pencil.

Dearest Children:

What has become of you? Our house on Nicolaevsky Street is now the publishing house of the university. And Anton Nicolaevitch tells me they put the torch to our beloved Marino. Not all was burnt, but a lot. I am a washerwoman. Can you imagine? Poor children, I wish I did not have to tell you this. We have had such times here as I could not put onto paper. I am old and very tired. I pray for you every day. Do not forget me.

Your Praskoviya.

'Oh, Lapin,' Asya squeezed his hand. 'Can't we find her?'

'I have made all possible enquiries,' he said sadly. 'No forwarding address. Possibly she slipped the letter to a foreign businessman and he posted it for her in Berlin. Impossible to trace.'

'We must do something,' she insisted.

'There is nothing we can do,' Botynsky said firmly. 'She would not want us to find her now. It would put her in danger.'

So there it was, this arrow from the past aimed straight at her heart. What a fool she had been ever to have thought she had put it all behind her. What a fool she had been to suppose she was free.

And Marino burnt. It was one thing to have heard it rumoured, to have thought it possible. How very different to hear it from Praskoviya, to know that it was true. Vandals looting the rooms, stripping the furniture, prying the floorboards up for kindling, strangers roaming the brocaded rooms with crowbars in their hands. And then the flames.

'Will we ever go back?' Niki asked.

She did not know what to reply. In the darkness of the back of Razumkin's car, as the beams of the oncoming headlights cut across his face, he said, 'We will.'

ASYA PACED IN front of the windows of the sitting room in the rue de Solferino, rubbing her upper arms through the sleeve of her jersey, and watched the dark October clouds scudding over the roofs of Paris.

She was always waiting now, either for Niki or for Sergei. How had she got to this moment in her life? She went to the mirror and considered the evidence. 1935. Autumn. Thirty-five years of age. How had she come by those new furrows on either side of her mouth? Everything had stolen up on her without her knowing: these little signs of ageing, this troubled gaze.

He was away so much. She couldn't even remember where it was this week. Was it Prague and Warsaw, or was that the week before? It wasn't oil any more. It was industrial machinery: a whole steel-rolling plant.

Large expanses of his life were unknown to her: those hotels, those Eastern European meeting rooms, even the offices of the Eastern Trading Company, she had never visited. In the old days she used to know some of the names of the men he dealt with. Now she did not even know the names of his closest partners in the company.

When she asked, he deflected her questions. He was tender but absent. The map of their marriage was scored with invisible lines of demarcation. She knew that were she to redraw the lines and insist on sharing his secrets, the result would only be his laying down of some new, unseen barrier between them.

She should have joined him more often on his travels, but whenever she did she hated the hours alone, wandering through the streets of strange cities waiting for Sergei to emerge from those smoky masculine rooms where he put together his deals. In the end she preferred to stay in Paris, working away at the clinic, and let him go. He would simply disappear, then reappear with an absurd story or two to tell, and always making more and more money, which he treated with casual indifference.

The truth was that she had let it all happen. For she did love the unapproachable part of him and the look that said, My dearest, these are the facts – I am alone, and so are you. And for his part, didn't he love the same thing? His favourite word for her was 'incorrigible'. She liked it when he said that. It acknowledged the existence of a dark region of herself which she often lost sight of: an unteachable and unreachable core.

Had he been unfaithful to her? Were there women in those hotel rooms, in Riga, in Prague, in Berlin? She could not be sure. He was the kind of man who would take care to efface any hint of perfume or smudge of lipstick. Carelessness would have offended his meticulous nature. He was never careless, and he never allowed anything to happen that he had not intended. He never missed a change in her mood, never failed to read her mind. So if he did not want her to find out, she never would. She was more than resigned to this. She was almost admiring. She knew that Sergei assumed, without ever saying a word on the subject, that she would be as meticulous in her secrecy as he was. He was ruthless, and he accepted that she might be too.

He had never said a word about Botynsky, and he had even made a substantial anonymous contribution to the editorial expenses of *The Russian Voice*, anonymous because Botynsky would have refused it had he known its source.

The clock in the sitting room struck six. Rain had begun to streak the French windows. Where was Niki, she suddenly wondered. He was supposed to have been home from school two hours ago. She grabbed her coat, dashed down the stairs and ran through the crowds in the rain-slicked streets. She followed the route Niki usually took. People stared at her and she ran on, absolutely sure, in that place at the centre of herself where the tocsin sounds, that something terrible had happened.

Up ahead, a crowd of people, their faces lit by the light that streamed from a café, clustered around something in the road. She elbowed her way into the middle. There, in the centre of the circle of wet shoes, lay a white-faced figure breathing rapidly, like a frightened animal. She bent down. Among the crowd, observing the wounded figure with the same neutral curiosity as everyone else, was Niki.

'What's the matter?' Niki wanted to know.

'You were late!' she shouted, and strode off towards home leaving him to straggle behind. She was furious with herself, because she had always believed that she would know when he needed her protection. It seemed unspeakable to her that her protective instincts had misled her. What would happen if he really was in danger? Would the tocsin sound inside her then?

'What's the matter?' Niki said again when he came through the door of their apartment.

'Your father is away too much. I get jumpy.'

'Mother . . .'

'I know. It's ridiculous, but I suddenly had this feeling you were in trouble somehow, that you might be injured . . . when I saw that crowd I was absolutely certain you were . . .'

'Mother, I'm sixteen.' And he put his arm around her, his sleeve wet from the street. She leaned her head on his shoulder. His upper lip was dusted with a comical moustache. His eyes were grey like hers, and his body was compact and muscular like Sergei's. Yes, almost an adult. Incredible.

She took his hand and placed it against her cheek. 'I have these premonitions. But I was wrong. Here you are, safe and sound. I am being ridiculous.'

He stroked her arm.

'I have not been a good mother. Botynsky. Razumkin. Sergei. All these men. All my running about. You have been very patient with me.'

'Mother, what is the matter?'

'Where were you?'

'With Sonichka.'

So that was it. Asya drew away. Botynsky said that the girl's father, old Dimitriev, was a perfect candidate for the Black Hundreds: pious, fanatical and unreconciled. 'The type who was happiest in the old days smashing Jewish shop windows in Kiev.'

'We drank tea,' Niki said, 'and we talked.'

'Who is this "we"?'

'We had a meeting. Loyal officers, people my age, too.'

'Who?'

'You know perfectly well.' And he left her and went to his room.

Young Russia. That was the name of the organization Niki had joined. At Sonichka's bidding.

'And I suppose I am old Russia,' she had said to him.

'No, no,' he had replied, but she knew that he thought she was: resigned to exile, collaborating with loss, while they were young and vigorous, held parades, denounced the Bolsheviks, smuggled in Bibles and portraits of the royal family, and God knows what else. 'At least we are trying to do something,' Niki said.

She knew that the whole milieu was enraged and futile. Niki shouldn't be mixed up in it. The head of the Union of Veterans, General Kutiepov, had been kidnapped in the street right in front of his office, and had last been seen in a pine box – so rumour had it – being wheeled up the gangplank of a Soviet freighter in Le Havre which set sail for Leningrad. For weeks no one in the Russian community had talked of anything else.

'Niki,' she had begged him. 'Keep away from these people. It is too dangerous.'

'What is dangerous?'

'Botynsky says some of the Young Russians are spies and provocateurs. Who knows what they get up to?'

But the danger lured him ever closer.

Sonichka was to blame: all shrill adolescent conviction. 'Remember General Denikin's remark about Stalin,' she said once. 'Like a radish. Red on the outside, white on the inside.'

'What is that supposed to mean?' Asya had said, struggling to be polite.

'The purges are destroying the Bolshevik party. Stalin is doing our work for us.' Sonichka and Niki shared a triumphant look. He actually seemed to believe this. It was too depressing.

Sonichka was sexual, too, in a confident, rapacious way: the eyeshadow, the deceitful use of her mother's rouge to make herself look older, the brassière which lifted up her small, pointed breasts. The whole effect in a young girl was appalling, Asya thought. And

Niki believed he was in Heaven; shy Niki, so awkward and unformed.

And, on top of all this, Asya was sure Sonichka was setting Niki against Sergei.

'You should not trade with the Soviet regime,' Niki said in a pompous way that was so unlike him.

'You should not waste your time with adolescent reactionaries,' came Sergei's reply.

It was so obvious now what had gone wrong. It wasn't the politics. After all, who cared about politics? It all went deeper. Why hadn't she seen it coming? She went over the accursed ground, combing her life for clues, tracing everything back to the very first moment, when Sergei returned. Staring up into his father's face for the first time, Niki must have decided, in that fatal instant when everything is decided, that Asya loved him only because he stood for this beloved absence, because his hair, his eyes, his skin, had kept this stranger's memory alive in her heart. It was not true! But she knew that something had been broken between her and her son in that instant of return, and that nothing she could ever say would mend it again. And there was something in Sergei's claim upon her that could not forgive the years in which she had lived alone with Niki. Botynsky was not the issue. Razumkin was not the issue. Both could play the devoted but impotent admirer. The person who stood between him and her was their son. When Sergei made love to her, when he gave her such intense pleasure, when his hands tore the sheets beneath her, when his kisses stung and bruised, she was suddenly afraid. Then she knew that he was not what he seemed, the dispassionate foe of all jealousies. In his heart, he raged to possess her alone.

She cursed what lucidity she had, for lucidity could not stop the fatal unravelling already underway. She had once loved family Sundays, but now she dreaded them.

Sergei would be carving the roast, Botynsky and Razumkin at the far end, Asya and Niki on either side of the big dining-room table. Pointing with his carving knife in Niki's direction, Sergei would say, 'Now, my boy. The capitals of the Baltic republics.'

'Riga.'

Pause.

'Revel.'

Pause.

'Kaunas.'

'Excellent boy.' And a large slice of beef would be proffered, held between carving blade and fork.

Often that would be as far as it went. Niki wanted to do his best. His eagerness to please would make Asya ache for him.

But then one Sunday the game went too far. She had felt the pressure in the house rising all morning. It was damp, and Sergei's shoulder ached. He had pulled away when she offered to massage it. Then he had gone into his study in his dressing gown and pyjamas to listen to the news from Radio Moscow on the crystal set. Because of the deafness in his left ear, he listened with his head cocked. Usually she found this comic, but this morning he was not in a mood for jokes. He winced with irritation at the news coming through the deafening intercontinental hiss. The Soviet Trade Commission in London had been expelled for spying; the Paris commission had been purged. Unusually, Sergei had talked about these things.

'Our luck is running out.'

'Why?'

'We have entered the era of "socialist construction and the five-year plan". God knows what they shall want to purchase from us.'

And she left him bent over the radio, trying to decipher the clues. When she returned, bearing a cup of coffee, she asked him what the radio had been saying.

'Construction of the White Sea Canal, north of Leningrad. Where I was in prison. Two hundred and fifty thousand workers, they say. They are reporting Kalinin's speech on the subject: all the usual lies. "Great socialist achievement" and so on and so on. Actually it's all slave labour. You can imagine what it must be like. And they're saying no foreign machinery. Not one kopek of foreign exchange. Proud as punch of that. So, you know what that means? The poor devils will build that canal with their hands. In the permafrost.'

'Botynsky is right. You cannot deal with these people. You must stop.'

'Asya, why are you talking to me like this?'

'Because we always tell each other the truth.'

'Botynsky is the source of truth?'

'You are jealous.'

'The truth. What do either of you know about the truth?' He turned away and stared out of the window, rubbing the square wound on his shoulder.

At lunch he carved the joint, as usual, and then announced: 'And now, a little contest . . .'

Razumkin groaned.

'Five members of the Politburo. Any five.'

'Enough, Sergei Apollonovitch,' Botynsky said.

Razumkin looked down at his plate and stuffed his napkin into his shirt. 'Too difficult,' he said. 'They're all being purged. Who can keep track?'

'That's enough,' Asya said.

Sergei ignored her, and pointed his carving knife at Niki. 'Now, my boy . . .'

'Stalin.'

'A good start. Next?'

'Kalinin.'

'Very good. Next.'

Niki looked straight ahead, wondering who would rescue him.

'Next!' Sergei's carving knife was motionless in the air, pointing at his son.

'Gorky.' The boy faltered.

'Wrong. For his services to the Revolution, for all the lies he has told, he is resting quietly on the island of Capri. A cunning fellow. Next.'

'This is ridiculous.' Botynsky rose, threw down his napkin and pushed his way through the double doors into the salon.

'Tukachevsky?' Niki's voice was cracking.

'Wrong. Candidate member only. Deputy Commissar for War, my old opponent in the Civil War. Next!'

'Stop this at once,' Asya hissed.

Niki threw down his napkin, shouted 'Trotsky!' in a voice twisted with rage, and left the room. Asya followed him.

Only Razumkin was left now. Sergei lowered the knife and said quietly, 'Wrong. Trotsky was purged in November 1927, deported to Alma Ata, exiled to Constantinople on the 12th of February 1929. Currently hiding in Norway.'

'And you think Niki doesn't know that?' Razumkin said, not looking up from his food.

'Of course he knows,' Sergei said, sitting down and slicing into his meat.

When Asya returned they ate in silence, and then Sergei said, 'You protect him too much.'

'I cannot protect him from anything.'

'Exactly. So why do you try?' Sergei was at his most glacial. 'Who protected you? No one, thank God, and you learned to fight. Which is why I love you, but him –'

'You talk about him as if he isn't your son.'

'Don't be absurd.'

'He is a boy, for God's sake!'

'He is sixteen years old.'

'I want him to have a childhood.'

'Did I have a childhood? I was in the officer training school at sixteen.'

'More's the pity,' Asya said.

'I want him to know something a little more useful than "*nos ancêtres les gaulois*", or whatever they teach him at the lycée.'

'And I won't have him turned into your dancing bear. Never again, do you hear me?' She enunciated every word with cold fury.

'Niki,' she called over her shoulder. 'Please return to the table.' The boy did as he was told, and they finished the meal in silence. Out in the hall, Botynsky pulled on his coat and slammed the apartment door.

That evening, Seryozha went riding alone in the Bois de Boulogne, and she stayed at home. Niki remained in his room. Asya roamed from dining room to kitchen to living room and back. She looked out of the windows at the night sky. How had she let this happen? Why was she so helpless to stop it?

When Niki was asleep, she went out to meet Botynsky at the Café Voltaire. A Russian evening. The great singer Plevitskaya, wife of General Skoblin, would sing. But, above all, Russian worker poets would read, direct from Moscow.

When she came through the door, Botynsky waved to her from a table near the little stage. She had to make her way past the Russian taxi drivers downing vodka at the zinc counter, past the mild penurious Russian couples sharing a glass at little tables at the back, past the lady poets with neglected grey chignons and yellowed teeth who sat alone at tables with their manuscripts in front of them, tattered offerings, Asya imagined, to press into the worker poets' hands. As she moved between the tables towards the stage, past all the watching faces, she felt ashamed of her sable, a trophy of Sergei's latest deal at the Soviet fur sales: poverty seemed to be mocking her good fortune. Worse, there was a couple sitting with Botynsky, a fashionable young man and woman. She sat down flushed and unhappy. I shouldn't have come, she thought, as Botynsky kissed her hand and made the introductions.

Louis was a young man, perhaps twenty, whose leather jacket was open on a blue workshirt and who pushed the long golden hair from his forehead with a theatrical gesture. One of those bourgeois communist poets, she thought. If only Botynsky weren't so ready to endure such people. But Gaby was more interesting: red lips burning through the smoke like a shop sign, a strong pale face and sharp black eyebrows, her straight blonde hair cut clean and sharp against her neck. Botynsky introduced her as a *mannequin mondaine*.

When Plevitskaya opened the evening with what she called a bouquet of Russian songs, it was all Asya could do to remain in her seat. Black eyes, hands clasped, bosom rising, voice quivering — her shameless sentimentality epitomized everything about the Russian milieu that Asya despised. She sunk into her sable, willing the wretched woman to vanish from the stage.

After Plevitskaya had milked a final encore from her long-suffering audience and had minced away into the wings, one of the worker poets appeared from behind the red curtain, to deafening applause. He was not five metres from where she sat, and she recoiled from everything about him: his brutal size and his heavy lips, his black boots and black costume. The way he came to the podium, the way he stared them down, everything was mannered: all the tedious poses of a futurism now mocked by the future. She hated the way he insisted that everyone pay him the tribute of awed silence. He planted his feet wide and began to recite, his head thrown back, declaiming the harshest and most intransigent syllables of her mother tongue. She was close enough to see the veins on his neck standing out, to see his saliva jetting through the spotlight, the sweat beading on his forehead. All the intensity of will of the Revolution seemed concentrated in the deep furrowed line between his eyebrows, in the clenched set of his mouth and jaw, in his burning eyes. She thought: He is Soviet, I am Russian, and we have no words in common. The best is here. And there? Only terror and lies.

But the voice held her back. He had begun to recite lines from Mayakovsky, and stillness descended on the room. Into the silence flowed the voice, at first loud and harsh, and then sombre and low, sonorous as a tolling bell.

> You wouldn't understand why,
> cold as an ominous sneer,
> I am carrying my soul to be slaughtered
> for the dinner of impending years.
> Rolling like an unwanted tear
> from the unshaven cheek of the square,
> I am probably the last poet.

As the voice washed over her, Asya gradually gave herself to him and let the sound of his voice carry her to every one of the unvisitable places where her grief was stored.

The poet shut his eyes and softly recited Mayakovsky's words:

> I am a poet.
> I've erased the difference
> between the faces of friend and foe.
> In every mortuary, I looked for sisters.

When he had finished, she rose to her feet. Everyone around her was applauding while Asya remained transfixed, staring at the flickering red curtain. Gaby rose at her side and whispered, 'I didn't understand the words, but I knew what they meant, just looking at your face.'

Asya took Gaby's hand. 'I would like to see you again.'

Then she turned and pushed her way out, past women calling out the poet's name.

Botynsky caught up with her outside. It was damp and cold.

'I'm sorry,' she said, and he took her arm.

'I want to go back home,' he said, running his finger along a black railing.

'Everyone in that room wants to go home, but they can't.'

'What do you mean, can't? Mirsky went back, Svetlanov, dozens of others. All now busy working for RAPP, and the Writers' Union, and God knows what. The journals I get are full of their stuff, most of it unspeakable. Dearest, the Moscow train is full these days.'

'So why aren't you on it?'

Botynsky stopped to wipe his glasses, and sighed his infuriating sigh. 'Haven't you been listening to the radio?'

'Seryozha listens to Radio Moscow, not me,' she said. 'I can't bear it: that awful Russian, the brutal way they speak.'

' "That awful Russian." So what if they speak awful Russian, as Sergei would say.'

At the sound of his name she shrank down inside the collar of her fur. Then he said, 'I detest their Russian. I detest them. But I miss my country.'

Botynsky began walking with one foot in the gutter, limping up and down, up and down. 'Painted picket fences and village roads, bluebottle flies dozing between the panes of the storm windows, the kvass cart on the corner, the steam in the public baths . . .'

'Birch trees, balalaikas, the smell of charcoal in the samovar,' she mocked him. 'So go home.'

'You know perfectly well . . .'

'So go.'

'There's you,' he said.

'What about me?'

'I'm in love with you.'

'Don't talk nonsense,' she said firmly, digging her hands into her pockets.

'I love you,' he repeated.

She took his arm. 'Remember, in Aigues Mortes, in that hotel room, with the terrible stained wallpaper, remember?'

'You were waiting for him to come back. I was an interlude.'

'Stop it.' And to change the subject she said, 'Who was that beautiful girl?'

Botynsky uncurled the glasses from his ears and stretched his arms out to the night sky in a ludicrous gesture of yearning.

Asya began to laugh. 'Is she allowing you a bite?'

He bared his teeth, which like everything about him were long, thin and sharp. 'Not so much as a nibble.' And then, in his drollest manner, he said, 'You women all think I am so companionable, so inoffensive. All I want to do is tear you to pieces!'

She laughed. 'Oh, Botynsky, my only friend.'

'I don't want to be your friend,' he said, 'I want to be your husband.'

When they were at her door she said, touching his lips with her glove so that he inclined his forehead against hers, 'I still love you.'

'No you don't. You love the monster upstairs.' And with that he kissed her, pulled his collar up around his neck and slipped away into the fog.

She loved the monster upstairs. She couldn't understand why she had submitted to his malign enchantment. She wandered through the rooms of the apartment, still in her sable, as if unable to decide whether to stay. She went in and sat by Niki's bed. Poor thing, she thought, poised at the brink of adulthood, hovering at the lip of the waterfall of disappointment. She had never imagined it would be so painful to watch a child grow up.

She slipped into their bedroom and began undressing, with her back turned to Sergei, who watched her over the top of his reading bifocals as her slip slinked to the floor, as her stockings were rolled down to her ankles, as she rubbed the red line where the elastic dug into her thigh. He tossed a pile of business reports onto the carpet.

'How was your poets' evening?'

She did not reply.

She felt his eyes sweeping over her and she wanted to pull him out of the prison of his body, to obliterate the distance between them so that they would be one person, one set of eyes, hands, thighs, sweat and bone.

'Why do you love me?' she asked, and when he reached over to cup her long grave face in his hands she drew away.

'Why the question? Because of lunch, that scene with Niki?'

'You are so hard. I can't stand it. You will crush everyone in this house.'

'I won't crush you,' he said evenly.

'You mustn't crush your son. You mustn't. He wants to love you, can't you see?'

'Wants to?'

'You humiliate him.'

'No, I teach him.'

'For you it's the same thing: teaching, humiliation. All the same.' She rolled over to her side of the bed, and lit a cigarette. 'Why do you love me? Answer.'

'Because you are as unlike me as it is possible to be,' he said, and then, coming close and passing his little finger softly across her upper lip, he whispered, 'Why do you love me?'

'Because you are as unlike me . . . because you are from somewhere I will never understand. From the Solevetsky, from the Polar darkness, from the Stolypin wagons. I don't know . . .'

'You should have married someone like yourself, someone like Botynsky, for example,' Sergei said.

'I was waiting for you. Remember? I loved you, dammit,' and she stubbed her cigarette out and turned her back to him.

'Loved?' The past tense echoed in the darkness.

Next morning she phoned Botynsky. 'I need Gaby's telephone number.'

'An alliance of women. I'm not sure I should encourage this.'

'Exactly. I am hemmed in by men. An alliance of women is just what I need. Give me the number.'

'What is a *mannequin mondaine*?' Asya asked when she and Gaby met in the upstairs restaurant of the Brasserie Lipp on the Boulevard Saint Germain.

'The designer puts the clothes on our backs and we are paid to go to parties to show them off. I am a sort of walking sandwich-board for my designer. You don't think I'd wear these damn things by choice, do you?' she said in a strong Toulousan accent, smoothing the violent red silk down her hips.

'Botynsky says he wants to . . .' and then Asya stopped.

'Come on. Say it.'

'Bite you. Just a little bite. There, on your shoulder.'

'Botynsky is ridiculous.'

'I was in love with him once,' Asya said.

'I know.'

At once Asya said, 'He shouldn't have told you that.'

'Yes, he should respect confidences. Only women know how to keep secrets.'

'Who was that man you were with last night? That poet. Louis something.'

'Disposable,' Gaby said, so briskly that Asya began to laugh.

Gaby looked away across the room to return a man's stare and Asya gazed at her apricot-coloured shoulders, her collarbones and the cleft between her breasts, and then caught sight of her own drawn, white face in the wattled mirror behind Gaby's golden head. Sitting with Gaby, a woman in the fullness of her powers, Asya felt weak. Not with jealousy, but with panic at the murderous acceleration of time.

Gaby turned and gave Asya a smile of complicity, as if she understood everything, as if she even understood the horror that can overcome an older woman when she gazes at a younger one's dusky skin. 'I've heard a lot about your husband,' Gaby said softly.

'From whom?'

'We have the same doctor.'

'Razumkin?'

'Indeed. The rascal.' Gaby lit a cigarette. 'I was working in a place. He was a client there. I needed an abortion. He obliged.' She exhaled and smiled affectionately. 'Why shouldn't I tell you?'

'I didn't know,' Asya said, faltering.

'Abortions? Of course. The best in Paris.'

'But it's risky.'

Gaby smiled again. 'Razumkin is well protected, I assure you.'

It was best not to reveal how shocked she was by the news. 'And what does Razumkin tell you about my husband?'

'The Eastern Trading Company. I know all about it.'

'You know more than I do,' Asya said, uneasily.

'Perhaps,' Gaby said. 'But I know how to be a friend.'

'I need one,' Asya said.

Soon Gaby was as much a part of the family as Botynsky and Razumkin. On Sunday afternoons, after lunch at the rue de Solferino, she would accompany Sergei and Asya on their ride through the Bois de Boulogne. As Botynsky said, it was a sight to melt the hardest heart to see Gaby striding into the bar of the Jockey Club after their ride together, tapping her black boots with her whip, the hairs at the base of her chignon slightly moist from perspiration, and her arm coquettishly resting on Sergei's. There was an erotic edge to their friendship which they all enjoyed. The frankness of Gaby and Seryozha's interest in each other seemed to be a kind of joke which Asya was invited to share. When Sergei lit her cigarettes, Gaby's hand rested on his, and then they would both look at Asya as if to say: This is a game.

Gaby had too much acuity in matters of the heart to misjudge her part in a ménage-à-trois. All the time that she flirted with Sergei, she managed to give unmistakable signs that her first loyalty, perhaps even her first love, was to Asya. This became clear the night Asya and Gaby stole away together to Pigalle.

Gaby thought it would be amusing to go out together, just two girls, to see a strip show. They fought off two frightful German businessmen at the next table who kept sending them bottles of champagne, and danced with two quite presentable Englishmen from Derby with large red hands, who took their refusal to go back to their hotels with barely disguised relief. At about two in the morning they tired of the ostrich plumes and sequins. Gaby said they were in need of some real lowlife. She led Asya to a downstairs bar where a girl walked naked along the zinc in high heels, and all the men at the bar gazed up at her. The stupid look on their faces — the glazed fascination, the infantile hunger for the repetition of the same vulgar gestures — suddenly sent them both into helpless giggles. They laughed and laughed and knocked over their glasses, and the patron came up and scolded them for distracting his customers. This set them off laughing even more. They stumbled out into the night together and shared a taxi home, resting in each other's arms, Gaby's nipples hard in Asya's hands, her tongue licking her ears, her lips, her shoulders. They both came to the edge, and then they both pulled back.

When Asya let herself into the apartment that night, Seryozha was waiting for her in his dressing gown, writing letters, and when she said she had been with Gaby she could see that the thought inflamed him. He lifted her up in his arms and took her into the bedroom. Soon Asya felt his lips upon the places Gaby's had touched.

Asya and Gaby never repeated that night together, but they never disavowed it either. It was their secret, their conspiracy against the men of the world. Which was why Asya could say one day over lunch at the brasserie, 'I should be worried about you and Sergei, shouldn't I?'

Gaby put back her head and laughed, and Asya was seized by a fierce desire to kiss her lips again, to feel her darting, liquid tongue.

'I like you together,' Gaby said, her smile fading into a half-serious expression. 'Nothing like it in Paris. A ruthless man and a decent woman who stands up to him. Very good. Very rare.'

'Why ruthless?'

She considered for a moment, running her fingers over Asya's gloved hand. 'There is nothing he wouldn't do, if the matter required it. I don't mean that he has no conscience, but that he is hard. Once his mind is made up, he wouldn't lose sleep over anything. Am I right?'

Asya nodded, feeling the warmth of Gaby's hand in hers. 'Have you ever been in love?'

Gaby thought about it for a moment, looked at her carmine nails and then shook her head. 'No,' she said. 'Too risky.'

Gaby seemed to live entirely in the present, unencumbered by memory or regret. So envious was Asya of this that she day-dreamed about Gaby's seductions, saw her stretching back naked upon her bed and whispering, 'Come here.' Yet Asya also believed that there was something about the depth of human attraction, about lasting the course together, that Gaby would never understand. Gaby knew what pleasure was, but not what happiness could be. But then, no sooner had Asya thought this than she recoiled from her own pride. For did she, Asya, really know what happiness was? Did she know where her own had gone?

ON THE 14th of June 1937, Asya organized a party for the whole 'family' to commemorate the thirteenth anniversary of Sergei's return from captivity. Gaby flew in from a modelling job in Munich. Olga and Dimitri came up from Saint Rémy. Lapin took the boat train from London. Niki, who had been studying at Heidelberg for a year, returned for the weekend, bringing with him a German friend called Manfred. Sergei came back from a meeting in Berlin.

In the morning, they all went to the Exposition Universelle at the Trocadero. Every nation, every region of France, every industry – from cheesemaking to aeronautics – had its own pavilion. Crowds surged from one side of the Seine to the other and then rested in weary clusters around the spectacular new fountains on the Trocadero side. It was a study in excess, Asya thought, and the people who streamed past her in their thousands had the irritable look of those who were gorged on the absurd superfluity of it all.

What the 'family' came to see were the two gigantic pavilions on either side of the Trocadero bridge. On the left was the German pavilion: a gross modernist tower in the spare sub-Bauhaus style, nearly thirty metres high, topped with the eagle and swastika. There were burning sconces on either side of the doorway, as if to herald the entrance to some Teutonic grave. The outside was hideous enough, but the inside, Asya knew, would be beyond endurance: incomprehensible machine tools, pharmaceutical devices in glass cases, blown-up photographs of the Führer patting the heads of blond children, shining youths building the autobahns, and quotations from Goethe and Kant to encourage the belief that all this crude philistinism flowed from the purest sources of German national genius.

The Soviet pavilion opposite, a Stalin skyscraper topped like a layercake with a worker and collective farm girl fifteen metres tall striding into the future holding aloft a hammer and sickle, was no better. Inside, Asya knew, it would be much the same as the German: a different leader patting different heads, quotations from Pushkin instead of Goethe and Kant, but the same abundance of shining youths and the same solemn, mendacious atmosphere.

Asya planted herself on a park bench between the two pavilions, pulled back her skirt to expose her legs to the sun, and said she was staying right where she was. They all tried to change her mind. Sergei said that she might even meet the new Soviet man on display, a Stakhanovite coalminer specially exported for the occasion. Manfred observed that while the German pavilion might be vulgar, it was nonetheless symptomatic and therefore interesting. Niki simply looked embarrassed and irritated with his mother, while Botynsky pleaded ironically: 'The radiant future awaits you on either side. This is no time to play the pathetic old émigrée on a park bench.' But Asya would not budge.

She waited for them outside, watching the families from the provinces – the men carrying their jackets over their shoulders and mopping their brows with handkerchiefs, the women in white blouses, fanning themselves with the exhibition programme – drifting from one radiant vision of the future to the other.

'Didn't I tell you, Olga?' Asya said when they returned to the rue de Solferino and were seated at lunch.

'One pavilion is as vulgar and self-important as the other,' Olga said.

'Exactly,' said Asya. 'Power worship. I hate it.'

'So much for the great ideological struggle of our age,' said Razumkin, sucking on the bones of the stew.

'Mother has no politics whatever. Only aesthetics,' Niki explained to Manfred, and Asya told him not to be so damned condescending.

Manfred, a tall, freckled twenty-year-old with a pair of glasses which he kept pushing up the bridge of his nose, said he agreed with Asya. 'If a political movement supports principles of ugliness – in buildings or painting or whatever – it is a reliable sign that their politics will be ugly too.'

'Wait a minute,' Lapin said. 'The English have appalling taste in public buildings, or rather they have no public style whatever, but they have the best politics in Europe.'

'Best politics in Europe? Neville Chamberlain?' Sergei made a face of mock amazement.

Gaby cut in. 'I thought Speer's monuments in Nuremberg, that great stadium especially, were quite impressive,' she said. 'That's the trouble.'

'Yes,' Manfred said, 'that's the trouble.'

'So you like Speer's aesthetics,' Sergei said, 'but don't like his politics?'

'Like?' Gaby shrugged. 'No, I don't like. The trouble is that it *is* exciting. The searchlights. The vast arenas filled with people. The big banners, the pillars lit with light.'

'Brrrh,' said Asya.

'Brrrh. But still, exciting. That's the problem, isn't it, Manfred?' And Gaby leaned over and took Manfred's hand for an instant as he held his lighter to the tip of her cigarette.

'Yes,' he said. 'The spectacle takes possession of you.'

'Have they made you join the Hitler Youth, Manfred?' Asya asked brightly.

'Mother,' Niki said, irritated.

'So far I've kept my distance,' Manfred said, looking down at the table.

'So far,' Razumkin muttered to himself.

'What?' Niki said sharply.

'Nothing, boy,' said Razumkin, busying himself with the cheese.

While Asya and Olga cleared the table, Sergei said, 'The Soviets are without shame. I shipped them four tons of German textile equipment three years ago, and in their pavilion the very same equipment is on display, restamped on the shafts and presented as the pride of Soviet technology, made in Minsk.'

'Typical,' said Dimitri.

'It is absurd how things Russian affect me,' Olga said, coming out of the kitchen with the coffee. 'There was a little display of white wooden toys in the Soviet pavilion, you know, the old type, now all machine-made and horrible, but still with the old designs, and I stood there,' she put the coffee down on the low table in front of the sofa, 'and all my childhood came back. Looking at the two chickens pecking for grain, the bear banging the stump with a piece of wood, I burst into floods of tears. Such a spectacle. All those guides in their smart blue uniforms and cropped haircuts kept coming over and saying, in Russian, Are you all right, madame? Perfectly, I said, perfectly all right, and my heart was breaking.'

'That's why I wouldn't go in,' Asya said. 'I thought: I am going to succumb.'

'Despite myself,' Olga said.

'Exactly.'

'The electric cars were rather good,' Botynsky said to no one in particular. 'Gaby and I hired one, and I lost control of it, and it banged into the *fromages de France* pavilion.'

'So we bought some cheese and it all ended very well,' Gaby laughed.

'A toast,' said Asya, rising to her feet and holding up her glass of cognac. 'To Sergei. To his homecoming. Our anniversary.' And everyone drank his health, and he smiled, and everyone said he must, he simply must, and he refused, and Asya insisted, and he disappeared and returned, not in his white shirt, ascot, grey flannels and brogues, but in the faded and patched boilersuit and boots he had been wearing on the Sunday morning thirteen years before, when he had arrived on the sixth floor of the tenement in the Square des Batignolles.

'It still fits,' he said.

They all stared at him. Gaby had never seen it before, and got up to feel the material between her fingers. 'Incredible,' she said.

'Were you on a work detail?' Manfred asked.

Sergei smiled. 'If I had been on a work detail, I wouldn't be standing here. No one lasted more than three months in the quarries; and on the woodcutting detail, maybe six months at most. Up to here in the snow,' he indicated his chest, 'cutting down timber for railway ties. I did a month of that and lost twelve kilos.' He smiled again and shrugged. 'I was an officer, a brain, as the criminals say, so when I got out of the camp hospital they put me in the administration. I was one of the few who could read and count.' He put his arm around Asya. 'Your husband was a regular little functionary. I kept the files. By the end, I knew all the secrets.'

A sudden chill desended on the company at the sight of him sitting there in that blue uniform.

'I am still the same person,' he said, and Asya looked away, wondering whether this was true.

'How did they let you out? You've never told me,' Niki wanted to know.

Sergei replied in the same equable tone, 'There was a general amnesty on Lenin's death. I am here thanks to Lenin. And thanks to being the camp clerk. I made sure my file was among those sent to Moscow before the amnesty proclamation.' Sergei peeled the wrapper off a Havana, clipped the end and lit it.

'And they just put you on a train,' Niki said.

'They just put me on a train,' Sergei replied, exhaling smoke in a high, thin stream.

As was his custom, Botynsky lay down in front of the fireplace and rubbed his heart. Flat out on his back, ignoring everyone else. Every Sunday lunch he reclined in this manner, and every Sunday Razumkin sipped his coffee and told him not to make a spectacle of himself.

'You are my doctor. I have angina,' Botynsky said, staring up at the ceiling.

'Exactly. I am your doctor,' Razumkin said, looking away from Botynsky with distaste. 'And massaging your chest makes no difference whatever.'

Botynsky ignored him. Gaby sat on the sofa beside Razumkin and, while sipping her coffee, kicked off her red moroccan high heels and rubbed Botynsky's ears with a stockinged toe.

When Manfred looked embarrassed, Niki said, 'It's like this every Sunday. This is what Asya calls "the family".'

Sergei got up and went into the library. 'Radio Moscow. No capitalist can do without it,' he said as he closed the doors behind him. Through the closed doors, they could hear the hissing of transcontinental radio traffic from Sergei's new RCA radiogram.

'We're great fans of the show trials in this house,' Niki said to Manfred. 'It's our favourite sport, listening to Vyshinsky on the radio.'

Asya gave Niki a sharp look. Every time they mentioned the trials there was a fight. Throughout the last week of August the previous year, Sergei had stayed at home to listen to the trials on the radio. For an entire day the shrill voice of Andrei Vyshinsky, the state prosecutor, had echoed through the apartment, until Asya thought she would scream. It was one of those appalling performances, the affectation of hysteria by a mediocre actor, calling for the death sentence against Radek, Bukharin and Kamenev, one-time heroes of the Revolution and pioneers of Soviet power. Then came the confessions, the flat, wooden syntax of men already dead, being forced to make one last sacrifice for the Revolution, the sacrifice of simple truth. But Sergei listened by the hour, with a rapt and untroubled expression on his face, as if what interested him was how the thing was done, how the souls were broken.

'For God's sake, Seryozha,' Botynsky had cried. 'This is extermination. Of the opposition. Of a whole class.'

Seryozha threw his copy of *Pravda* across the salon. 'Botynsky, I was in the Tsar's army. I saw old Russia crushed by military defeat. By backwardness. By hopeless, genial Russian bumbling. A whole culture was destroyed by . . . people like you. It must never happen again. Do you think I *approve* of Stalin? How can you be so stupid?'

'But you are carrying this ethic of toughness to the point of obscenity, Sergei Apollonovitch. I can't bear it.'

'Do you think it is just an ethical question? Do you think fastidious distaste about his methods matters in the slightest?'

'It matters to me.'

'Exactly. All you care about is having clean hands, so you take refuge in outrage.'

'Refuge from what? I –'

'Refuge from the facts. You cannot run a war economy with the tender liberal politics you dream about. He is destroying his enemies so that he can secure complete control of the apparat.

Come, now. I only know one thing. The steel mills they are building – the ones I send them rolling plant for – will win them the next war. And unless the Soviets win the next war, you, Botynsky, and all of us, will be exterminated.'

Asya had sat between them, Botynsky all rumpled decency and indignant conviction, Sergei all elegant urbanity and incisive hardness, and felt that each spoke for the divided sides of her own character.

After that argument, Botynsky had rushed out vowing never to return. But of course he *had* returned. Where else was there for him to go? Here he was again, lying on the carpet in front of the fire, as ever, while Gaby sat grazing his ear with her toe.

Sergei came out of the study, still wearing his prison uniform. He stood still for a second, watching them. Asya stopped pouring the coffee.

'They have shot Tukachevsky,' he said. 'And eight other generals. A decree of the Soviet supreme court. They've just announced it. My opponent at Perekop. The cream of their general staff. The man who took the Red army to the gates of Warsaw in 1920. They have shot him as a German spy.' Then he laughed, a thin, bitter laugh. 'He and his co-conspirators are being called poisonous pygmies, reptiles of fascist espionage . . .' Sergei slumped onto the sofa and ran his hands through his thinning hair. Asya could see that, for the first time in their life together, he had lost his composure.

After a long period of silence, Botynsky said, 'Sergei, now even you must admit that he has gone too far. This is more than class war, more than weeding out the enemies. This is suicide.'

Sergei for once said nothing. He paced in front of the window. Then he said softly, 'I revered Tukachevsky. He was the symbol of the continuity between the old army in which I served and the new one created by the Revolution. He was the best military tactician in Europe.'

Niki broke the stillness that followed. 'They are tearing themselves apart.' He was smiling, a cool, infuriating smile of the sort his father sometimes affected.

'Yes, they are tearing themselves apart, and we are the ones who will pay,' Sergei shot back.

Niki and Manfred were standing together, framed in the light of the French window which gave out over the rooftops of the city.

Sergei stared at them as if they were complete strangers. 'You do not seem to understand that there will be a war in Europe. Then it will be of absolutely no consequence that you and Manfred studied philosophy together, that you like each other, that you are both liberal, civilized people. Get it into your heads. A war with Germany. And if the Germans win, if you win, my dear Manfred, Europe is done for.'

Manfred was speechless, but Niki clenched his fists and said in a high, tight voice, 'And who in Europe is going to do something about Bolshevism? Who? Not Blum, not Daladier, not Chamberlain, not Beneš. I'll tell you who will: Adolf Hitler.'

Botynsky sat up suddenly. Everyone else was quite still.

Sergei said quietly, 'So that is what you have learned from a year at Heidelberg, is it?' He strode to within an inch of his son. 'If that is what you believe, we have nothing more to say to each other,' and he left the room.

Asya looked helplessly about her, at Botynsky, at Gaby, at Razumkin, but they all looked away. Niki made to go, but she seized his hand and he sat down on the sofa. 'Enough,' she whispered.

After Niki had left to spend the night at Sonichka's, Asya sat up late with Sergei while he read his files, making ticks in the margins with his silver pencil. She watched him, his head and eyes in shadow, the light bathing his hands and the files on his lap.

'What are you thinking?' he asked, watching her watching him. His voice was gentle.

'I was thinking about how you looked when you came back in '24. Your eyes. How shocked you were, how young. Something terrible had happened to you out there in Solevetsky, and there was nothing I could do to help you.'

'Nothing so terrible,' he said, removing his glasses and rubbing between his eyes. 'I just reached my limit. I found out that they could get to me.'

'You must tell Niki what happened.'

'It's too late. He has found me guilty. I am convicted. Do you think anything I could say would make any difference now?' He said it matter-of-factly, and she felt her heart sink.

He sat beside her and held her hand, and she leaned her head on his shoulder.

'Niki and I cannot be reconciled. We are on opposites sides. That is all there is to it, my dearest. It hurts me, but there is nothing I can do.'

'It doesn't hurt you at all.'

At this, he took her face in both hands, and said in a voice that left her in no doubt, 'You will just have to believe that it does.'

And she did.

Her life had now split in two. Her husband traded with the Soviet regime, while her son devoted the time left over from his studies in German language and literature at the Sorbonne to working at the offices of Young Russia on the rue de Colisée. There was nothing she could do: he was eighteen. He was too old to be forbidden; too young to be reasoned with.

Young Russia's sworn enemy was the Union of Return to the Motherland, a Soviet organization whose purpose was to persuade the émigré community to return home. In the émigré quarters, in Clamart, in Passy, in Clichy, the Motherland organization convened meetings, and threadbare families longing to go home came to municipal halls to be given lectures by young Soviet officials about the welcoming embrace of the Soviet people. Niki and Sonichka would burst through the door, hurl leaflets and shout at the huddled families, 'Don't believe them! You will be murdered!' before being thrown out by stubby men in suits.

Once Niki came home with a cut over his eye and refused to tell Asya how it had happened. But she knew. There had been a fight at a meeting. A chair had been thrown. Botynsky told her what was going on. Now she felt ashamed of her indifference to politics. Now she understood how it was tearing her family apart. She read everything, gathered up the newspapers and émigré journals, devoured them. The atmosphere was vile. The pages were full of murders, disappearances, assassinations, plots. Stalin's agents were killing Trotsky's men across Europe. For weeks the papers were full of the Reiss case. Ignaty Reiss, a Soviet agent who renounced Stalin and declared his allegiance to Trotsky after the show trials of '36, was gunned down on a country road in Switzerland in September 1937; later in the same month the secretary of Trotsky's Fourth International was found under a bridge in the Seine with his head cut off.

One morning in February 1938, Asya was at work in her clinic when a patient was brought in from an ambulance and wheeled along the corridors on a stretcher, closely followed by two men who posted themselves at the door of his private room. At first they would not let anyone but her in to see him. She was not even allowed to know his name, but because she had been there for almost twenty years the clinic director whispered: 'Leon Sedov.'

'Who?'

'Trotsky's son.'

He was a thick-faced young man in his thirties, with a heavy line of beard, and he was suffering from a serious abdominal complaint. Dr Sharaevitch and Dr Lopatkin came and went and could not determine what was wrong with him. Trotsky's son stared up at the ceiling, looking grey and emaciated, and then called for his guards, who bent right over next to his face to hear what he was whispering. Asya sat with him one evening and watched him sleeping. The son of the great outlaw, she thought, the creator of the Red army, the victor of the Civil War, the one who had masterminded the battles that had sent her into flight and exile. The genius aboard the armoured train. Hadn't Botynsky once told her that Trotsky kept editions of French poetry to read in his bunk at night? Mallarmé, things like that? The most civilized kind of barbarian, she thought. A literate Genghis Khan. An educated Attila. She felt nothing, really, about all this, merely a sense of pity for this son, always in the shadow of the outlaw father, lying there struggling for breath.

When she came back on shift next morning the men outside the door were gone, and the bed was empty.

'Poisoning,' the clinic director confided. 'Only don't tell anyone.'

'Why not?'

'The clinic will be under suspicion.'

'Did they poison him in here, under my own eyes?'

'Of course not, dear, of course not.'

But she didn't know any more. Anything was possible.

It was all part of the same slowly encroaching vileness: this man poisoned by persons unknown, perhaps in her own clinic, by these agents everyone spoke of, these killers no one could name.

Botynsky was thin and gaunt with worry. The émigré organizations were accusing each other of complicity in these plots. Each would claim that the other was either a fascist, a Soviet plant or a Trotskyist front. Everything was now a front for something else. There was no simple truth left anywhere in the world, Botynsky said sadly, running his hands through the remains of his hair. They were even fighting each other at his magazine, he said. Gaby, who had 'her sources in the Ministry of the Interior' – meaning the young chef de cabinet she had taken up with – would only tell Asya that, if Russians were killing each other in France, what business was it of the secret police? Gaby's habit of knowing everything, of being unsurprised by anything, sent shivers down Asya's spine.

Niki was being drawn into this web of sordid intrigue. She found leaflets in his room: crude mimeographed sheets accusing the Motherland organization of being running dogs, lepers and insects. A language of contagion was infecting him with its poison.

Then, one evening in September 1938, he phoned. 'Can I see you?'

'I'm your mother. Of course. Come home.'

'No. The café on the rue de Colisée.'

'What's the matter?'

'Wait until I see you.'

It was in all the evening papers: General Miller, head of the Russian All-Military Union, had disappeared.

'Stalin's agents. No other possibility,' said Niki, smoking a cigarette. Asya watched him in disbelief. When had he begun to smoke like this? What was happening to her child?

'What do you know? Niki, tell me!'

General Skoblin, Miller's deputy, had also vanished. The suspicion was that Skoblin had connived at Miller's kidnapping. The police had arrested Skoblin's wife, Plevitskaya.

'The woman who sang the night the worker poets came to the Café Voltaire?'

'She was up to her neck in the Miller business.'

'Niki, what is going on?' She begged him to escape from this milieu before it was too late. He promised, because he was scared, but she knew he was slipping out of her orbit. He slept at the Dimitrievs' flat with Sonichka. There were weeks when he joined Manfred in Germany. Everything was spinning out of Asya's control.

In December 1938, Plevitskaya was put on trial in Paris for the kidnapping of General Miller. Asya and Sergei read the newspapers in a stupor. While General Miller's body had not been found, the supposition was that he had been shot and his corpse loaded on board a Soviet freighter at Le Havre. Just like General Kutiepov years before.

'Why?' Asya asked Sergei.

'It's all quite simple, and quite disgusting,' Sergei replied. Miller had discovered that his deputy, Skoblin, had approached the Gestapo with a plan to frame Marshal Tukachevsky as a German spy and pass the information on to Stalin. Using documents supplied by the White Russians in Paris, the Gestapo had forged evidence of Tukachevsky's secret negotiations with the Germans, to make it appear that he was seeking their support for a plot against Stalin. In effect, the Gestapo and sections of the White Russian community in Paris had collaborated to destroy the ablest commander in the Soviet army. When Miller found out about the plot, he was liquidated.

Asya had never seen Sergei so upset.

'I worshipped that man,' he mused. 'His father had an estate in the same province as ours.'

'Tukachevsky?'

'He was three years ahead of me in staff college. The best of my generation. The very best. I should know. I fought him in '19, and we had nothing to compare with him. Nothing. And now what does Stalin have? Voroshilov as Commissar for War. Toadies, lackeys, pygmies, every one of them. It is unbelievable.'

He stood up and went to the window. 'And my own son worked

for the people who framed Tukachevsky. Our son.' He turned and looked at her, and shook his head.

'What do you mean?'

'Where did the Gestapo get the material to frame Tukachevsky? Right here in Paris. From someone in Young Russia. Who?'

'No,' she whispered.

'Let's find out.'

He ordered Niki back home for dinner.

Pacing back and forth in front of the large windows of the sitting room on the rue de Solferino, Sergei said, quietly and distinctly, 'And so you think it is acceptable to collaborate with the secret services of the fascists in order to betray an officer of the Red army? Is that what you think?'

Niki said nothing.

'In your adolescent mind, you suppose that your enemy's enemy is your friend?'

Niki said nothing.

'You suppose that striking a blow against the most brilliant commander in the Red army will be a blow for the eventual restoration of a White regime in Russia?'

Niki said nothing.

'You suppose it is acceptable to collaborate with fascist intelligence services in a murder?'

Niki said nothing.

'Answer me!' Sergei suddenly roared.

Niki looked him straight in the eye and whispered: 'Better than working for Stalin's secret police.'

Seryozha clenched his teeth and said in a whisper, 'Are you accusing me?'

Niki's eyes said it all.

'Please leave the house this instant.'

And Niki did so, with an appalling smile on his face, exalted, self-satisfied, repellent. Asya did not stop him. She listened to him throwing the remainder of his clothes into a suitcase. She heard him pull on his coat and she heard the door slam shut. She did not move. It was now too late to do anything. She sat in the sitting room and watched Sergei pacing by the window.

'How can he believe such things about you?'

'You've heard the rumours.'

'I've lived with them ever since you came back.'

'What do you believe?' He was staring up at the ceiling.

'I would not be in this room if I thought they were true. But . . .'

'But what?' he said softly.

'Seryozha, you keep too much from me.'

And so he told her. Yes, it was no longer Baltic timber and Baku oil. There were arms shipments, medical supplies. Razumkin gave him a hand with the medical side.

'Razumkin?'

'Why are you so surprised? His practice has been in difficulties. He has a very good head for business. Only too glad to assist, as he puts it.'

'Where to?'

'The east.' He found his cigarettes, lit two, and passed one to her.

'Where, Sergei?'

'At the moment, Poland. I want to help Poland. That is where it will begin. They must buy us some time. They are so absurd, the poor Poles. They have a magnificent cavalry. The best stables I have ever seen are in Lodz. I rode with them two weeks ago.'

'So that is what you were doing?'

'Wonderful mounts. But can you imagine? Against tanks? So I must give them some help. No one else will. My dearest, you have the misfortune to have married the last man in Europe who really believes in a free Poland.'

The next day he left for Warsaw again, and he was gone for two weeks. The apartment seemed desolate without him. Asya stood in the doorway of Niki's bedroom, surveying the wreckage left by his departure. She did not have the heart to clean it up, so she left it as it was, the bed strewn with books, the cupboards open, the empty hangers on the rail, the drawers pulled out of the dresser. She could not bear to call the Dimitrievs' apartment, where he must be staying, so she wrote Niki a letter. But she got no reply. It was March 1939. German troops had entered Prague. Darkness still fell early, and she ached for spring.

She developed a cough and a low fever, and Razumkin arrived to listen to her chest.

'Why are you working with Seryozha? I thought you were a doctor.'

He smoothed the coil of hair on the top of his head. 'I help on the medical side. Only too glad to be of assistance.'

'So he says. But why, Razumkin? Why?'

'We are going to have a war, dearest. Indeed, the first skirmishes have begun.'

She climbed the stairs to Botynsky's little flat in the rue de Moscou. The books, the manuscripts, the bottles of glue, the blue dressing gown hanging on the back of the door were still the same, but it now seemed quite impossible that she had ever made love on this bed, that the shelf had ever tumbled down upon them both. Some other life, not hers. There were two sharp lines on either side of Botynsky's mouth, furrowed as deep as a scar.

'Niki won't reply to my letters.'

'He won't see you until you break with Seryozha,' Botynsky said. 'You are a collaborator. His words.'

'Collaborator,' she repeated. 'It has come to this.'

Botynsky nodded, blowing on his coffee and looking out at her through his glasses.

'Never,' she said. 'What Niki did was unpardonable.'

'But not unprovoked.'

She exploded: 'You are so weak, so anxious to understand everyone! No wonder Sergei calls your magazine a sandbox. You are a child. It is impermissible to have any part in an organization which betrays a man like Tukachevsky and sends him to his executioners. Impermissible. That is all.' And then in her vehemence, she began coughing.

Botynsky watched her recovering her breath. He stood, and walked up and down on the faded carpet. 'I do not know what you know. I do not know what you have willed yourself not to see. But I have it on good authority that Sergei was recently seen on the Moscow train.'

'Of course. It passes through Warsaw. He is in Warsaw.'

Botynsky shook his head. 'No, he was seen leaving Warsaw station in the Moscow train.'

She suddenly felt cold. 'Who saw him? Who, Botynsky?'

'I did.'

'What were you doing there? Were you spying on him?'

'Asya, please. I was in Warsaw for the sake of what he calls my sandbox, persuading a Polish poet to publish with me. I just happened to see Sergei on the platform. How can you think I was spying on him?'

'I don't believe you. I don't believe it was him.'

'Asya, you are very good at believing what you want to believe.'

'So I am to believe you rather than my own husband? He never travels to the Soviet Union. He would be arrested and shot at the border. You know that.'

Botynsky shrugged.

'I will tell you what he was doing,' she said briskly. 'The Moscow train goes through Lodz. He was going to Lodz. To the Polish army riding school. There. That is all there is to it.'

Botynsky said nothing, but his eyes seemed so plaintive, so remote behind the concentric circles of his lenses, that she stroked his cheek.

'Thank you for telling me, Botynsky.' He leaned his head against her shoulder, like someone very tired, like someone wanting to sleep.

Yes, that must be it. He was going to Lodz. He would be back on Friday. She would ask.

Sergei was weary when he returned home, and she massaged his shoulder, kneeling astride his back in her nightgown, kneading the little scar between her fingers, running her thumbs up and down the tight tendons on his neck.

'Botynsky said he saw you in Warsaw station. Boarding the Moscow train.'

She could feel a momentary spasm pass through his neck muscles. He opened his eyes.

'I was on my way to Lodz,' he said.

'That's what I said,' she purred, bending low to kiss his neck, her breasts brushing the tips of his shoulderblades. 'You didn't go to Moscow.'

'I never do.'

'I know,' she said.

As he turned over and drew her down upon him, Sergei said softly, 'Botynsky should not circulate rumours about me.'

The next morning he made some phone calls and brought her a cup of tea in bed, and said he had a surprise in store.

'London. For the weekend.'

'Now?'

'This instant,' and he smiled and kissed her.

She hugged him. Yes, an escape. They both needed it.

When the Golden Arrow had deposited them at Victoria station and they had checked into Brown's Hotel, their first port of call was to a little shop in Jermyn Street, where Sergei bought himself some badger-bristle brushes and some shaving preparation and special cologne. They lunched at Wilton's and strolled through Green Park, and were just walking through Piccadilly Circus on the way to the Criterion for tea when a street photographer burst in front of them, snapped their picture and held out a card.

'Delivered right to your hotel! Just furnish me with its address.'

Sergei gripped the man tight. 'What are you doing?' he whispered.

'Hands off, guvnor, just a photo.'

Sergei relaxed his grip and wrote Brown's address on the card, paid five shillings, and they walked on.

Next morning the photograph, miraculously, was brought up to their room with their breakfast. It showed them arm in arm, their feet in step, together, a smile on their faces. 'You were about to thrash him,' Asya said.

'I don't like surprises,' he said.

They spent the whole morning in bed. The papers were brought in and soon Sergei had them spread all over the covers. The guarantee that Great Britain would go to war for Poland had been given in the House of Commons the night before. He read Asya bits and pieces as she nibbled on her toast.

'Mr Hore-Belisha, Secretary of State for War, declares that if we are involved in war our contribution will not be half-hearted.'

'Sounds pretty half-hearted to me,' she said.

'Isn't exactly dying to die for Danzig, is he?'

She wanted to know what Danzig was like.

'Half-German, half-Polish, dirty port town on the Baltic. Poland's outlet to the sea. Standing between Germany proper and East Prussia. Standing in the way of Hitler's dreams of a greater Germany.'

'I know all that,' she said, handing him his toast.

'Hitler supplies the Germans in Danzig with arms, and . . .' he took a large, satisfied bite of toast, 'yours truly supplies the Poles.'

'How?'

'Through Le Havre. Best French machine guns.' With that he kissed her. 'Never forget I was born in Chelm. I'm half Polish. The Poles need all the help we can give them.'

'Why?'

'To give us time. We're next, I'm sure of it.'

He picked up her tray and put it on the floor, swept the papers onto the carpet and, after removing the piece of toast from her hand, made love to her.

In his arms she was transported back to the time when they were still strangers, when their bodies were young. But now, even as he cupped her breasts in his palms and then caressed her thighs, she could not stop herself wondering whether some portion of his mind was taking merciless note of every place where she had aged. She longed for complete forgetting but she knew that time had stolen it away.

But she was happy when she awoke, happy that they were in this hotel room, alone together, safe from the world. She went into the bathroom, looked at herself naked in the mirror and began laughing. 'Look at me! Look!'

And there she was, in the doorway, smiling, drops of wetness falling from her, her body smeared with the dark smudges of his newsprint-stained hands. With a suddenly serious expression on his face, he came over to her, sank to his knees and began to sponge her body clean, removing the stains of time.

They spent the rest of the day in that newspaper-strewn room, calling down for food, listening to the radio, once making a little sortie to Green Park, past the kiosks, for more newspapers, and then returning to jump back into bed and extend, by as many hours as they could, their escape from the world. When night came and they were settled into their bunks on the Golden Arrow sleeper back to Paris, Asya said, 'I feel guilty about not seeing Lapin.'

'Sometimes it is better just to escape,' Sergei said.

When they arrived at the Gare du Nord, and stepped out onto the platform, the papersellers were bawling the news: '*Conscription! Conscription! Mobilisation des réserves!*' She wanted to turn around and burrow back into the crisp white sheets in the burgundy-coloured compartment of the wagon lit, but Sergei gripped her arm and they passed the barrier, searching for Jacquot, the chauffeur. He was there, looking runtish and criminal even in his chauffeur's cap. And Razumkin was there too.

He took Asya's arm, wiped his face with a handkerchief and looked doleful.

'Whatever is the matter with you?' she said, giving him a kiss.

'I think you should sit down.'

'Don't be ridiculous. What is it?'

'Botynsky. His heart. I did my best, but I got there too late.' Razumkin took her hand and kissed it. Sergei pressed her to him.

'When?'

'This morning.'

'There, there. Cry,' Sergei said as she buried her head in the lapel of his camelhair coat.

'I want to walk,' she said, and pulled away.

Sergei snapped his fingers. 'Jacquot, follow.'

She left them and pushed her way through the crowds streaming out of the station. Jacquot hung back, but she could hear the motor of the Citroën purring, a block behind her. She walked until she came to her beloved Clichy, to the rue de Moscou where she stopped for a piroshki and ate it, standing up, hearing Botynsky say to her, 'While it's hot! While it's hot!' and pushing the crumbs of pastry into her mouth. She climbed the stairs to the room with the sagging bookshelves and the blue dressing gown on the hook behind the door. There were men there, one of whom was dusting a cup for fingerprints.

'Madame?' a policeman said.

'I was his friend,' she said. And when she saw the overturned chair and the pile of manuscripts that had slid from it onto the floor, she sank down on the bed and began to cry.

'Who found him?' she asked at last.

The policeman consulted his notes. 'Dr Razumkin. This morning at seven.'

'His heart was always bad. He was always massaging it,' she said. The policeman nodded.

'Where did you find him?' she asked.

'On the bed, where you're sitting, with his arms folded. Just as if he died in his sleep.' He paused. 'What kind of man was he, madame?'

She looked around the room, at the gummy bottle of glue on his desk, at the sagging, dusty shelves. 'He was a poet. A Russian poet,' she said.

At the Russian church on the rue de Crimée, the coffin was open, framed with lilies. Without his glasses, without that squinting, quizzical stare through the thick circles that separated him from the world, Botynsky in his coffin was unrecognizable, a confection of the embalmers.

'Where are his glasses?' Asya said, in the stillness of the church. Razumkin, behind her, whispered: 'Couldn't find them.'

At her insistence, Niki and Sergei shouldered the coffin on either side, their faces stony masks. Razumkin held it up from behind, and after him came Gaby, in a black suit and veil, holding a single white rose. When they reached the cemetery she dropped it into the grave.

Asya put her arm around Niki and whispered: 'Come home,' but he shook his head and remained where he was, staring down at Botynsky's casket in the earth. As she walked away from him, between the jagged gravestones, she felt all the light that had once streamed towards her from the long corridor of the past go out.

Black doors closed behind her, marooning her in a lightless present.

Two months later, in mid-June 1939, Sergei left for Danzig. He was personally escorting a shipment from Le Havre.

'Why do you have to go?' She knew it was useless to ask.

'This shipment must get into the right hands.'

'What is in it?'

He put his finger to his lips. 'I'll tell you when I return.'

She watched him pack the pigskin case with the green silk lining. He was so neat, so economical. Every space was used. Just two changes of underwear, two pairs of socks, light summer trousers, two shirts, his brown leather shaving bag and a spare pair of his Lobb shoes on top. He snapped it shut, turned the key, smiled at her.

At the Gare du Nord pigeons wheeled under the dirty glass panels of the roof and scraps of newspaper drifted underfoot. A few listless soldiers going off to their mobilization points snoozed on empty mail trucks, their helmets in their hands, their knapsacks in a pile.

'Take care of her, Razumkin,' Sergei said.

'Of course,' Razumkin answered, and then Sergei took her in his arms, moved her black hair off her cheek and kissed her and caressed her face. He waved at her until the train was out of sight.

His office phoned her a week later to say that the ship had berthed safely at Danzig. Two weeks passed. He was overdue. She telegraphed his hotel. His reply read: 'Not to worry.'

She lunched with Gaby at the Brasserie Lipp. The newspaper billboards were so full of Danzig that there was nothing to say.

'You should never have let him go, dearest,' Gaby said.

'You couldn't have stopped him either,' Asya retorted, smoking furiously. Then she laughed bitterly. 'He said he was the last man in Europe to believe in a free Poland.'

'Not the only one,' Gaby said. 'This time, even the French will fight.'

'Is that true?' Asya said.

Gaby put a shiny, bright-red fingernail to her lips. 'One of my state secrets.'

July gave way to a hot, airless August. Asya sent telegrams and received two short replies: 'Not to worry. Delayed' and 'Returning Imminently'. She tried to phone and was told that the lines to Danzig, which passed through the German Reich, had been severed. The newspapers reported that the Germans were smuggling arms and provocateurs into the city. Nazi gangs were beating up Poles in the streets. Some communist workers in the shipyards had been kidnapped, trucked across the border and interned in concentration camps. She read and smoked and coughed and read until her fingers were black with newsprint. Every morning she phoned Sergei's office and was told that they had received telegram traffic in the night. He was well. He sent his – and here the secretary would pause and read in a prim voice – 'his most affectionate greetings'. She asked whether she could join one of the ships sailing from Le Havre and the secretary told her that Danzig was now blockaded by German warships.

One morning she phoned the office and there was no answer. The phone rang on and on, echoing in her ear. She decided to go to Passy herself. She found the building. The offices were on the third floor. A plaque was on the door: Eastern Trading/Compagnie de l'Est, in burnished brass, but the door was locked. She bent down and looked through the keyhole. She could see a black telephone, the edge of a calendar hanging on the wall, a typewriter covered with its grey-green shroud. When she heard the phone begin to ring she pounded on the door, but no one answered.

'What do I do, Gaby?' she said, when she got to a phone.

'Leave it to me.'

Next afternoon, Asya was in a long, vaulted room at the Quai d'Orsay, listening to a polite young official assuring her that he would make immediate enquiries with the French consul in Danzig.

'I think he has gone to fight for Poland,' she said.

'We shall look into it for you.'

The next day when she called on him, he said, 'Nothing, madame. He is not at the hotel. That does not mean he is not in Danzig. God only knows what is happening in Danzig. I am afraid your husband has disappeared.'

She walked home, stopping to buy a paper. There in cold type she read the news that Hitler and Stalin had signed a non-aggression treaty. She realized that the official had known this and had seen fit not to tell her. She dropped the paper and walked along the quais. The tide was running under the bridges, and when she stopped and looked down she could hear it sluicing against the arches, like the Vasousa in spring, ripping away the earth around the roots of the willows, pouring across the lawns, flooding the gardens. She watched the river, aware that she had turned cold and clear as she always did when disaster struck. She recalled every fragment of the last time she had seen him, on the platform of the Gare du Nord, the smell of gloves on his naked hand as he caressed her, the light and open smile that said he would be back in a twinkling of an eye, the pressure of his lips upon her face. She thought, with bleak lucidity: I have lost him once again.

Niki returned from Germany on the last Saturday night of peace, arriving on a packed train from the Alsace border. Jacquot drove them home through the milling streets, past the newspaper billboards which screamed the news: 'War! War!' and she felt, as she looked at the young faces streaming past her, that she alone knew what desolation was in store for them all.

'He has gone to fight in Poland,' she explained.

'He has gone to fight for Stalin,' Niki replied.

'He has gone to fight for all of us. To buy us time.'

'You believe that?'

'I do.' As she said it, he knew there was nothing more to say.

'Niki, please stay with me now.'

He shook his head, and put his hand on top of hers.

'Father has destroyed your life.'

She looked out at the crowds on the quais, every face alight with the carnal excitement of a city about to go to war.

'Do you remember the folk tales we used to read together?'

He nodded.

'The one about the king who died and all the people assembled in church carrying unlit candles?'

'And he whose candle lit first would marry the queen and become the king,' Niki remembered.

'Yes. And the stranger, someone nobody had ever seen before, entered the church with a candle, and immediately it burst into flame. And the boyars tried to·put out the candle and drive the stranger away.'

And Niki said, turning to her, 'And the queen cried: "Don't touch him! Whether he is good or bad, he is my fate."'

Asya began to weep. 'Whether good or bad,' she repeated, looking out through the windows of the car at the city on fire with the prospect of war: 'he is my fate.'

PART THREE

RAZUMKIN BENT CLOSE to her face to catch what she was whispering. He pressed her hand.

'What did you say?'

Asya whispered: 'I have been conducting an experiment in dying.'

The experiment had been going on for months. In all the years he had known her, this was the first time she had manifestly given up. The cough became bronchitis, the bronchitis became pneumonia, the pneumonia became TB. And she had let it all happen. 'I am wasting away like the heroine of a bad romance,' she would say, and cough and smile.

Razumkin thought: They have all abandoned her, except me. She is dying, and I have her to myself at last: *son chevalier sans peur et sans reproche*. He sighed and wiped his forehead with a handkerchief. He could see the stars through the hospital window. Asya's fingers were grey against the white sheet.

'Why should I be required to live?' she said faintly.

Razumkin opened his eyes, took a biscuit from the bedside table and bit into it disconsolately. Crumbs descended onto his waistcoat.

'I'm your doctor. I won't let you die.'

'You can't make me live.'

'I can't make you do anything.'

They spoke in whispers, in Russian, heads nearly touching. The curtains were drawn around the bed. In the ward, bodies turned in their sleep.

'It hurts your feelings that I should wish to die.'

'Exactly so.' Razumkin took another biscuit from the table and snapped it between his teeth. There were bulbous mounds of flesh between the joints of his fingers. His suit was stained, his collar yellowed: there was an air of ruination and neglect about him.

Someone was groaning in the darkness. Down a long hall a naked bulb swung in the night draught. A wisp of cigarette smoke was floating through a cube of light across a linoleum floor.

'Where am I?'

'Bordeaux. You weren't in any position to argue.'

He had sedated her, carried her down the stairs at the rue de Solferino with the help of the concierge, and bundled her into the back of Jacquot's Citroën. How light she had been, how her skin had burned, as he carried her in his arms.

No reputable doctor would have moved a patient in her condition. But then, he thought with a certain morose pride, he was not a reputable doctor. Left alone, she might have died in that flat, and if she hadn't the police and the Germans would have paid their call and the poor thing wouldn't even have known what they were questioning her about.

'The Germans are in Paris.'

'What?'

'You've been here about a week.'

'And Niki?'

In Paris, doubtless putting his German to good use. Better to say nothing. 'No word,' he said.

She stared up at the ceiling. 'I want to go to Olga and Dimitri.'

'Better not.' Saint Rémy would be the first place the police would come looking. 'Trust me.'

She looked away and was soon asleep again. He felt her forehead. Still feverish.

The journey had been unspeakable, bumper to bumper on the country roads through the cornfields, with the endless line of families wheeling carts and baggage wagons and prams. Mothers banged on the roof as they inched along, and cursed him for having a car. And then, above the creaking of the carts and the crying and the tramping along the dusty road, there rose another sound, a whine which grew in pitch until everyone was looking up into the vacant sky. He saw a flicker of black light in the rearview mirror, then a roar and a line of machine-gun fire splattering the dust, everyone screaming, hurling themselves into the ditch. Then a diminishing snarl, then silence, then children crying.

A mother clambered out of the ditch beside the car, holding her little boy.

'Take him! Save him!' she screamed.

The car was moving and she ran along beside him, holding out the child, who bobbed in front of the window, with terror in his eyes. All Razumkin could do was look straight ahead down the dusty road, along the endless columns of those in flight, and say in his coldest voice: 'The woman in the back seat is tubercular. Highly infectious. I am her doctor. I cannot take responsibility for your child.'

There. Done with. In his most officious hospital-ward tone. One's training had to be good for something.

As he accelerated and lurched past a haycart, piled with furniture, he caught a glimpse of the woman in his rearview mirror, placing her hand to her face and dropping by the wayside, her child clutching her around the waist. A distressing sight.

Razumkin rubbed his eyes, sighing deeply. He had kept it all at bay, all those frantic scenes, and now he was beginning to unwind. He looked around to get a grip on himself. The sea-green walls were stained and neglected, the lightbulbs glared down under their tin shades, the tree in the grimy courtyard scratched against the streaked windows, and down the corridor, past the vacant nurses' station, a tap was dripping. In all those years of work in private clinics, he had forgotten how sordidly neglected a public charity hospital could be.

How hollow-eyed Asya was. Shrunk to this, he thought, all shrunk to this. Yet another example of Russian self-destruction. It was his speciality. There was a science to it. He could have demonstrated, for example, the correlation between the mortality rate among his patients and the declining fortunes of the White movement. What had only been a nagging bronchitis in 1919 became a fatal pneumonia in 1926. And as the 1920s turned into the 1930s, he would mount the stairs of the tenements – each year, it seemed, a storey higher, as poverty chased them up into the eaves – and find them in some filthy room, piled with Russian newspapers, unwashed cups of tea and grimy icons flickering above candle stumps. He would listen through his stethoscope to the irregular thrashing of their hearts and to that sound in their ribcages, like the tearing of cloth down a dark well. The fury at their dispossession that once gave colour to their cheeks and a fevered energy to their plotting now began to feed upon their flesh. These were people dying, not just of poverty, but of rage. They lay on stained sheets in dirty dressing gowns, hacking away into their handkerchiefs, staring by the hour out of the streaked windows at the lead-grey sky of the city of exile, bitterly resolved to die. There was the same stubborn resolve in Asya's self-destruction.

It was his job to understand, not to approve. It was his speciality, after all. But approve of it? Never. Survive. At all costs and by all means, as Sergei used to say. At first, when Sergei had left for Poland, Asya had played at being indomitable. She kept up with her work at the clinic, she continued her lunches with Gaby, she even let him take her out for dinner occasionally. But he was not fooled. He could see from the clenched way she held herself, from the masked quality of her imperturbability, that she was merely going through with one of her gallant performances. Of Botynsky, not a word. Of Seryozha, not a word. Of Niki, not a syllable. It was gallant all right, but this time the performance had been too much for her.

He warned her about her bronchitis. He advised treatments, sanatoriums. She nodded. She fingered the bottles of pills. She left them unopened. Classic signs. He warned her, 'This is not like you.'

'What am I like?' she replied angrily. 'What does that mean? I don't know any more.'

When her collapse came, she lay in bed in the rue de Solferino through the winter months of the *drôle de guerre*, letting self-neglect slowly claim her: her hair uncombed, her nails uncut, her lips unpainted, her nightdress left open, indifferent to the point of catatonia. He advised a sanatorium. She refused, and he could tell that she wanted to remain at her post in the rue de Solferino, in case Sergei returned. By March 1940 she was so ill she had to be admitted to her own clinic, but to his intense annoyance she discharged herself again as soon as she could walk.

'Let me die,' she had said, quite calmly. 'I am curious about what happens next. Let me go.'

She had said all this, but he did not believe her. His hours by the bedsides of declining patients had taught him that their hold on life was often stronger than they knew. Just now, at his side, her face was not in repose. She had all the strained attention of a saint at prayer. By day, Asya said that she wanted to die. By night, in her sleep, she seemed to be struggling to live.

Razumkin shook himself like a seal and looked at his watch. The first rays of sunlight were streaking across the dismal courtyard and lighting up the branches of the tree against the window. Asya's face seemed almost translucent in the light. Where was everybody? Had the nurses and orderlies deserted? This place was like a ship abandoned on the high seas. Its lights were burning in the night but the wheelhouse was empty. Razumkin called out. No answer. God, they've all hopped it. In the bed opposite, a body stirred with a muffled groan.

If only he could find Gaby. That morning in Paris, as Reynaud pushed her into the back seat of the minister's car, she had shouted, 'Bordeaux, you fool!'

'But where shall I find you, which hotel?' Razumkin had asked. But the car had roared off, drowning her reply.

Gaby was made for times like these. Her flesh gave comfort. She had been the only one who had not ridiculed him for abusing his place as a gynaecologist. She worked on the assumption that no doctor could see her lying with her feet in stirrups without feeling impaled by the force of her carnal presence. 'It takes all kinds,' she said, the gold bracelets tinkling on her wrists as she drew him towards her. Gaby, ridiculous Gaby, *élan vital* herself, where are you? A politician's mistress in times like these was the key to every door. She would know what to do, who to bribe, in order to get them out of this appalling place.

Down the long corridor, a mop was being slopped across the linoleum. The sound, sloshing wearily to and fro, was oddly reassuring. This might be the end of the world, and everyone else

– doctors, nurses – might have taken flight, but this old woman was still at her post. And so, by God, was he, thought Razumkin. Still at my post. He had promised Sergei he would look after her, and he had. In the damnation that now cursed everything he had ever touched, this promise was the one clean and honest thing left to him.

He caressed her face, moved a strand of hair off her cheek. His watch was over: she would sleep like this, he knew, for hours.

Through the open window he caught the faint but unmistakable smell of baking bread. A good omen. One of life's little miracles coming to the rescue. He roused himself and set off outside in search of that smell.

It was about seven in the morning: clear and bright with an edge of chill to it which revived Razumkin as he walked down the cobblestoned streets. By nature a pessimist, Razumkin also trusted to life's capacity to save him when he had run out of ruses. A morning such as this seemed full of promise. The sunlight glowed on the walls, the cobblestones glistened, shutters were being opened at the upstairs windows of the narrow street, and the smell of coffee issued from the kitchens.

At the baker's, however, the queue stretched halfway down the street, a line of anxious women, each determined to buy the place out before the bread supplies vanished. Razumkin joined the back of the queue.

'What's the news overnight, madame?' he asked the woman ahead of him, in her bedroom slippers and a housedress, clutching a string bag in her hand.

'And who are you?'

'A French citizen like yourself, madame,' Razumkin said, with a bow.

'The town is so full of foreigners.'

So, it has come to this, he thought. Identity checks next. Arrest of foreigners, internment. He could see it all coming.

'The Germans are at Tours,' a woman said.

'We're next,' said another.

The baker was limiting each customer to six loaves, and already the women were wheedling.

'But I have six children!'

'I know her, she just has her father to feed.'

'It's not fair!'

'Make an exception.'

The baker, in flour-dusted shorts and a singlet, played judge in a tribunal of rough justice. 'If I start making exceptions I'm done for,' he shouted. When it came to Razumkin's turn, the baker shook his finger.

'Only my regulars.'

'But . . .'

The woman behind him was already nudging him aside with her elbow.

Razumkin held on to the counter with both hands.

'I am a doctor. I have a patient at the hospital. I must have two loaves.'

The baker looked Razumkin up and down, took in the dirt-stained collar, the rumpled suit, the grey unshaven face and the oily hair snaking across the bald forehead.

'Poor bugger,' the baker said, and handed him one loaf.

Razumkin fumbled in his pocket and placed the worn bills meekly on the marble counter. 'Next!' the baker shouted, and Razumkin was elbowed aside into the street.

He stopped at the corner and leaned against the wall to regain his breath. The world was unravelling, and all he felt was shame, endless shame. He walked on towards the railway station, chewing disconsolately from the heel of the loaf. People were running in every direction, women with children and babies in arms, soldiers and policemen, everyone in flight. The station concourses were jammed with baggage and porters and people shouting for each other. He felt disengaged, as if in a film: panic in every face, a vortex sucking them all under – it could not be happening. But it was. Razumkin breasted his way through the crowd towards the station hotel. A Calvados was what was needed.

The alcohol seared its way down his throat. He looked at himself in the bar mirror: poor bugger. Must change the shirt and the suit. Must pull myself together. His suit front was covered with baker's flour. He dusted it away, straightened his tie. If only this dread could be stilled.

At that instant a man and a woman skipped down the steps of the hotel entrance. Razumkin leapt to his feet and rushed after them.

'Gaby, help me!' he cried.

Gaby was just stepping into the back seat of a black Citroën. She fingered his filthy lapel. 'You and everyone else, dear old man. Look at you. You mustn't let yourself go to hell like this. It is at just such moments that appearances count for everything.' Hers was the only face not twisted with panic.

A finger tapped impatiently at the Citroën's window. 'Can't stay. The plane is waiting.'

'Where to?'

'The cabinet is flying to Algiers.'

'Take me with you.'

She considered for an instant.

'Not me, I mean us,' he said.

'Who else?'

'Asya too. She is in hospital.'

Gaby shook her head, but she was reaching into her handbag.

The hand rapped hard at the window. She waved the irritation away with a flick of her wrist.

'Here,' and she handed Razumkin a set of keys. 'Nice, 14 rue Masséna, flat 4. My hiding place. Take her there. And Razumkin, be very careful. There are rumours about you. Don't get caught by the Germans.'

She touched his cheek with her glove and slipped into the back seat of the car which pulled away from the kerb and began forcing its way through the crowds. People pounded on the roofs, spat on the black bonnet. 'Deserter! Traitor!'

Razumkin stood on the steps, watching her receding profile, so elegant in a veiled hat, in the oval rear window. She turned and gave him a cheerful wave.

He opened his hand and looked down at the long pewter key to what must be the porte-cochère, and at the little one for the flat itself, and he thought: Now I really am in trouble. Being an official's mistress, Gaby heard all the rumours first, and as rumours went, hers were bound to be of top quality.

The problem, Razumkin realized when he had found the quiet backstreets again, was *which* rumour. With the Germans in Paris, no one would bother with his little delinquencies. So there were grounds for hope. But the world was now upside down. You could never be sure. Razumkin sat down on the nearest park bench. He felt like an old stick snagged at the edge of a rushing stream. The river of people flowed by him: he watched them, distant, disconsolate. He took a deep breath, studied his shaking hands and willed them to stop. Right to the end, Gaby would have said. To the bitter end. The mistake would be to run for it or blurt it out before they had cottoned on. Calm down, she would have said, rubbing the space between his eyebrows with that ironic look women reserve for panic in men. They would go to Nice, they would find a boat or a train to Spain.

'Right,' he said in a whisper as he got up. 'Right to the end.'

ASYA SAT ON the sofa by the open window, wearing a pair of Gaby's silk pyjamas and her pink peignoir. Gaby had done her best to take her shadow with her, yet there was the print of her soles in a pair of shoes in a cupboard, and the musky odour of her body in the folds of her peignoir. Otherwise, all trace of her had been expunged. The apartment on the rue Masséna was as bare as a convent cell.

Josette sat opposite, her knitting needles clicking to and fro. It was hard to tell how old Josette was, she could have been any age between her late forties and early sixties. She wore brown woollen socks beneath her housedress and glided soundlessly across the parquet of the apartment in thick felt slippers. She had a thin, pinched face and a moustache of fine black hairs on her upper lip. She was both the concierge and Gaby's maid. She had adopted Asya from the night they had arrived, feeding her soup from a spoon, changing her nightdresses, turning her over in bed, and carrying her to the bathroom. In the shadowlands of fever, they had become intimate.

When the knock on the door came, Josette got up calmly, gestured for Asya to hide in the bedroom and went to answer. Asya held her breath and pulled the covers up around her chin. Josette returned, put a finger to her lips and waited for a full minute, until the footsteps on the stairs had receded.

'The police?'

'Of course. They wanted to know if Madame was here. I said she was not.'

It was frightening to put your trust in a stranger like this, but Asya had no choice.

When Razumkin returned that night and she told him about the visit, he began pacing up and down in front of the windows. 'A disaster to come here,' he muttered, ramming a cigarette into the pearl holder he always used. 'We should have tried for the Spanish border right away.'

'But what do they want, the police?'

Razumkin rubbed his cheek. 'Vichy has ordered the deportation of all foreigners found within twenty kilometres of the French coast. We are subversives, my dear, didn't you realize?'

That was sufficient explanation for the moment, Razumkin thought. Let's not agitate her.

Then he laughed, a mirthless chuckle. 'You are fortunate to be ill, my dear. Hang on to illness. They do not intern the sick. They haven't the facilities.'

'We are at the mercy of the barbarians,' she said.

He led her through possibilities she had never imagined. Their safety in the apartment depended, he said, on the ecumenical dimensions of Gaby's adventuring in the upper reaches of the Third Republic. If Gaby had contacts only with the officials who had taken flight in June, Asya and Razumkin were done for. But if she had also 'made herself available' – Razumkin's phrase – to the men now taking up posts in Vichy, the police might have second thoughts about storming into a bedroom where their *patron* might be taking his ease.

Asya, needless to say, had not understood this. 'Thank God I am in the hands of a rascal like you,' she said, and took one of his cigarettes.

'At your service,' Razumkin said, cleaning one thumbnail with the other. He allowed her one puff and then pulled the cigarette from her lips.

'And our papers?'

He smoked gloomily. 'The port is a veritable bazaar. Everything can be had for money. I have found a most accommodating Greek at the Portuguese consulate. In office hours, no visas to be had. After five o'clock, in the café round the corner, this Greek sold me two very presentable visas for hard currency.' Razumkin reached into his pocket and pulled out a little packet of papers.

'There.'

She inspected the flimsy document in her hand.

'Why am I not Gourevitch? Why Galitzine again?'

What was he to say?

'I thought it best not to draw attention to ourselves. There is some slight chance that the French border police might ask you questions about why Sergei is not with you and so on. I thought we should avoid this.'

She nodded. 'So you have reinvented me.'

'Exactly.'

'How did you get this picture?' She looked at her former self, framed in the tightly permed look fashionable five years before. 'I can't have looked like this. It's impossible.'

Razumkin shrugged: no one looked the way they once had. 'I took the liberty of removing your passport photo and having it copied.'

'Ingenious.'

He gathered up the papers. 'I am nothing if not ingenious.'

She kissed him on the cheek. 'I am at your mercy,' she said.

Several days later Asya woke up from her afternoon nap, came into the kitchen and found Josette sitting there with Razumkin and a small, wiry man in blue work overalls and jacket.

'My brother,' Josette said.

He was a railwayman, based in Perpignan. He had the self-contained air of a man who lived alone. He said he lived in the country, and she imagined what it must be like: the bachelor's bed, a clump of olives in a stone-girt field, chicken coops hemmed in by old bedsteads and wire, with mangy dogs braying on chains. He ate with them, as taciturn as Josette, methodically running his bread around the empty bowl of broth.

During a long silence the brother looked up and said, 'You want to get across the border?'

Razumkin said nothing.

'I do the train to Cerbère on Thursdays; I know the customs people there.'

Asya got up and cleared the dishes. As she stacked them in the sink she took a deep breath, readying herself for the leap into the dark. When she turned around Josette was watching her, the brother too.

'Yes, we do,' Asya said. 'As soon as possible.'

'How much will it cost?' Razumkin asked.

Josette and her brother exchanged a glance.

'It will cost you nothing,' Josette said.

After her brother had gone and Josette had withdrawn to her lace-curtained sanctum by the porte-cochère, and Asya had shut her bedroom door, Razumkin opened his medical bag, scrutinizing each tuck and fold, each packet of surgical dressing, each phial. He could not tell whether Josette had searched his things or not. Everything was in place, including the Biretta at the bottom. He sank back on the couch.

He lacked faith. If you knew yourself to be untrustworthy, then such offers of help were laden with menace. Asya was able to throw herself on the mercy of strangers. It was an element in what he called her goodness, that she could have faith in people, that she did not rely only on their weaknesses. She was ready for those moments when you could trust only in their best. Unfortunately, she lacked the necessary saving suspicion. Josette was a concierge, and there wasn't a concierge in the world who didn't know more than she should.

Razumkin pulled off his clothes and lay down on the sofa in his undershirt. It was hot and airless in the room. He threw open a metal shutter. No better. The quiet was uncanny: water running in a gutter, pots being moved in a sink behind the shutters opposite, but no cars, no voices. Curfew: a whole city withdrawn behind its blinds.

He lit a cigarette and smoked it between forefinger and thumb from below, in the old Russian way, like Mother, squinting at him through the smoke around her patience board while she played the cards out and glanced at him with that thin, mean look. That was all he had left from her, her way of holding a cigarette. That and the Meissen figurines. Nothing else remained. All dissipated. All those years watching or assisting the self-destruction of his class, he had never seen that it was happening to him, too. It was too late now to trace all the streams of his self-betrayal back to their origins. He could blame others. He could say he had made a pact with the devil, and could blame the devil. But no, that was a lie. It had all begun before, the unwinding, the complacent surrender of his best self. No more alibis. He was sick of alibis. All that was left was to cling to appearances, to his semblance of worldly good manners and, of course, to his cunning.

And there was Asya. He could cling to her, too. She was the old, untraduced past, the good, authentic world his life had betrayed. He had given his word. He would make sure she was out of harm's way. That promise might even be his redemption.

He sat up. There was a cry, then another. He got to his feet, wrapped a towel around his bulk and padded into her room. She was sitting up, staring straight ahead at the streetlight slicing through the shutters. Her mouth was wet and she was trying to say something. He sat down and put his arm around her, pulling his towel around his middle. Anguish was pouring out of her. The sight of her eyes set the tuning fork of Razumkin's own fear sounding deep inside him.

She shook herself, rubbed her face with both hands and shuddered. One side of her face was red and lined from the pillow. In a garbled voice a dream tumbled out of her: she was seeing him, just as he was, walking briskly up the street.

'Who?'

'Sergei,' she said. 'In Paris, right past the Café Weber where I was sitting. I couldn't seem to move.' He could tell that she had wanted to leap to her feet, to rush through the café door, to fling herself into his arms, but in the prison of dreams she had stayed rooted to the spot. The phantom had vanished into the crowds on the rue de la Madeleine.

'He heard me calling his name, but then he looked right through me. He saw me, knew who I was, and turned away.'

Razumkin stroked her hair. What a river of suffering still flowed deep inside her! She shivered, staring at the light through the blinds, possessed by her phantom. Sergei would always be there, walking past on the other side of the café window, always beyond her reach.

She was still going over the accursed ground in her memory. Oh, it was so clear, and so dangerous. Love could no longer be counted on to ensure her self-deception. Some part of her, deep in dreams, still sought the truth. She was like a blindfolded child, searching a room with her fingers. One day, her hands, blindly tracing their way, would close upon the silent stranger pressed flat against the walls of her life.

Razumkin sat beside her on the bed and took her pulse. She looked desolate and beautiful, shadows in the hollows of her eyes, and her cheekbones dusted with light from the shutters. He made to get up. She whispered, 'Stay.'

So he stayed, and absently stroked her hand. Clad only in his towel, he felt ridiculous, like an old gentleman who had taken the wrong door out of the steamroom and ended up in the street. How had he managed to slip into this ruin of middle age? Gingerly he put his feet on the bed and arranged the towel over his chest and stomach.

'I've let myself go,' he said.

'So have I,' she said.

'We're going to have to get you into shape. The Pyrenees are steep,' he said, squeezing her shoulders.

Since Bordeaux she had not talked of dying. The sunlight and the quiet Josette had woven around her had begun to do their work. She had regained her grasp on life, but she was still weak.

'I'm no mountain climber.'

Razumkin gestured at his bulk. 'And I'm no guide.'

She took his fingers and kissed them.

'Lapin said I was mad to remain in Paris,' she said. 'But that is Lapin — caution itself — and I am the way I am. I let the Germans come; and Lapin as always was right. So now we will go to him. The hard way.'

In twenty years as her disreputable but indispensable 'uncle', Razumkin had never been alone in the dark with her like this. She lifted her face. Her lips touched his. He could scarcely believe it. Her hands explored his chest. He could not imagine it was possible. But then, suddenly, he wanted her to make all his accumulated shame disappear. She lay back on the bed and let him move the folds of the nightgown apart. She let him touch and kiss her. She pulled his head down upon her breasts and, like a man at last granted his most cherished wish, he buried himself in her body and knew that she felt just like him, that she would do

155

anything to forget, even for a second, the weight of her loneliness.

When Asya woke the next morning, Josette was sitting reading *Nice Matin* at the breakfast table. Asya came up behind her and looked at it over her shoulder. There was a picture of Pétain on a visit to Toulouse, his liver-spotted hand poised over a jet of outstretched children's hands. It was not true, she thought, that he was everyone's lovable grandfather. The face was vain, coldly observing the children's tribute. Their eyes gazed up at him, round with awe at the sorcery of adult power. Asya's heart tightened, for she thought irresistibly of her own son staring up at his father's face on the morning of his return. She shook herself. These backward fugues must stop.

The smell of Razumkin was sharp about her. 'Josette, I must wash,' she said. While she bathed, she watched Josette throw back the coverlet of her bed, flatten the sheets with a brisk stroke of the hand, pause for an instant and then strip the stained sheets and bundle them up in her arms.

It was wrong to be embarrassed. Embarrassment was a form of condescension towards one's own feelings. Always a mistake. She felt a surge of tenderness towards Razumkin.

'What day is it?' she asked as Josette passed by.

'Sunday.'

'The?'

'Fifteenth of August, madame.'

'Oh, Josette,' Asya said, 'call me Asya.'

Josette paused before the door and looked in at the pink body in the tub.

'Yes, Madame Asya.' She bent over and picked the soap out of the water. 'The last bar of real soap. They are only selling carbolic in the market now.'

'I'm sorry.'

'Enjoy yourself. Make yourself smell nice. Why not? You won't have another chance.'

As Josette swathed Asya in Gaby's luxuriant peach towels and rubbed her back and legs, Asya said, 'It is my father's name day. Saint Vladimir's day. I should light a candle to his memory.'

And so they became conspirators in evading Razumkin's strictest instruction, which was never to leave the flat. A Russian on a Nansen passport in a banned coastal port. She should stay hidden until things sorted themselves out.

In the street Asya clutched Josette's arm. She had lost the habit of walking in shoes. They turned off the Promenade des Anglais for fear of meeting Razumkin. In the airless backstreets people seemed to avoid her eyes, the cafés were listless, the barmen moodily wiped their counters with a cloth. Asya paused in front of a chemist's window. Among the dusty trusses, bandages and bottles, propped up against a tower of carbolic soap, was a dusty mirror in which she caught sight of her own reflection. She was shocked at how gaunt she was, at the way her lipstick glowed against the pallor of her skin.

There had been long periods in her life when time flowed flat and slow, like a gentle brown river, so slowly that she had to concentrate on such things as the imperceptible lengthening of Niki's face to see the river's movement at all. Life had been like that in the thirties. At such moments, taking tea in the flat on the rue de Solferino, watching the dusk settling over Paris on a leisurely afternoon, she could look back along her life to its beginning, and she could see it vanish beyond the bend ahead. It was then that life gave her an instant of serenity. But now, seeing how much her face had aged in the reflection of the dusty chemist's window, she could feel time begin to plummet downwards into a tight gorge. She leaned against the wall to get her balance. Above her head rose dark houses, shutters hung with washing and a sliver of sky.

Josette took her arm and they walked along the shadowed street. Suddenly the church was there, two slate-grey onion domes framed by the dark funnel of the street. She stood staring at the church where her mother and father had been married, and she felt a memory stir inside her and begin to climb up the dark well towards the surface of her mind. She remembered how once she had climbed into her mother's closet, how the mahogany door had swung shut behind her, and how, among the darkness of her mother's clothes, she had closed her hand

157

upon a sere, sharp thing, and how on blundering out into the light she had found herself standing in the bedroom with her mother's bridal veil in hand, a withered rose entwined within it.

'Do you ever cry, Josette?' she whispered.

'Not if I can help it,' said Josette briskly, handing her a handkerchief.

The old women, the church mice, who usually clustered in the courtyard benches muttering and twittering among themselves, were nowhere to be seen.

Passers-by looked at them suspiciously as they rang the doorbell. The door opened a crack and an old caretaker with a yellowing beard and a stained jacket peered out at them. No, the church was shut: no services, the priests were gone.

'My mother and father were married here.' The caretaker's face remained a blank.

'It is my father's name day,' Asya persisted.

Josette shoved a small wad of francs in front of his nose and blocked the door with her foot. The caretaker looked at the notes driven like a wedge into the air between them. Then, with a furtive glance to left and right, he let them edge past him through the door.

He would not turn on the lights for fear of attracting attention, and so the candle which Asya lit before an icon of Saint Vladimir gave the only illumination. She knelt in the flickering darkness and the stones felt cool beneath her knees; the silence seemed to flow into her, and as she began to say her prayers, she was entirely at peace, in a still place where past and future met.

> 'I will not betray thy secrets
> to thine enemies
> With a kiss like Judas.'

Saint Vladimir's coal-black eyes shone down upon her, harsh and austere. She crossed herself and prayed that her memories would never be dimmed by time and forgetting. She could not have said whether she believed anything at all. But she prayed nonetheless: her prayers had become the spells she chanted to restore the desecrated past.

> 'But like a thief I will acknowledge thee.'

Time's undertow carried her back to the family chapel, to the sight of her father bearing the icon from the sanctuary, his face overcast with grief. That had been one moment at least, she knew, when her sceptical mind had finally been subdued, when she had submitted herself to her prayers, when she had felt all the brevity of her time on this earth.

> 'Not unto judgement or unto condemnation
> But unto the healing of my soul and body,
> Amen.'

The candle flame glowed still in the darkness. She crossed herself and rose, aware that she must stop this backward flight, that she must attend now to these humid stones, to this oval flame, to this caretaker approaching, to Josette taking her arm. She turned at the door and looked back for the last time at the single candle in the gloom and the cheap Saint Vladimir in its niche. She knew the caretaker would snuff the candle out as soon as she was out of sight.

Out again in the sunlight, she took Josette's arm and they began walking swiftly. They were within sight of the apartment when Josette drew up and stopped. The porte-cochère was opening and several policemen were halfway through it. Josette pivoted Asya round and nudged her into a café, then walked briskly towards the building.

Asya made her way to a corner table. She ordered a diabolo menthe and, when it came, sat quite still, wrapping her hands around the cool green glass to stop them trembling. Had she covered her traces? An extra toothbrush in the bathroom, odour in the sheets, the coffee-cup on the table by the open window: anything could give them away.

Just then, Razumkin passed the window, walking with careful deliberation. He came in, took her hand, kissed it and ordered a cognac. He said they must hurry. He downed the cognac with a convulsive gulp, dipped into his vest pocket and, placing a note on the table, offered her his arm. His gallantry was alarming.

They walked the airless streets until she felt she would collapse. When he was finally sure the men had gone, he led her through the entranceway, closed the porte-cochère behind him with a click and hissed, 'Don't ever do that again.'

Josette drew them into her room behind the yellow curtains. Asya sat down on Josette's bed. It was a tiny room: a bed, a cross above it, a statue of the Virgin, a clothes cupboard, a pair of slippers, a glass on the night table.

The police had searched the apartment and had found nothing. Except, and here Josette looked at Asya, 'There is a problem. I do not wear lipstick, madame.'

Asya imagined a policeman's thumb rubbing its way curiously across a red smudge, like a scar, on the lip of her coffee-cup.

Razumkin and Asya sat dumbly on the bed and let Josette take charge. The police would be back. They had to leave tomorrow. Josette would sleep upstairs, in Gaby's bed, in case the police came to test her story that she was occupying her mistress's flat in her absence. To Razumkin, Josette simply gestured 'Outside'. He was to meet her at the station, the five thirty train for Marseilles.

Josette lit a candle and bundled Asya through a door down into the cellar. A bed had been prepared on the floor. Asya knelt and opened the bag that Josette had packed: inside were Gaby's nightdress and some underwear that could not possibly belong to Gaby: plain, practical white cottons, a slip, some stockings. Josette had plundered her own wardrobe for Asya's sake.

'Why are you doing this for me?'

Josette said sharply, 'Why are you hiding?'

'Because my name is Gourevitch. I married a man who went to fight with the Poles and may even be a prisoner of the Germans. Because we do not want to be interned.'

'And Monsieur Razumkin, why is he hiding?'

'Because he is a Russian too.'

'Those police, madame, were not from here. I know the local ones. These were from Paris.'

'I don't understand.'

'Madame, if you were just two foreigners in the wrong place, or with the wrong papers, it would be an affair for the local police. Paris people wouldn't bother with you.'

Paris might mean the Germans, the Gestapo.

'That man is not telling you everything he knows.'

Asya didn't know where the doubt began in Josette's mind, so she started talking in a blind rush, her face burning with shame. She knew Razumkin as well as she knew herself, but as she spoke she realized that this was not true at all. Yes, he had been disbarred, defrocked, or whatever happened to doctors for that abortion business, but he had recovered his practice, and she and Seryozha, and Botynsky – and here she was conscious that she was losing all sense – were practically like brothers and sister.

Josette cut her short. 'The people from Paris do not care about abortions. They would not come down here for that. You must ask yourself what the Sûreté in Paris wants with this man.'

Asya was speechless. Josette's reflection, lit by candlelight, flickered against the low, black walls of the cellar. So, she was Razumkin's accomplice. But if she was, what had been their crime? It had all seemed like child's play when he had spread the new travel papers across the table: she to become Asya Galitzine of old, he to become Dr Gabriel Pinceau, accompanying his patient to Perpignan and then to the Portuguese sanatorium. All those reassuring stamps and signatures so dearly bought, all those papers began to swim in front of her eyes. What had seemed like a game of make-believe now seemed mined with all the lies of their situation. And at the bottom of it all was the memory that she had slept with him. Her mouth was dry.

'I have been very foolish, Josette.'

Josette disappeared up the cellar stairs and then returned carrying a bowl of broth, its vapour tumbling and turning in the light of her candle. Asya sipped at her soup, and Josette watched her as they sat together on the little palliasse on the flagstoned floor. Asya wanted to put her head on Josette's lap, to fly from this narrowing present to the bright clearing of her past. She knew she must fight this, now more than ever.

'Why do you do this for me, Josette?'

Josette's reply was so soft Asya could barely hear it. 'Because you are an innocent.'

I T WAS STILL dark, but the station concourses were already thronged with unshaven soldiers in oversized demob raincoats, women and children dozing on top of their tattered belongings, men in berets waving their papers at railway officials, porters crying 'Passage, Passage,' the newsagents rolling up the shutters and shouldering in the bundles of *Nice Matin*. As they made their way through the station, Josette whispered, 'He is lying to you.'

What could she do, Asya thought. She had no husband, no parents. Olga and Dimitri were too old to protect her. She only had Lapin, and he was in England. Who else could get her there but Razumkin?

Razumkin was by the barrier, beside the ticket collector and the gendarme checking the papers. He lifted his old panama hat and bowed in a courtly manner to Josette, who ignored him.

It was impossible to embrace Josette, to say everything that had to be said. Asya just extended her hand and said, 'Thank you.'

'Another time, madame,' said Josette. In that instant, Asya saw her as she was to remember her all her life: her cold, dry hand extended, her stern face framed by grey hair in a kerchief, with a hint of a moustache on her upper lip and a wintry smile. Another time? What other time would there be?

Razumkin took Asya's arm and they walked along the platform. As she stepped up into the carriage she turned around, but Josette had gone.

The carriage was crowded with soldiers going home and families on the run, everyone isolated in their fearfulness. Razumkin slipped her glove below her wrist and took her pulse. His hands filled her with distaste. Suspicion had seeped into every pore of her body.

Josette was right. She had been innocent, to an appalling degree. She felt she had been born in a better time, and was unfitted for the mean world that had come to pass. But now that would change: she knew it must.

As the train stormed along the south coast, roaring in and out of tunnels, then swooping down to the bright water's edge, she could sense, from his acrid bulk beside her, that Razumkin was afraid. Good, she thought. I will use that. As the train drew to a halt in the thronging quais of the Gare St Charles in Marseilles and the other passengers filed from the carriage, she hissed at him, 'The men who searched Gaby's were from Paris. They wouldn't have come just for the sake of some Russians. So you tell me, Razumkin, why these attentions?'

Razumkin wiped his face with a handkerchief, ran his finger around the stained band of his panama and looked up at her with red-rimmed eyes.

'You know me. It is not a good story. I am not proud of it. There are many things those men from Paris could want me for. You don't need me. It would be safer if you left me behind. Here.'

And he took out his wallet, removed her papers, and handed them to her. 'Go.'

She had not expected this. Having prepared to do battle with dishonesty, she was disarmed by truth. She knew he meant it, knew that he was, this time, beyond pleading. There was something about his plaintive shame, the way he stared down at his hat, running his hands sadly round the brim, that brought back all their years together, all his unrewarded devotion. 'Don't lie to me, Razumkin,' she said, relenting.

'I swear,' he said.

Razumkin followed her out. She was regal as she stepped down onto the platform, pivoting on ankle and heel, her gloved hand touching the back of her chignon. The platform seethed with bodies; to Razumkin she alone seemed calm and detached. They were swept along towards the barrier by the crowd. The whole of France, Razumkin thought, was funnelling through such choked weirs, and at every one men in raincoats waited to pull a struggling creature or two from the water. Allied soldiers on the run, Dutch, Belgian, anti-Nazi Germans, anti-fascist Italians, Jews, criminals, demobilized soldiers, all pushed their way towards the barrier, eyes down, shrinking behind their collars; Jews pretending to be gentiles, Germans pretending to be French, and everyone pretending to be an inoffensive nonentity. The dispassionate eye would have seen Marseilles' Gare St Charles as a theatre in which a thousand melodramas were being played by desperate amateurs for the benefit of a few bored policemen in raincoats. The only one, Razumkin thought, who seemed to be playing no part at all was Asya. She walked ahead, and he prayed that her imperturbability would save them both. At the barrier, she turned and waited while he fumbled with the tickets, watching calmly while their papers were checked. I will stick with you like a dog, he thought, as they boarded the train for Perpignan.

It was hardly an innocent destination: it was known as everyone's jumping-off point for the escape over the mountains. Already the carriages were full of people, watching each other for potential accomplices, potential betrayers. As they took their seats, it occurred to Razumkin that they were still wearing the clothes they had worn on the flight from Paris, Asya's a grey worsted suit and topcoat, his the usual doctor's pinstripe, now creased and clammy with sweat. They were conspicuous. Eyes in the carriage dwelled on their clothes, scrutinized their faces.

Razumkin had gambled on the chaos of the moment, but what was uncanny was the insidious way in which normal life had returned. The train left on time, the *controlleurs* made their rounds through the cars and everywhere the great machine of life resumed its turning. Only the newspapers people were reading gave any sign that they had entered the shrill, hard atmosphere of the new European order. The headlines screamed: Hitler's warning to Britain; new rationing regulations; a photo of Pétain and Laval shaking hands. The public world was blaring so loudly that it reduced every private conversation to a whisper. Everyone in the carriage avoided their neighbour's eye.

As soon as the train was rolling through countryside again, Asya made her way down the corridor and locked herself inside the lavatory. She had to get away from him, to take stock. She leaned against the wall and pinioned her foot against the pedestal of the washbasin as the train hurtled around a bend. Her face was white

165

in the mirror and the handkerchief in her hand was slivered with tiny flecks of blood. The world outside roared by; light and shade spattered the translucent glass of the lavatory window, and hot dry air whistled through the transom. Breathe in, she said to herself. Breathe out. Trust him.

The train was swaying. As she walked back down the corridor the orange curtains were flapping madly in the open windows. The train whistle screamed, and when she sat down beside him her heart was racing. He pressed his fingers to her pulse, found a pill in his bag and made her swallow it. As she did so, the old woman opposite looked up from her knitting, and Asya knew for a certainty, from her dull, flat stare, that she could watch them being arrested without dropping a stitch.

The flatlands of the Camargue passed on endlessly, the cane brakes torn by the mistral, the horses planted in the bare, burnt fields. On the edge of the horizon, Asya caught a glimpse of the thin metal line of the sea. On a white road skirting the railway embankment she saw a man and a boy in a donkeycart, blurred by dust. A departmental roadsign flashed by. Aigues Mortes, 10 kilometres.

The towers of the walled city, marooned by the tide, were now just visible from the train window above the battered, weeping fronds of the cane. Razumkin nudged her shoulder gently. She knew that he wanted her to remember the beach at La Tour des Sphinguettes, but she looked away from the window and shut her eyes. That day on the beach – the last day before Sergei returned – belonged to the sealed room of her past, and she would not open it. Razumkin looked over at her. Her eyes were shut, her thumbnail scratching at the underside of her wedding ring, her other hand a tight fist around her handkerchief. The train was tearing along the edge of the beach, past the sickle-shaped tidemarks rimmed with light. When he remembered how she had emerged naked from the sea, that afternoon, a moan rose within him at the memory of her glistening, animal well-being.

Asya woke with a start when the train came to a stop in Perpignan station. He walked her across the platforms to the connecting train. The line to Port-Vendres skirted the sea. It was late afternoon. They were alone in the compartment and Razumkin began talking, as if being alone had lifted a weight from him, but she could not follow what he was saying. He pressed her hand, took her pulse, held the mineral water to her lips. Water dribbled down her neck and the front of her dress. He dabbed at it with his handkerchief and fanned himself with his panama. She felt herself falling in and out of sleep, to the howl of a train horn. The carriages swerved past beaches streaked with black shadow.

She knew that they had arrived and that she had been helped into a car. She could smell thyme and the cool rush of evening through a window. Then she was being wheeled along a corridor and someone was taking off her clothes and laying her between sheets. There was a nauseous tumble of images in her mind: Niki with a kite on the beach; Sergei lying on the sand under the umbrella, observing her over his bifocals; Botynsky looking at her through his pebble-thick lenses imploring her to speak, to reach across to him through the darkness. He wanted something, he needed her help, but she couldn't speak.

Light, like a bright scar, shone under the doorway at the foot of her bed. She knew that Dr Feldman had come at last. His beard smelled of mint and his cool hand lay upon her forehead. But she also knew that this was not Dr Feldman and that she was not really in her father's house. With weary curiosity, she wondered whether she was dying.

'Out of the question to travel.'

'Of course, out of the question.' Razumkin's voice.

Whispers now. She could not hear.

It was a long time before she opened her eyes. A man, no older than Niki, was sponging her arm.

'Who are you?'

'I am Majiec. From Lodz. Are you Jewish? We're all Jewish here.'

She shook her head.

He went down to the end of the bed, pushed back the covers and began soaping her feet. He did everything with deliberation, like someone deep in thought, or suffering from shock. He wore a white hospital coat over a pair of dun-brown army fatigues and dusty boots. He was small and wiry, and there was a week's growth of beard on his thin, white face.

'My husband was Polish. I mean he was born in Chelm,' she said.

Majiec was towelling her feet. 'But you are a Russian woman.'

'He was a Russian who went to fight in Poland.'

'He is dead now?'

She nodded.

Majiec said nothing. He handed her a newspaper. She looked at the date. So, she had been there a week.

'Where is Razumkin?'

'Doctor? In Perpignan. Back tonight.' Then he reached over and pointed at a column in the paper. 'Look at this.'

Asya read the decree from the Hôtel du Parc in Vichy. It took a long time before she realized it was a decree of the Vichy government removing French citizenship from all persons of Jewish race, or married to those of Jewish race, nationalized as citizens of France after January 1932. Majiec was philosophic. 'They are bastards.' He continued to observe her.

After a while he said, 'We same trouble.'

When she was his age, she had never believed that any harm could come to her. That was what it meant to be young. But now, at forty, with the newspaper and its odious decree lying across her bed like a stain, and the stinging pain in her lungs, and this runaway stranger, so reduced beside her, she felt she was just a frightened middle-aged woman whose chances of survival were no better than even. In a dry, tight voice, she did not recognize as her own, she said, 'We are in the same trouble.'

It was easy for her to imagine the path this boy had travelled: scrabbling on all fours past the armoured columns, sleeping in ditches and under hedgerows, gnawing turnips and stealing from rubbish bins, fetched up here at last, beyond exhaustion, in a sanatorium ten kilometres from the Spanish border. He pulled the hospital nightgown over her feet again, settled the sheet over her and went to empty the water from the basin. He went from bed to bed, treating all the women with the same proprietorial attention as he bathed their slack limbs, wiped them with towels, rearranged their linen, plumped their pillows.

She lay awake the rest of the day and watched the sun make its transit of the sky.

It was a real sanatorium all right: white walls and blinds, a long ward of beds, a nurse's cap just disappearing around the corner and Majiec's white orderly's jacket. There were four women spaced out in beds along a green linoleum corridor. They stared at the ceiling and rose only to shuffle towards the bathroom with the listless gait of the hospitalized.

Two beds away lay a woman with thin, olive features whose small hands continuously smoothed her coverlet. Once she took out a pocket mirror and applied dark red lipstick with a brisk gesture and then lay back again, staring at the ceiling. At the end of the day she padded past Asya's bed and stood looking out at the sea. When she returned she suddenly whispered, 'Good evening,' in German.

It made tears start in Asya's eyes to hear the language spoken that had once been the common property of cultivated people in a lost continent called Europe.

Darkness fell, but no one in the ward seemed to sleep. The four women, separated by empty beds, kept their silence, and lay awake together, listening to the night, their common anguish communing in the darkness. Then she heard his footfall, his creaking shoes and his laboured advance down the corridor.

Razumkin removed his hat and mopped the red rim on his forehead. He pulled from his coat pocket a bit of sausage wrapped in paper, and handed her a slice on the end of his pocket-knife. They ate in silence. She handed the paper to him and pointed to the decree. He nodded.

'I thought you might have bolted,' she said.

'That you should think such a thing,' he said wearily.

Razumkin shifted in his seat. 'I've found Josette's brother. There is a train. The *contrôleur* is a friend, the *douanier* is a friend.' He added, 'No problem,' in a tone of ironical and cheerless disbelief. How much had he spent, she wondered, to get them this far, and how many notes remained in the pouch in his inside pocket? On his face was written the strain of furtive meetings in the Palmarium, in the Tintin, in the Café de la Gare.

169

'When?' she asked.

'Thursday, five thirty.'

'Go without me,' she said.

'Out of the question. I made a promise.' Razumkin turned the newspaper over: 300 planes over London, total destruction of the docks. She had better not see this: Lapin was there, standing beneath the open sky, and the high explosive was falling like rain.

'What are you talking about?'

'I promised Sergei.'

'You never told me.'

'So I am telling you now.'

Administer hope, he thought. Give her just enough, the correct dosage. He added quickly, 'You cannot think about him, you cannot afford to be distracted by anything. By your memory, anything.' His voice rose from a whisper to a throaty pleading.

'They are rounding up communists in Paris,' he said, to bring her back sharply to the operational mode. 'That's the rumour in Perpignan.' He did not say he was sure the *rafle* included Jacquot. He turned and looked at the German woman two beds away.

'From Cologne,' he whispered to Asya. 'Pneumonia. She'd been sleeping in culverts for six weeks. By the time she got here she could hardly walk.'

Across the whole continent, Asya knew, there were people on the run – this woman from Cologne, Majiec, perhaps even Sergei – sleeping in ditches, running down the open roads, fear and hunger in their guts, and the anticipated moment of betrayal frozen in their minds like a film's climactic frame stuck in the projection gate. And behind them all, rooms abandoned in flight, a clock winding down, milk turning sour on a window-sill, a telephone ringing off, drawers of clothes, dresses in a wardrobe, a toy on a stair, a pen open on a writing desk, ink drying in the nib, time suspended, awaiting the boot splintering the door.

What, she wondered with weary indifference, were they doing to the rue de Solferino? And then she thought of something that did matter, intensely.

'Where is Niki?' she whispered.

Razumkin felt too tired for subterfuge. Truth was like a heavy parcel he had been carrying too long and wanted to lay down.

'In Paris, at the German Embassy.'

'With Manfred?'

Razumkin nodded.

'What are you talking about?'

'As *Dolmetscher*.'

As interpreter. From the language of the masters to the language of the vanquished, from the language of the captors to the language of the captives. She sank back on the pillow and stared out at the night.

The embassy Germans, Razumkin thought sourly, would have confirmed all Niki's innocent preconceptions. They were all like Manfred, well-educated boys who kept clear of the nasty business going on in the basement of the Hôtel Lutetia.

He sat with her for a long time, while she lay and stared into the night. What was it like, he wondered, to bear a child as a woman did, to lie beside them as they slept, to inhabit their world of ghosts and games, to watch them grow inexorably beyond you, to search their faces for the faint traces of oneself, to hear in their adolescent voices one's own vanished confidence and courage? To have seen, as she had, this fissure opening between her son and herself, to see him go wooden with resistance and conviction, must have been like feeling her own body splitting in two. And now he had gone over to the enemy.

As Razumkin watched her, he realized that one of his own fantasies of redemption had died inside him. He had always wondered whether children of his own might have saved him, might have made him a decent man. But no woman had ever considered having his children, and looking at Asya's forlorn and abandoned expression he realized what a blessing that had turned out to be. He rose to his feet, pressed her hand to his lips and turned into the corridor. She listened to the squeak of his rolling gait on the linoleum, heard him descending the stairs.

She was obsessed with the details, like someone bent double with a huge weight on her back and able only to see the stones, the blades of grass, the ruts at her feet. Would Niki wear a uniform?

would he have to click his heels? Would he have to give that obscene salute? She covered her face with her hands.

All those baffled mothers she had read about in the papers who had stood up in the witness box in court, looked across at their sons in the dock and said, to the silent derision of all, that he was a good boy, really, a good boy. She understood now. She could see now how incommunicable a child's goodness was, how incorrigibly a mother would believe in it, in defiance of all the facts. Goodness was in the smell of his skin, the brightness of his hair to her touch, the odour of sleep when she lay beside him. She wanted absurdly to plead these facts in extenuation so that he might be forgiven.

She looked at her hands. Some scars bleached away, faded back into the skin, and one could search in vain for their traces. But this one would always be there, a clean, white mark of time on her body. She felt old now, wounded and depleted. All her losses lay there beside her.

As she stepped into the cab which would take them to the station for the journey to the frontier, Razumkin knew she had put Niki out of her mind. She had this capacity for ruthlessness, for cauterizing her own emotions. When the taxi glided into the station forecourt past a table of men in black, dusty boots, drinking pastis at the Café de la Gare, past these old Catalans who knew that no journey from this station was ever innocent, Razumkin felt himself gripped by her cold exhilaration.

He could have chosen the route by foot; safer, but arduous. Majiec had even offered to take them. The trails were well marked and one of those men in the café would have led the way, for a fee. But Asya was too weak for the mountain climb, and he had promised to stay with her, to get her to safety, to separate her from her son. He had kept his promise. Whatever else they might say about him, he would do this honourable thing. Ahead, rounding a corner, stretched the undulating reaches of Spain. He could just begin to imagine his life for the first time as a blank sheet of paper. He would practise again. He would be without stain. Patients would flock to him; like baptism, the frontier crossing would redeem him in their eyes and in his own. Even if the English made him do the medical exams again, he would pass them. He was young, not yet fifty. Harley Street beckoned. He would have a brass plate, faint and bright with polishing, by the door. Asya would love him. Other nights like Nice, lying together under the slatted light from the blinds, opened out before his eyes.

Cerbère was approaching. The track was being funnelled into a tight place between the sea and the hillside and then the train was swallowed up in tunnels. The compartment was black, then propelled into brightness again. The cliffside at the track's edge was sheer, pebbly and loose, as if one false step would produce a landslide.

The train ground to a halt. They were on a railway bridge that passed over the port town, squeezed between the rocks of a crescent bay. Out of one window they could see the shale cliff, while from the other they looked down on a hotel, a bar, two palms, a dusty square, a sliver of beach: Cerbère, Cerberus. There was no one in the streets. It was late afternoon. The shadows were faint, the sky grey, heavy.

Razumkin tugged at her sleeve and pointed.

Josette's brother was walking slowly along the bridge. He came level with the window, gave them a quick nod and then bent down to check the brakes beneath their window. Just behind him they could see a border guard, walking up and down the bridge in his cape.

The compartment door opened.

'Your papers.'

The revolvers at their hips were smaller than the ones she had seen in American movies, the brown leather holsters shiny from much handling. One seemed to be Spanish, the other French. The peaks of their caps covered their eyes. It was difficult to make out what kind of men they might be.

'The patient Galitzine?'

'Yes.'

'For the Sanatorio da Gama in Lisbon?'

'Yes.'

'Your brother is awaiting you there?'

'Yes.' A lie.

'Naturalized the 30th of April 1928?'

'Yes.' Another lie.

Asya watched the stamp rise then descend upon her papers like a kiss. The men touched their caps and were gone. She looked out of the window. She wanted to send Josette's brother a fugitive wave of gratitude, but he was nowhere to be seen. Razumkin mopped his brow, let out a long sigh and pulled at his tie.

The train inched forward and shuddered to a stop beneath a dusty glass canopy. A cracked blue enamel plaque opposite read 'Gare de Cerbère'. Razumkin rubbed his face with his hands and looked down at the floor. Asya watched the customs officers, French and Spanish, leave the train and walk along the platform. One removed his kepi and scratched his head; the other lit a cigarette. Coming off duty. She looked up and down the platform. No buffet, no coffee wagon, no paper stand. The glass panes of the station roof were streaked and grey. Her mind played with a word. *Voksal*: the Russian word for station. *Vauxhall*: a pleasure garden on the south bank of the Thames in the eighteenth century. The name of a British railway station. A suburb of London. Or so Nanny Saunders had said. She would soon be there, safe in Vauxhall. She looked up at the blurred glass canopy of the station roof. A pigeon was whirling, claws outstretched, settling down on the lip of a broken pane. Opposite her, on the platform, a man with a cardboard suitcase and a bicycle wheel wrapped in paper stood waiting. Where was he going with that bicycle, she wondered. Why did he look so dejected?

The compartment door slid open.

A man in a suit reached into his inside pocket and pulled out a wallet with a badge. 'Police. You will come with me.'

Razumkin rose to his feet and carefully fitted his hat upon his head. He held out his papers.

'What are you doing?' she said. She could not see the policeman's face beneath his hat brim.

He said, 'You are free. The train to Barcelona and Lisbon leaves in an hour.'

'I am travelling with my doctor.'

'He has questions to answer.' Razumkin was in the corridor, grey, sweating, holding his hands out in front of him, as if he were already in manacles. There were other men in the carriage now. They took the bags down from the racks and led the way into the stationmaster's office. The faces in the train watched their procession: Razumkin, the two men on either side, just touching his elbows, and Asya following behind. She caught sight of Josette's brother, between cars, checking the connection. He stood there, six feet from her, his gloved hands gripping his train iron, his face averted.

In the stationmaster's office they repeated that she was not needed. She was free to continue her journey. She forced her voice into the groove of command.

'I cannot continue without my doctor. What are you doing with him?'

No one answered. Razumkin was slumped in a chair in an inner office. The two men in suits stood on either side of him. One was making a phone call. Through the open door, Razumkin looked up and whispered soundlessly: 'Go.'

She shook her head.

They took him away, down a steep iron spiral stairway to the street below. From above, she saw the dusty palm fronds and then Razumkin, bare headed, his hat in his hand, held on either arm by the two policemen. He disappeared inside the gendarmerie across the square. She looked around the office: a typewriter, a Michelin calendar. A short man she had not seen before leaned in the doorway of the inner office watching her. The phone rang. He picked it up, listened, looked at her, took a pull on his cigarette, and stubbed it out. He came towards her.

'Your papers, madame?'

'I have shown my papers.'

'Police, madame.'

He could have been any age between thirty and fifty. The hands that examined her papers were clean and pale. There was a light film of dust on his polished black shoes. His features did not come into focus. His hair was close-cropped, his moustache looked as if it had been applied with a pencil, and there were black onyx studs on his cuffs.

'Some questions. Follow me.'

'You said I was free to go.'

'A few questions.'

He followed her down the iron staircase into the street. Her heel caught in a step. He waited behind her while she disengaged her shoe. Beneath her, visible through the iron grating, she saw the top of a palm tree.

In the empty street, he walked beside her. 'I've been looking for the two of you for some time.' She said nothing.

'I've even paid a call on your friends, the Ourousoffs.'

She turned, furious. 'I have no idea why you want to question us. But whatever it is, those two old people know nothing. You should leave them alone.'

He looked amused and held the door for her as they entered the gendarmerie. A long corridor, linoleum gleaming under the light of a single bulb, the smell of bleach, a door, the sound of her shoes, the sound of her heart, footsteps just behind. A hand opened the door in front of her and she entered.

He slipped by her and seated himself behind a desk. He searched for paper, a pen, opened a new file, and cracked the binding with satisfaction. He had come from Paris, just for them. Behind her, next to the filmy window looking onto the street, she sensed that there was another policeman watching her. On the wall behind the desk, Pétain's portrait stared down at her.

'You are the wife of Sergei Gourevitch?'

His pen was poised above the paper.

'Yes.'

'But you are travelling under the name Galitzine.'

'My maiden name. My husband is dead.'

'Your husband left France on the 16th of June 1939.'

She could not lie, because they would catch her out, but she could not tell the truth because, though she did not know how, that would incriminate Razumkim.

'He went to fight in Poland. I have not seen him since. I presume he is dead.'

'I see.' The pen remained poised over the file. 'What does the name Ignaty Reiss mean to you?'

Nothing, apart from the paragraph in the émigré press. 'Ignaty Reiss was murdered on the outskirts of Lausanne in 1937. He was a Soviet agent who refused an order to return to Moscow. I read about it, as everyone did.'

The pen was still poised, the paper still blank.

'Your husband, where was he when you read the news of Reiss's death?'

She could hear the crackling line, Sergei's voice: 'I'm in Geneva.'

'What?'

'You know me.'

'I know you,' she was laughing.

'Something came up, the possibility of a deal, so here I am in the Grand Hôtel du Parc. Back tomorrow night.'

'I was worried. I didn't know where you were.'

She remembered every word of this, the crackling of the line, his voice, light and amusing, pleased to hear her. She could feel her own heart beating.

'I insist on a Swiss watch. As reparation. I insist on it.'

It was a joke. She couldn't have cared less about a watch.

'Done,' he said, and suddenly in Russian, 'I kiss you.' And then click and crackle and she was holding the phone.

'Where was he?' the question was repeated.

'He was away on business.'

'Where?'

'In Riga first for the timber business, I think, then in Munich.' She felt stupid: the man already knew the answers.

'And in Geneva. He phoned me from there.' And she added, feeling ashamed, 'He gave me this watch.'

The inspector leaned over indulgently to take a look at the watch. 'I see.'

She could not stop her mind hurtling to a forest clearing where the snowy ground was mottled with boots and a powder-burned body thrashed about, legs splayed, and executioners watched the hands clawing the ground.

'It is not possible.'

'What is not possible?'

'What your questions imply.'

'They imply nothing, madame.'

He was evaluating her nausea, her astonishment. Good, she thought. Now I must use my nausea. I must use my fear.

'You think my husband's trip to Switzerland has a connection with the murder of Ignaty Reiss.'

His gaze remained calm. He waited for her to speak.

'It is not possible. You see, I would have known.'

For we were so close. There could not be a secret between us. I slept by his side for twenty years. I knew the very words he murmured in his sleep. I knew every line, every hair on his body. I watched him age, I watched him doing his exercises every morning, watched his face taut with exertion. I knew how much damage had been done by his life, what was reparable, what was not. I knew everything. We could spend a day without speaking, reading side by side on the couch by the French windows, and minute by minute I could sense his mood, his engagement in what he read from the way he turned a page, the way he would look up into the distance. Our faces were as transparent as water to each other: we could see every stirring of the depths. My first love, my soul mate. No. It is not possible.

'Very well.' The inspector changed the subject. 'You knew Vladimir Isaacovitch Botynsky well?'

'He died in April last year.'

'Exactly, madame. My question was: did you know him well?'

He knew the answer. But how?

'We were friends. Particularly when I first arrived in Paris in 1919.'

'We have seen the letters.'

'What letters?' She blushed, fingered her watch, her wedding ring.

'The ones you sent him. The ones he kept.'

'They were not a police matter.'

'Of course not, madame.'

She could see the letters now, in a biscuit tin perched on top of those crazy sagging shelves in that dark room at the top of the stairs, a tightly-bound pile, not very many of them, twenty years old. They would be in order: the envelopes would be attached. Botynsky was meticulous with small things, but baffled by everything larger, like his life. They had evidently taken the apartment to pieces. She could imagine this policeman in front of her pulling Botynsky's shelves apart, ripping books in half, rifling drawers. Such searches must be gratifying to men like this, a bestial diversion from office routine. Good. She was angry. Anger helped her to focus, to see this office in the Cerbère gendarmerie, the grey-green walls, the stained light from the dirty window slanting across the carpet, this man's pink, close-shaven face, the cropped moustache, the utter

nondescriptness of him, his contemptible calm, his posed polite-
ness.

'You would have been distressed by his death?'

'You know the answer to that question. You have read the
letters.'

He looked pleased that she had risen to the bait.

'And you were surprised by his death?'

She could see Botynsky sprawled out on their living-room floor
after Sunday lunch, on his back, breathing in and out slowly,
while Sergei sat back on the sofa, ignoring him and turning the
pages of *le Matin*, and Niki snaked a train around Botynsky's
legs.

'His heart was always bad. No, I was not surprised.'

He was writing now, then paused and looked at her, with a
thin smile. 'We, on the other hand, were very surprised. Disagreeably surprised.'

She hated the way he shot his cuffs and leaned forward,
savouring what he was about to say.

'Monsieur Botynsky had been of material assistance to us. He
had been very useful, so naturally we were very surprised. You
didn't know that he assisted us?'

He didn't need to ask. It was written all over her face.

Oh, God, no. Not possible. But against her will she saw him –
her Botynsky – cupping his hand over the receiver of a phone and
whispering into it in some dingy café, the aqueous eyes behind
the lenses flicking to and fro.

'I don't believe you.'

'As you wish, madame, but I can tell you that your Monsieur
Botynsky was particularly helpful in the matter of Ignaty Reiss.'
Here he tapped a file. 'You would be foolish not to believe me.'

The hook was in her mouth. He was reeling her in.

'And Dr Razumkin?' he continued.

'My doctor. For twenty years.'

'And Monsieur Botynsky's too, it seems.'

'Yes.'

'It was in fact Dr Razumkin who was called to pronounce
Monsieur Botynsky dead at his apartment.'

'Yes.'

She felt suffocated. The light had faded from the windows. Across the street, in another world, she could see a lone couple in the Café de la Gendarmerie. Ten metres away, they were having dinner. Through the open window she could hear the clatter of forks, the rattle of a glass on a table.

He was reading now from another file. 'Razumkin, Ilya Ilyonovitch, born Paris, December 13, 1894, no military service, sole support of ailing mother, graduate of the École de Médecine, 1917, at twenty-two. Very young to qualify – a distinguished beginning.' The policeman was enjoying his ironies.

'He delivered my son.'

'So obviously you are attached to him. Quite right. But now there are some difficulties. The 24th of April 1926, at the Tribunal of the First Instance, Paris, the complaint of Madame Gaston Dulhumeau, a patient, assault. Case dismissed for lack of proof. And this.'

'The abortion business,' she said quietly.

'Ah, so you knew? I see. Yes, the abortion business. Understandable perhaps, as a gynaecologist, that he should get involved in this matter, but unfortunate that the girl should have bled, that her parents should have made a complaint. It cost him his licence to practise. For a time.'

Here he looked up. 'And so he sold drugs. You knew this?' He was curious.

She lied. 'There was a rumour.'

Looking up from the file, he smiled. 'The rumour was true. A pharmacist, that is what he became, a pharmacist to Parisian society. You are familiar with cocaine, with heroin?'

'I am familiar with the words.'

'He was familiar with the things themselves. And he gave us a little help from time to time as well.'

She could now see the stain that had spread across his life. Everyone's favourite uncle, the indefatigable friend, chubby joker, family pet. He had been blackmailed. Once the police saw that a man was disgraced, they knew they could use him. It would not have taken very much to turn Razumkin. She knew this, she had even allowed some portion of her mind to think it. He knew strange people, he told stories at the table which had an unclean smell to them. And there was his sidekick, Jacquot, whom Sergei had taken on as a driver and who always had the furtive air of a small-time crook. What was Razumkin doing with such a person? All the evidence was there, but . . .

'I am loyal to my friends,' she heard herself say in a chilly voice.

'Indeed you are. No questions asked.'

'You have your loyalty, I have mine.'

He snapped the folder shut.

'Indeed I do. I am very loyal. I take care of my own. And that is exactly why we are having this conversation. You see, Monsieur Botynsky was one of my own. In my business, I cannot afford to let my own be harmed. I cannot let this go unpunished. I mean, where would a detective be without his sources? Where would I be if any little hoodlum thought he could eliminate someone who works for me? I am sure you understand. For you are an intelligent woman, and perhaps even a truthful one. We have had a useful discussion, and now I am sure you would like to see your friend again.'

She turned as they led Razumkin through the door. He came towards her, holding something in a handkerchief. They sat him down beside her. Razumkin did not look at her. There was a small smear of bloody saliva on his lips. He looked down into his hands. He was holding his front teeth in his handkerchief.

She stood up. Razumkin mumbled, pulling at her coat to make her sit down, but she banged her fists on the desk and shouted. 'You have no right! Stop this at once! At once!'

The inspector understood her perfectly, understood that her fearlessness came from her name, from her past, from her enduring illusion that no mere policeman could ever make her afraid. So he said, quite calmly, 'Where do you think you are? Why do you think I should listen to a word you say? Sit down,' and motioned away the man who was preparing to force her into her seat. He knew she would sit.

'That's better. Now, let us review the situation. I want you to see this matter as I see it. Our interests, those of my current employer, no less than my previous ones' – and here he began to pace and made a gesture, at once mocking and respectful, towards the portrait of Pétain – 'are quite precise. It is a matter of indifference to us that the secret services of the Soviet Union should wish to despatch, in various European countries, over a period of five years, the leading members of Leon Trotsky's organization, including his son, Leon Sedov. Nor do we care in the slightest that they should wish to kill Ignaty Reiss, or any other agent who suddenly develops scruples about the great Soviet experiment. That is their affair, and we are happy to leave them to it. If Russians are killing each other, so much the better. Our interest is solely to guarantee that those who are working for *us* do not also happen to be working for *them*. And that is our problem here. As you know,' and here he gestured to Pétain's portrait again, 'our new employer places very great importance on the extirpation – that is his exact phrase – of communist influence in our new political order.' He was enjoying himself. Such opportunities did not occur every day. The trip down to Cerbère had been a great success.

'You can readily understand how concerned we would be if such infiltration were to be discovered at the heart of our own organization. That, you will now appreciate, is our concern with Dr Razumkin. An old friend of mine.'

Razumkin's head bobbed from side to side. He had his handkerchief cupped over his mouth. His clothes were not torn or dirty. He had received a single blow.

'Now, as you can see, Dr Razumkin has lost two teeth, and yet he continues to tell us that Monsieur Botynsky died of a heart attack.'

The inspector was standing in front of her. He was smaller than she had thought. He smelled of eau-de-Cologne: his elegance was evidently a matter of importance to him. She thought she was going to be sick.

'Madame Galitzine, your friend has been foolish. As you yourself seem to understand, it is better to tell the truth.'

She said very quietly: 'How do *you* know the truth?'

He reached into the pocket of his blue double-breasted suit and unwrapped an object from his handkerchief. He laid it on the desk in front of her. A pair of wire-rimmed glasses, bent by an impact, shards of glass hanging from the rims.

'Do these belong to Dr Razumkin?' And here he opened them out before Razumkin's bowed face. 'Of course not. Your doctor's face is too broad, too fleshy. So who can they belong to?'

Oh, my poor Botynsky, fumbling in the dark as your attackers break down the door, groping for these glasses in the dark as they fall and splinter under a heel and you scream.

'I am puzzled by this mistake, doctor, genuinely puzzled. What compelled you to keep such an incriminating piece of evidence wrapped in a rag underneath the sink in the lavatory of your apartment? Why bother to keep the dirty secret?'

Razumkin wept noiselessly, holding his bloody handkerchief to his mouth.

'You had it made. We had nothing. You had returned, cleaned up the place, erased the signs of struggle, returned the chair by the bed to its upright position, straightened out the carpet on the floor, rearranged the body, returned it to its sleeping position. A charmingly thoughtful touch. And then you called the concierge as your witness, took the pulse, pronounced the patient dead, looked at your watch to note the time, phoned the police, waited for us to arrive, answered all the questions, filled in the form, and went on your irreproachable way, right under my nose. Because I was there, was I not?'

Asya wept, bent over, covering her ears.

'So I do not understand these glasses. Why you kept them. Were you secretly trying to incriminate yourself, ensure your eventual punishment? Such things happen.'

Razumkin wiped the blood from his mouth, and looked at the red smear on his hand.

'Are you sentimental? You were Botynsky's closest friend, as well as his doctor. So are they a little keepsake, something to remember him by?'

The inspector was looking at Asya as he talked. She had buried her head in her hands.

'Fat men are easy to pity. Fat men are easy to be sentimental about. Even their failures, their scrapes with the law, add a certain pitiable allure, do you not agree?' The inspector turned to Razumkin. 'It is natural to think of yourself, doctor, as a sentimental person. You are Russian, after all. You cry easily, as I can see. But – '

Asya looked up, and wiped her tears on her sleeve. The inspector leaned close to Razumkin's sunken face.

'Doctor, you are not a sentimental person. The glasses are not a keepsake, and you are much too concerned about your survival either to make such a mistake or to wish to incriminate yourself. So there is only one reason why you would keep such a vital piece of evidence stowed away in your lavatory.'

Razumkin staggered to his feet, and laid his bloody hands on the desk.

'Sit down, Razumkin. I repeat, there is only one reason, and that is so that you could blackmail those who ordered his murder. If need be. If they began to threaten you. Am I right?'

Razumkin mumbled through his broken teeth. 'Let her go. There is no reason to torture her with this. She knows nothing. I swear it. I swear she knows nothing.' He was at bay, staggering, clutching at the straws of his honour. If the truth were to be knocked out of him, she must remember, when this was all over, how hard he had fought, right here, at this instant, to save her.

'This is touching, Razumkin, your desire to protect her.'

Razumkin put his bloody hands on the desk and said in a whisper made indistinct by his missing teeth, 'Marceau. We know each other. We've worked together. You are not a sadist. You are too ambitious for that. You want results. I am telling you, there is nothing to be got from her. Let her go.'

They had Razumkin by the neck and jerked him down into his seat so hard that he howled like a beaten dog.

'Stop it!' Asya begged.

Marceau waved the two men away.

'Sit down, madame. Now, you tell me, what do you know about all this?'

She slumped in the chair, covered her face with her hands, and shook from head to toe. 'Nothing,' she whispered.

Marceau cupped his hand behind his ear and bent low towards her, all the while observing Razumkin. 'What was that?'

'Nothing.'

He lit a cigarette, paced about the room, looked out of the window at the café, turned back, surveyed them, and went on pacing. A minute passed. Then he said, in a musing voice, 'No marks of struggle, no contusions. Our pathologist went through that body from top to bottom. Nothing. Death consistent with coronary occlusion. So what happened, Ilya Ilyonovitch?'

Razumkin was slumped in his seat. The two men were right behind him. He said nothing.

'Did Jacquot put the fear of God into him, or did he need your help?'

Razumkin said nothing. Marceau came up behind him, bent over and whispered: 'The air-filled syringe? The bubble into the bloodstream?'

Razumkin shook his head from side to side. One of the men made to hit him. Marceau waved him away. 'Details. It doesn't matter.'

More silence, followed by the sound of Razumkin's breathing and Asya's tears.

'This is a pathetic sight,' Marceau said, looking at the two of them on the chairs in front of his desk. He came around the desk and knelt down in front of her, so she could not hide her face from his.

'Your former lover informs for the police. Your doctor conspires in his murder. Your – '

Razumkin grabbed Marceau by the arm. He gave a hoarse cry. 'Marceau! Stop! I'll tell you everything.'

The two men grabbed him and squashed him back on the chair. Marceau stood up, brushed his sleeve where Razumkin's hand had been, and walked slowly back behind the desk.

'Let her go,' Razumkin whispered. 'I'll tell you everything if you let her go.'

Marceau looked at him. 'Why should I? We're doing quite nicely as it is.'

'She knows nothing. That was always how it was. Let her go. I will tell you everything if you put her on the train.'

Marceau looked at his watch. He lit a cigarette and blew smoke up into the air so that it clouded the portrait of Pétain. 'Why should I, Ilya Ilyonovitch? Why shouldn't I let my men remove the rest of your teeth? That seems to get results.'

Razumkin whispered, 'It will be faster my way.'

Marceau smiled and walked around the room. Another minute passed, while he paused and considered Razumkin's proposal. Addressing Asya, who still sat huddled in her chair, hands covering her face, he said, 'You are lucky, Madame Galitzine, that Ilya Ilyonovitch and I know each other so well. I know him better than you do, because, unlike you, I usually know when he is lying and when he is telling the truth. And, madame, today you are in luck, because he happens to be telling the truth.' He snapped his fingers at the men standing behind their chairs. 'Take her to the train.'

She did not resist when they lifted her up and escorted her to the door. She turned. Razumkin sat slumped in the chair in front of Marceau's desk, his back to her, his head sunk on his chest. Marceau stood behind the desk, leaning on his hands, his fingers splayed out like a predator's claws after a meal.

The door shut behind her and she was led down the dark hallway into the street. Up above the square, on the platform at the top of the spiral staircase, stood the express, steam pouring from its funnel. They escorted her up the steps, carried her bags from the stationmaster's office, placed her in a compartment, handed over her papers and, as they left, raised their gloved hands to the brims of their hats.

The compartment was empty. She sat rigid, staring straight ahead, her left hand gripping a handkerchief, her ticket and passport in her right hand. The train began to move. She turned and looked out of the window. There was Josette's brother, holding a trainman's iron, his eyes following her until she passed from sight.

The train entered a tunnel and gathered speed in the dark. She pulled open the compartment door, felt her way down the corridor under the faint yellow light, found the lavatory and locked herself in. She was sick into the washbasin. Her body was convulsed by contractions and sobs, her mouth and nose plugged with vomit. Her knees shook violently, and she slumped down on the toilet seat, gasping for breath, gripping the metal handrail as the train howled in the darkness. Every time she thought of Botynsky's glasses, of Razumkin's bloody teeth, she was sick again.

It was many minutes before she was able to splash water over her face, towel the vomit from her blouse and make her way back to the compartment. Her whole body shook uncontrollably as she pulled herself along the corridor. The curtains flew at her and the train lurched from side to side in the tunnel.

She pulled the compartment door open, went to the window, sat down and closed her eyes. She wiped the smeared tears away. She was still shaking, still vibrating at an intolerable pitch. She knew that if she unclenched her teeth, they would begin to chatter. She knew she must hold on, keep herself together.

Suddenly she was aware, without having to open her eyes, that someone had entered the compartment. She saw the shoes first: brown alligators with metal heels and points, then the cuffs of a white linen suit several sizes too big, a grey shirt and a yellow silk tie with a palm tree on it. On his head, a straw panama with a black band.

Some kind of gangster. His first words were: 'You like my shoes?'

It was Majiec.

PART FOUR

S HE LIFTED HER nightgown and ran her finger along the scar on her hip. She thought of her scars as plaques to the passage of time: the faint mark on her forehead took her back to the exact spot on the gravel alleys of Marino where she had tripped and fallen at the age of seven; another brought back the moment when she had gashed her right thumb opening a tin of Niki's babyfood. The one girdling her left hip returned her to a summer holiday with Sergei in Corsica in 1934. The café owner had told her not to swim alone, the waves were too high, but she had dived through them and then been flung back against the breakwater. She was savaged like a doll in the jaws of a dog, and her last sight before going under was Sergei running towards her on the breakwater. Next thing she knew, she was between the sheets of their hotel bedroom and he was rubbing cream onto the abrasions on her thigh. He had loved her scars.

Now there were new scars, ones he might never see, puncture-marks between her ribs, surrounded by a circle of blue discolouration, where they had inserted the needles. As soon as she had arrived, the doctors came and pulled back her nightdress, searched for the right spot, jabbed her with a local anaesthetic and then forced the needle into a space between her ribs. A rubber tube was attached to the end of the needle and air was forced into the cavity between her ribcage and her lungs. Dr Lucas said they were just shutting down her lung for a rest. It had been resting for six months now. Time stretched behind her like a fallow field under an empty sky.

'Your visitor, madame.'

Asya spun around, letting her nightgown fall. Lapin was there holding a bouquet of flowers and looking embarrassed.

He kissed her on the forehead and she took the flowers.

'You are a magician.'

'A woman was selling them from a stall by the station. Aren't they incredible?'

They were cornflowers, just like the ones that grew in the fields of Marino, just like the ones in their mother's Fabergé brooch. Where was that brooch now, she wondered? She had pawned it in Constantinople, condemning it to a twilight existence, passing eternally from one pawnshop to another.

'*Eh bien, ma chère*,' he said, lowering himself into the seat, the brown leather of his Sam Brown belt creaking. He was tall and thin, and his uniform made him look more emaciated than usual.

'For Heaven's sake, what has happened to you?' she cried, and took his hand. There was a large white bandage protruding from under the collar of his tunic.

'Just a scratch,' he said, in his phlegmatic English way, 'from a blast fragment.'

'Tell me!'

And he did tell her, and she could see him sprawled in the rubble-strewn Edgware Road, in the long echoing silence after an explosion, his ears ringing, his mouth and nose full of dust, and blood running into his hands. She had seen the lurid glow of the night raids over London, forty miles away, above the treetops of the park. She felt ashamed of her safety.

'You poor fellow,' she said, and caressed his face.

Lapin had taken care of everything: secured their clearance from Lisbon, used all his influence to persuade the English consul that they were not spies after all, found the ship, paid her passage, met her at the docks, installed her in the sanatorium, visited her every weekend, even found Majiec his lodgings.

Majiec's attendance upon her in the sanatorium during the early months of her illness had been against all the rules. They tried to send him – as they put it – 'on his way', but he scaled the brick walls, forced a window, and they found him next morning asleep in the chair opposite her bed. He was insane on this one subject. Lapin explained to Dr Lucas what they had been through together, and Lucas relented, allowing Majiec to make up a bed in her room and to stay with her until she was past the worst. He fed her, bathed her, lifted her up and escorted her to the toilet. The nurses and doctors put his behaviour down to war trauma. He was a Pole, after all.

For his part, Majiec treated the medical staff with indifference, collecting Asya's towels from their linen cupboards, her thermometer from their trays, her meals from their kitchens. But when Lapin came for his visits, Majiec bowed and vacated the room with a click of his heels.

It was Lapin who persuaded Majiec to part with his stained Spanish gangster suit, worn all the way from Cerbère to Southampton, and to put on a new set of army fatigues. It was Lapin who took Majiec up to London to enrol in the Polish army in exile.

'I think your Majiec is in love,' Lapin said. 'I was in Portland Place on Wednesday on my way to the BBC and there he was outside the Polish legation with a woman, whom he introduced, very impressively, as "My Rachel: secretary to the Foreign Minister in exile."'

That sounded like Majiec.

Asya said, 'I'm jealous. Isn't it ridiculous?'

Lapin was at the sink, cutting the stems with his penknife and placing each cornflower against the lip of the vase. He pursed his lips exactly as Mother had done, Asya thought, when she went about the greenhouses of Marino trimming the peach trees with her secateurs.

'What day are we today?' Asya asked.

'The twenty-second.'

'Of June? Already? My God. In this place time just disappears.'

They walked along the corridor to the day room. It was a drowsy summer afternoon, overcast and heavy, with flashes of sun that shot deep shadows over the lawns.

Gladys was there as usual, in her peignoir, finishing off the *Telegraph* in the chair with the best view of the begonias. She was from Streatham, though Asya had no idea where that was, and her husband was in the desert. Asya had been shown a photograph of a windblown man in long khaki shorts standing by a tank, smiling like a sunburnt boy.

'And is your husband in the forces?' Gladys had asked when they first sat together in the day room.

'My husband is dead,' Asya had replied.

Gladys wore a lot of powder and had tightly-curled blonde hair. From Gladys Asya learned about life in England, or at least about life inside a semi-detached in Streatham. Gladys loaned Asya her *Picture Post*, and every evening they listened to Alvar Liddell on the wireless.

'News is on any minute. Draw up a chair.' Gladys turned on the wireless. As they looked out on the begonias of a sanatorium garden near Hastings, Lapin and Asya learned that the German invasion of Russia had begun.

The German radio was reporting prisoners taken in their hundreds of thousands and armoured columns within twenty miles of Pinsk. The Soviet radio was silent. When the bulletin had finally passed on to the weather for the Home Counties, Gladys reached over and switched it off. They sat silently for a minute.

Gladys said, 'Well, that's that, then.' She smoothed out the newspaper on her lap and looked at the begonias.

Lapin got to his feet. 'I must get back to London. We've been caught napping.' Lapin was in military intelligence. He knew the telephones would be ringing already in his deserted offices.

Asya rose, went to the window and stared out into the garden. It came to her, with the full force of certainty, that Niki must be in that invasion force, that he would have fought for secondment as translator, as driver, as anything, so long as he could be there in the van of the invaders, returning to his native land. She pressed her forehead against the window. All her remembering, all her stories, all her keeping faith with the desecrated past could only have led to this. He had made himself her avenger, and now it was too late to stop him.

When Lapin kissed her goodbye and rushed off to the station, Asya returned to her room and lay on the bed, and watched the midsummer dusk settling on the ancient wall at the bottom of the garden. There were no brick walls like that in Russia, and of all the things she had seen in England, this wall was the finest, bowed with the weight of ages, lime green where the sun did not reach it, the bricks umber-coloured with patches of bright weed growing in the cracks. The light skimmed over the topmost rows of bricks, then slipped away, leaving the wall in shadow, the lawn fading from green to grey, the sky to black. She lay for hours, motionless, watching the summer light slowly settle and die.

She awoke with a start. It was early morning, the lawn spangled with dew and the sun not yet over the wall. She pulled her towel robe on, padded down the hall to the day room and listened to the news: Brest, Malorita, Pripyat, a thousand-mile front, breakthroughs near Pinsk. Every name conjured up memories. She knew the Pripyat marshes: the trains to the Riviera used to pass through them, the vast, flat, reedy plains, frozen and deserted in winter. She wondered what they must be like in high summer: cranes wheeling up in flight from their nests among the reeds, the flat glare of high noon, and in the distance the black clouds of dust rising from the half-tracks. She could even see him in a mud-spattered uniform, peering over the top of the Daimler's windscreen into the diminishing distances of a homeland she had described to him on the edge of sleep. For an instant she was with him, on the road to Marino, and against her will she shared the full fever of his flight.

Asya sat and waited for the news bulletin at seven, then at eight, but neither added anything, and the glacial English tones of the announcer infuriated her, as if he were describing a duststorm on a distant planet.

When Majiec arrived for his regular Sunday morning visit, his mouth fell open when he saw her in her suit. She had dressed for the first time in six months.

'So,' was all he could say. 'You have heard? Now is your turn coming.'

Asya took his arm and they stepped into the garden. The smell of wet slate, moist flowerbeds and grass rose from the earth, and the air was pungent with the promise of the sea. Majiec wiped the dew from a white bench and they sat looking back at the converted Georgian country house that had been her home these past months. The news from Russia had made her lucid. She had to get better. She had to do something.

He put his arm around her and she remembered how they had crossed the interminable Spanish plain, sere brown in the October light, how she had slipped into sleep, his face next to hers. She had wanted to sleep forever, to escape the sight of Razumkin's bloodied teeth in his handkerchief and Botynsky's shattered glasses.

When she awoke her head was on his lap in the bedroom of a hotel in Lisbon. He was stroking her hair with one hand and eating an apple. She lay in bed with the shutters drawn, and the windows open. The room was chill and damp. They heard seagulls crying above the Tagus. So long ago.

He was talking about Rachel. The Polish Brigade, into which he had enrolled, was training on Salisbury Plain. He would soon be without any leave at all.

'You miss her. That's good.' Asya examined a viburnum trained to girdle the old brick wall. It was in flower: the fragrance of the buds was faint, at the edge of vanishing.

'Do you like to meet her?' Majiec wondered.

Asya smiled at him in exasperation. 'I don't think so.'

'You angry?'

She was not angry, just determined, suddenly, to awake, to 'put the past behind her', as Gladys would have said.

'Come on. I am going to walk you to the station.'

She had never been out of the grounds, but the staff nurse at the entrance could do nothing to stop her.

The walk to the station was along a country lane with hedges that rose above their heads on either side. There was a bright runnel of water in the ditches, and sunlight danced off the mica-flecked roadway. Above her, puffs of white cloud stood motion-less in the sky. Thousands of kilometres to the east, at that moment, the whole horizon would be lit with fire and the ground would be shaking with the thunder of armoured columns. She knew that she was both here, in a sunlit lane, and there, with her son, on the dusty road of conquest, past the torched and blackened villages, the lamenting women. She could not help it, her heart was pounding at the thought of his return.

When a hay wagon passed them both on the curve and the boys

on top turned right around and stared at her, Majiec could see her as they saw her, this European woman in high heels, with the straight line of her stocking seams running right up the back of her heels to her hem, the skirt with pleats and the tight tailored jacket, and the hair brushing her collar, and the bright red lipstick, and the straw between her teeth.

When the train came, Asya ran her finger along his cheek and walked quickly away. As the train gathered speed he saw her striding back to the sanatorium, deep in thought.

When Dr Lucas pronounced her well enough, Lapin came down and took her back to London by train. Somewhere south of Clapham, the train stopped on the line and she stared down at a dense patchwork of allotments. A man was pausing from his spadework; a boy in shorts was peering out from the corrugated bomb shelter in a garden; through the parted floral curtains of the house behind, Asya could see a woman washing her arms at the sink.

On the other side of the same street, not a single house had been left standing. The entire row had been flattened and left a tangle of blackened beams, wrenched windowframes, pulverized bricks and mortar. A gigantic hand had swept down from the sky and had wiped away one whole side of the street, while leaving identical houses and lives on the other side intact. The precision of it was fascinating. As the train slid past the devastated street and into the cavernous glass cave of Victoria station, she believed that such a fate, neither wild nor exuberant, but cold and precise like a surgeon's knife, was poised above her life and the life of her child.

197

GAZING THROUGH THE taxi window on the way to Lapin's flat, she could barely believe her eyes. Was this the city where she and Sergei had spent that weekend of escape before the war? This filthy expanse of hoardings, blind-eyed façades, gap-toothed fronts? The city was like a wound, the craters like lesions in her own memory.

Lapin enrolled her in the newsreader's training course at the BBC. Everyone said her deep, dusky voice was perfect for the microphone, and the Russian service took her on. For weeks she picked her way to work and back home to Lapin's flat in Seymour Street, behind Marble Arch. She struggled to find her bearings in the blackout, fumbled with coal fires whose heat only made the sheets of her bed seem damper, while the news on every billboard —the defeat in Greece, the fallbacks in the desert, the German advance to the outskirts of Moscow – grew steadily darker.

In the blitz of '40, Lapin said, there had been a certain exhilaration amidst the terror. Now there was only unrelenting routine, filthy streets, dust smarting in your eyes, rubble forlornly sprouting weeds, garbage-filled bomb craters, and grim exhaustion in every eye.

Late one night, on the top deck of a bus, she sat and watched a couple kissing in the seat in front of her. The soldier was rasping the neck of a rinsed-out blonde with his lips, while the girl had her hands deep in his uniform. Asya watched the boy's tongue darting to and fro, glistening with saliva. The bus hurtled through the darkness, heaving them to and fro. Suddenly the girl realized she was being watched. She turned and stared at Asya, cold hard pleaure in her face as the soldier buried his mouth on her nipples. Even when the boy let out a groan of abandon, spurting into her hand, the girl's eyes never left Asya's face.

She got off at the next stop, lost her way in the blacked-out streets, stumbled on some rubble, fell heavily against a hoarding and slithered down into a bomb crater. She sat there at the bottom, filthy water filling her shoes.

'Are you all right?' someone called.

'No.'

Then a man leaned down and pulled her out. He was an off-duty air raid warden in a siren suit, and she let him accompany her home. At Lapin's flat she ran upstairs, fed some shillings into the meter and turned on the bath. She peeled off her gashed stockings and soaking clothes, knelt in the tepid inches of water, looked down at the threads of blood eddying from her thigh and burst into tears.

When Lapin returned home at midnight, he found her wrapped in his dressing gown, asleep in the armchair before a dying coal fire. He knelt down and touched her hair. She started violently.

'Where have you been?'

His face was white with fatigue.

'They are fifteen miles from Moscow. We sit there looking at the maps, monitoring the radio traffic and wondering whether they are going to hold.'

'Forgive me.'

'What for?'

'I must stop at once,' she whispered, wiping her tears of relief at his return from her face. They sat by the fire, side by side, silent, brother and sister against the darkening world.

The next morning was glacial and bright, and she scraped a little porthole in the hoarfrost on the bus window. Everything that was desolate in London was now redeemed: frost shimmered on the grass-filled craters, the tin hoardings, the jagged and teetering façades and the tips of men's service caps.

Just before Christmas, she was pronounced ready to go on air. She was led down into the basement of Bush House through thick, padded double doors, past an instrument-filled control room, to an airless studio with its table, microphone and chair all in institutional grey. She had hoped she would be reading the news, or perhaps even Pushkin or Lermontov, but when the engineer eased up the sound bar on his instrument panel and the red light went on, her first words were: 'Camel Tango to Red Star Two Zero Three, Wedding is Postponed. Alpha Delta Pilot Six to MC Fourteen Two Zero Six Christmas Presents Late. Foxtrot Five Seven Delta Four, List is Ready for Shipment.'

Her voice beamed out over the frozen forests and rutted roads, the cupolas and domes of her homeland, and as she spoke it dawned on her that somewhere, in shattered ruins or deep in a bunker, a young German lieutenant listening on his platoon's receiver might chance upon a voice he would recognize, with a start, as her own. When she finished she pushed her way through the studio doors and made for the canteen, to get a grip on herself. She bought a cup of tea and sat alone by the window.

Would his boots be warm enough? Would the Germans have prepared their men for a Russian winter?

She banged her cup down on the saucer.

Stupid woman, stupid woman, she muttered to herself. Sentimental fool.

'Asya,' someone was saying. It was Gaby.

She leaned across the table, and as their lips met Asya thought: Here is the only woman in London who doesn't smell of Sunlight soap. Even the cut of her uniform, the tightness of the skirt, the slight flair in the pleats, mocked male military proprieties.

'So here we are: among the savages.'

'My God! I thought you were in Algiers.'

'I was. But I hate frightened men. It is so disillusioning, and believe me, Algiers was full of frightened men, preparing to make a deal with Vichy or I don't know what. So when I heard de Gaulle was here, I thought, Why not? And there was an English plane, and I got to know this man and so . . . here I am. And what are you doing here?'

'Broadcasting incomprehensible messages in my best school-girl's diction.'

'So am I!'

'I have a lot to thank you for, Gaby.'

'It's all on the bill.' Gaby reached into the breast pocket of her uniform and pulled out a packet of Senior Service. She lit one for each of them.

'Without your Josette, I would have died.'

'My Josette?' Gaby was laughing. 'How amusing.'

'What do you mean?'

'Josette is my mother.'

How could they possibly be mother and daughter: this luxuriant creature and the old woman in the pinafore and carpet slippers?

'I've come a long way,' Gaby said, blowing a funnel of smoke up into the lights.

'Why didn't Josette tell me?'

'She had to be careful around Razumkin. And she was right, wasn't she?'

Asya went silent, so Gaby just said, 'I warned him at Bordeaux. I told him they were after him. I didn't want you mixed up in anything.'

'I just couldn't believe he would do that,' Asya said.

'I think he was jealous,' Gaby said.

'Of Botynsky? Gaby, I can't bear it.'

Gaby observed her tenderly, and stroked her arm.

'I heard what happened at Cerbère.'

'How?'

'Carlton Gardens got the message.'

'Carlton Gardens!' Asya recovered and laughed. 'You are incredible! From the Algiers regime to the headquarters of the resistance in a single bound. I don't know how you do it, my dear, I really don't.'

Gaby smiled and blew a perfect smoke ring.

'I travel light.'

'But how does Carlton Gardens know what happened at Cerbère?'

'From the trainman.'

'Josette's brother?'

'You are hilarious. What do you mean, brother? That is my father.'

'No!'

201

'So now you know. There's a lot more you wouldn't believe.'

'Meaning?'

'Some other time.'

'Gaby.'

'Some other time.'

They smoked their cigarettes in silence.

'Back to work,' Gaby sighed. As she pulled back the cuff of her khaki to check the time, her eyes squinting in the cigarette smoke, Asya suddenly recalled how Josette had waved the small wad of francs at the caretaker of the Russian church. Like daughter, like mother. Both knew instinctively what was required to break down a man's resistance.

In the hallway, Gaby said that there was to be a party at her flat on New Year's Eve.

'Why don't you come? You might meet someone bearable.'

'You always said there were *no* bearable English men.'

'Who's talking about English men? They're banned,' Gaby said with a sweep of her hand. 'They'll all be French, except for a Pole and a Canadian or two. You don't mind a few Canadians, do you?'

'I don't know any.'

'And there's a Russian I want you to meet.'

'What kind of Russian?'

'Cultivated. Your type,' Gaby added, pecking Asya on the cheek as she moved to open the door of her studio.

'You're leading me astray.'

Gaby gently clapped Asya on both shoulders. 'That's what a war is for.' After scribbling the address on the flap of her cigarette packet, tearing it off and handing it to Asya, she was gone.

When Asya announced that she couldn't possibly go because she had nothing to wear, Lapin looked out one of the dresses his wife kept in the flat for her visits to town. Asya tried it on and made a face in front of the mirror. 'It's not me at all,' she said, smoothing the black velveteen over her hips, running her hands over the straps, turning her head this way and that with a disapproving grimace. It fitted her perfectly.

As soon as the door opened on the house in Walton Street, she was repelled by the frantic, student gaiety of it all, by the hall festooned with toilet paper, by the forlorn knee-high pine covered in paper decorations. A girl named Molly, with her arm around a gigantic Canadian soldier, told them to throw their coats in any of the rooms and get themselves a drink out back. It was a tall, narrow house, and they picked their way between couples sitting on the stairs. The noise from the gramophone was deafening, and the whole house seemed to be shuddering to the thud of dancers' feet. Lapin opened a door into a dark room on the first landing, and surprised a couple rolling around among a pile of coats.

Everyone seemed so young, so heated, that Asya retreated to the landing at the top of the house, leaving the groundswell of the party below her. She pulled the blackout curtain back a fraction and looked out over the tops of the trees at the darkened city stretched out beneath the half-moon.

'There you are,' said Gaby. 'Lapin sent me to find you.' She handed Asya a glass of punch and they both moved sideways as a soldier burst out of the bathroom buttoning his flies. He stepped over them with a grin and thundered down the stairs. Gaby sighed. 'Who *are* these people?'

'But Gaby, you live here.'

'Doesn't mean I invited them.' She shared the house with Molly from Winnipeg, Manitoba, a typist at MI 5, Florence from Nantes, Daisy from Trois Rivières, Quebec, and Rose from Paris. Gaby shook her head in mock disbelief.

'The incredible thing is that bidets do not exist in this country. What is a girl supposed to do?'

A muffled groan and a thud issued through a door on the landing.

'It doesn't seem to stop them, does it?' said Asya.

'Rubber goods. Brrrh.' Gaby shook herself and then jumped up and beckoned to a tall man on the stairs. 'Here, meet a friend of mine,' she said. He was tall and strongly built, with thin sandy hair and a moustache. There were maple-leaf flashes on his uniform.

'This is the Russian I was telling you about,' Gaby said, kissing him on both cheeks, and then patting the place beside Asya. He blushed and sat down on the stairs next to her.

'Excellent,' Gaby said, amused at their embarrassment. Then she clattered away downstairs.

'Captain Nick Isvolsky.' She shook his hand.

'You must be Lapin's sister. We work together.'

'Isvolsky?'

He nodded.

'From Kislovodsk?'

He nodded again.

'It's not possible.' She put her hand to her face.

He smiled, a big, wide grin. 'Why not?'

She threw her arms around him and kissed him on both cheeks.

'I was a kid at the time. Can't remember much, but you . . .'

'I remember!' she cried.

'I was probably out back playing with the neighbours' boy,' he said ruefully, not wanting to draw out the difference – ten years – in their ages.

'You had been playing outside, and you came running in halfway through tea.'

She could see old man Isvolsky beckoning him from the doorway, the comical bow the boy made, how he took a biscuit from the tray and clambered up onto the arm of his father's wicker chair, his bare feet dangling against his father's trousers.

'Can't remember a thing,' Nick said, shaking his head.

'Your Russian is as rusty as an old gate,' she said.

'That's what Canada did for me.'

'And your father? How is he?'

Nick looked down at his hands. They were strong and sun-burnt, with a faint shading of sandy hair on the knuckles and a thin gold band on the third finger of his left hand.

'He never practised law again. He sold electrical goods for the Philips company. The Montreal territory, as it was called,' he said, swilling an ice cube around in his drink. 'Every Monday morning he loaded boxes of electric shavers into the back of the Studebaker and set off alone to sell them to the better dry-goods stores in Chicoutimi and Trois Rivières.'

'Where's that?'

'The back of beyond. The north shore of Quebec, up a long, lonesome stretch of blacktop. Beautiful, though. He always said it reminded him of the forest country near Pskov.' Nick thought about this for a while, and Asya found herself realizing how good it made her feel to listen to his thoughtful voice. 'Here he was, a member of the St Petersburg bar, fifty-five years of age, selling shavers in Trois Rivières.' They sat quietly for a while, feeling the tremors of the dancers' feet two floors below.

'What happened?' she whispered. They were side by side. She could feel his body next to hers, muscular, substantial and warm. He offered her his drink. She took a sip.

'I was living with him while finishing university, and I'd make dinner for him when he came in off the road on a Friday night, wheezing up the stairs, pausing on the landings, with the unsold boxes under his arm, coming home to the fifth floor of the Victoriaville Apartments, calling for his glass of hot vodka and milk.' He looked down into his drink. 'Why am I telling you all this?' His breath was sweet with gin.

'Because we are nearly relatives, for God's sake. Anyone who survived Kislovodsk in '18 is my relative.'

He laughed. 'Dad would lie in the bath, drinking his vodka and milk, and tell me through the transom about Madame Demers in Chicoutimi, and Madame Richard in Trois Rivières. I think he used to sleep with Madame Demers. Anyway –'

'I liked your father.'

'Yeah.' Nick sat silent for a long time, swirling his drink around. 'What about you?' he said. 'Tell me the whole story.'

'Later,' she said. 'I want to hear what happened.'

'Anyway. One Friday I was cooking dinner, and Dad was sitting in his bath with his vodka, talking through the transom as usual, and then I didn't hear anything and so I called out.'

Nick looked at her. His eyes were clear and deep-set. She wanted to touch his cheek.

'I don't know why I'm telling you this,' he said.

She nudged him gently. 'Go on.'

He sat still for a while and then said in an abstracted voice, 'When I went into the bathroom, the vodka glass was rolling along the tiles. He was soapy as a seal. I couldn't get him out of the bath. All I could do was hold him up, so he wouldn't drown.'

They sat side by side, their bodies touching but their spirits far away, reliving the moment when they had watched the light fade and dissolve in their fathers' eyes.

She felt instantly that this stranger was the only man who had ever understood what she had lived through at that moment. She leaned close so that their heads were nearly touching.

'Your father was the only one who came to the cemetery. Did you know that?'

Nick shook his head.

She could feel old Isvolsky holding her at the grave's edge, his hand stroking her shoulder. Just then, she could see how much she had depended, at that moment, on his strength, on his hands caressing her shoulder, wiping away her tears.

'I must have drunk too much,' Nick said.

'You sound sober to me.'

Nick drained his glass. 'Are you married?'

She looked down the long, winding staircase that disappeared beneath them. 'He vanished.'

'Tell me.'

'Some other time.'

She looked at him and shrugged. It made him laugh. It was obvious from the gold band on his finger that he was married, so she didn't bother to ask.

He stood up. 'Would you like a dance?' He followed her as she stepped between the couples on the stairs into the room where the gramophone was playing. She turned around with her arms up in position ready to take his hands in hers, a smile on her face, and she let him lead her, feeling as light as air. He was a head taller than her, a big man. She pulled him closer, rested her head on the rasping stuff of his uniform. She could hear his heart beating. Out of the corner of her eye she could see Lapin in the doorway, watching them with a wistful expression.

'My turn,' Gaby said, and tapped Nick on the shoulder. He stood back, looking abashed, and let her dance away with Asya. Soon they were entwined together, fingers enlaced. How full and ripe and musky Gaby was. Asya kissed her cheek, feeling Nick and Lapin watching them from the doorway. 'He's not bad, is he?' Gaby said.

'I had tea with him when he was a little boy.'

'He's not a little boy now.'

Asya bit Gaby's damp, fragrant neck.

'Your sister is eating me up!' Gaby called out as she passed Lapin.

Then the music stopped and they went in search of a drink. Asya fanned herself as Gaby poured her a glass of punch. 'So now you have met Nicolai Dimitrovitch,' Lapin was saying, and Asya poked him in the ribs. 'Why did you keep this man a secret from me?'

'We are in intelligence,' Lapin said with a comic shrug.

'No excuse,' Asya replied.

There was a commotion outside in the hall, a rush of cold air, much shouting and foreign voices. A knot of people in greatcoats pushed their way onto the dancefloor.

'The Poles!' Gaby cried, and as Asya turned, there was Majiec coming towards her, with a bottle in one hand and Rachel shyly in the other.

He kissed Asya so hard that she grimaced and drew back.

'Wherever did you find that ridiculous moustache?' Asya exclaimed, holding him out at arm's length to get a better look. It was straight out of a Pathé newsreel.

'Is magnificent, you think so?'

'Magnificent,' said Gaby drily, and Majiec embraced her and handed her the bottle. Then he brought Rachel forward, and Asya shook her hand.

'Majiec saved my life, so you must look after him for me. You do realize that he is quite mad?'

'I know,' said Rachel.

'You are saying terrible things about me, I can tell,' Majiec said, and Asya raised herself on tiptoes and kissed him on the cheek, above his absurd handlebar moustache. Then he bowed to her, with a touch of sadness, and led Rachel onto the dancefloor. She seemed like a little bird carried inside his greatcoat, and as Majiec danced with her, treading all the while on her feet, Rachel gazed up at him with mute forbearance.

When midnight came, they all cried 'It's 1942!' and went outside and stood around breathing in the chill tang of the night air. A voice called out from a nearby house for them to shut up and go inside, didn't they know there was a bloody blackout. One of the Canadian boys started to climb the railing, declaring that he was going to teach the goddamn Brits some manners, didn't they realize the Canadians were all that stood between them and goddamned Hitler, but his girlfriend pulled at his trouser legs and got him down off the railing.

Nick went upstairs to fetch Asya's coat, and Lapin went prowling through the darkened bedrooms for his, while Asya stood in the doorway of the dancing room and watched Majiec and Rachel, now slowed down to a drugged swaying of their hips. Both of his arms were locked around her waist, and she seemed to have fallen asleep on his chest. When Nick came and stood behind her, Asya said softly, 'Goodbye, Majiec.'

It was brisk and shivery outside and she raced ahead of them down the street, her high heels clattering on the flagstones. Nick lit a cigarette and watched her skipping across the square, her shadow in the moonlight rippling along the iron railings before vanishing at the corner.

When they caught up with her she was leaning against the railings and they swept her up by the elbows and set her down like a child. Then she ran ahead of them again, leaving them to saunter, in their male way, with their hands in their pockets. When they reached Lapin's flat, and Nick said he was happy to keep walking, the night was fine, she suddenly kissed him firmly and whispered in his ear: 'Stay.'

WHEN ASYA AWOKE in the morning, there he was, tangled in the quilt they had laid out on the sitting-room floor, his head thrown back and his hair across his face, an arm draped along the carpet in front of the extinguished fire. She placed a cup of tea beside him, and when she returned from the bathroom he was dressed, cupping his hands around his tea and looking dazed with sleep.

On the second night they cooked together, side by side in the galley kitchen, slicing beets for the meatless borscht made from a recipe Nick remembered from his Russian nanya. He sucked the beet juice off his fingers, took a swig of stout from the bottle and passed it to her. He had a gift for living ordinary life that she had never seen in any other man. After dinner he took them to the pub to play darts, and when they came home and Lapin had withdrawn to his room and closed the door, Nick made love to her in front of the fire, cradling her head in both hands. Looking up at him, she said, 'You are like a brother,' and he laughed and bent down and kissed each collarbone.

'Not a brother, never.'

They had seven nights like that, and on the morning of the eighth day she woke beside him with a start and thought to herself – half guilty, half amazed – that she had not once thought of Sergei.

On the ninth day she and Lapin took a cab to King's Cross, met Nick on the platform and boarded a train for Greenock. It was a 'special', two passenger coaches and sixteen freight cars, and there were military police behind a barbed-wire barrier checking the papers of the sailors queueing at the gate. As the guard scrutinized the pass Lapin had procured for her from Captain Saunders, the head of the Russian section, Asya realized she was the only woman on the train. She had insisted on seeing the boat that was to carry Nick northwards into the ice, to Murmansk.

She had watched him pack his Arctic gear, and some of it had reminded her of the paraphernalia that used to be loaded into her father's sleigh when he went on winter hunts: the long underwear, rough flannel shirts, rolls of socks, fur-lined boots and gloves, which the servants used to pound with unguent until they were soft to the touch. All of these were familiar, but there were other, menacing items of standard issue: the service revolver in a heavy waterproof case, and the asbestos flash hood worn at battle stations to protect the face from fire, phosphorus and shell fragments. She asked him to try it on for her, but he shook his head.

'We have Molochkov with us, I see.' Lapin had taken some papers from his briefcase and was scanning the names on a list.

'Christ,' said Nick, staring out the window. 'That oily bastard.'

Lapin shrugged. At the last minute the inoffensive London deputy station chief had been replaced by his secret police superior, Vassily Petrovitch Molochkov. Who could fathom the Soviets?

'Saunders always says to me: "You're Russian. You should understand them,"' Lapin mused. 'I keep saying: "They're not Russian. They're Soviet. A new human type. I am the old human type. Hopeless. I am just as baffled as you." Naturally he says: "What the hell do we have you on the payroll for then?"' Lapin shrugged. 'At least I can speak their language.'

'I can't even do that,' Nick muttered.

'You can,' Asya said softly.

'I wish it weren't so rusty,' he said.

'I went to Saunders and asked him what we had on Molochkov,' Lapin said. 'Rumours, he says. Deputy station chief in Vienna and Madrid. That would place him in Austria in the days before the Anschluss, and before that in republican Barcelona.'

'Doubtless weeding out the local party,' Nick ventured.

'Doubtless.'

The minute you had their story, Asya said – the history that trailed behind them – you had the man. You were no longer fooled by the good manners.

'Damn it,' Nick said, 'If the British hadn't been so bloody casual about counter-intelligence before the war, there might have been a file on him.'

'If this had been France . . . ' Asya began.

'Exactly,' Nick said. 'There would have been a file, but Saunders said we hadn't really bothered with that sort of thing before the war.'

So they had damn all on the Soviets, damn all on their European network, damn all on the Murmansk lot.

'None of this bothered Saunders in the slightest. "Just gen up on them when you're there. That's what we pay you for, old boy."' Nick mimed his superior bitterly. 'Don't "old boy" me,' he said, looking out of the window.

The thought of a month on the high seas with Molochkov sank Nick into a silence that lasted till the train was well out of London. He took out his briefcase and, after making sure their compartment door was locked, unsealed the oilskin pouch containing his confidential orders. He knew the gist already: the visit had been initiated on the Soviet side. Code traffic between London and Murmansk was being intercepted, they said: they knew this from the German bombing cycle. German bomber command in Norway was able to anticipate flotilla arrivals, and their accuracy was becoming alarming. Losses were mounting in the Arctic approaches. The head of Murmansk depot wanted a face-to-face on home ground to discuss what to do. Why not in London? Saunders had countered. No, Molochkov had insisted, it must be home ground. All this led the unit to think that Nick was going over to bring back a high-level message. The orders belaboured the obvious: Insist meeting top man, local station chief plus Moscow lead. Nick passed the pouch over to Lapin, who shut it inside his briefcase: no need to take the orders on board.

Nick looked over at Asya. Shadow from her hat bisected her long, angular face and the ruby of her lipstick glowed in the compartment's gloom. He looked away and she knew he thought she shouldn't have come. He pulled back the blackout curtain:

they were approaching Birmingham. Sparks from the funnel sprayed past the window. Above the soothing music of the train was the thin, high drone of aircraft overhead.

There was a knock on the carriage door. Lapin snapped his briefcase shut, placed it in the net rack overhead and went to the door. When he slid it open, Molochkov stepped into the compartment. 'May I?' he asked.

He sat down facing Asya and pulled the compartment door shut with a practised shove. He had a high, receding forehead, steel-grey hair and clear grey eyes. Asya glanced at his hands, looking for some telltale sign of his past there, but they were white and unmarked, as blank as his face.

Just like his name, she thought to herself. When she and Lapin had been children they used to work themselves into helpless laughter, playing with people's names. She could see Lapin lying in the canopied garden swing under the pines, spinning out his droll variations while she swung them up and down, kicking against the frame with her shoe. And now, opposite them, sat the Milky One.

There were red stars on his epaulettes: otherwise the tunic was bare, functional, rather poorly cut, of low-quality stuff. The people's army. He was holding out a curved, gleaming cigarette case, which at a touch of his thumb opened to reveal a platoon of Dunhills, all at attention behind a line of gold braid. She shook her head. He passed the case to Nick. When he took a cigarette, the lighter was there instantly, the flame purling in the draught.

'So at last you are returning to your homeland.' Molochkov's Russian was the modern, harsh kind which grated on her ears. Lapin was right: a new human type.

'Vassily Petrovitch, do me a favour,' Nick said in English. 'We are going to be locked up together in that wretched boat for the better part of a month. We may even have the pleasure of drowning together. Spare me your jokes about my homeland.'

'But it is.'

'I'm a Canadian, Molochkov.'

'Well, it is *your* homeland, Princesse Galitzine,' Molochkov said, 'is it not?'

'My passport is French,' she replied as coldly as she could. Not exactly true, but why admit to this man that she had never had the heart to surrender her Nansen passport, that badge of un-reconciled Russian exile?

'Dear me,' he said cheerfully. 'I expected more congenial company.' He laughed, and they all watched him.

He was like a street magician she had once seen in Paris who had pulled a pigeon from Niki's pocket, and whose intense, smirking gaze had kept them rooted to the spot. So it was with Molochkov: as he grinned at her in his malicious way she half expected him to snap an ace of spades from behind her hat.

'We *are* struggling in the same cause, are we not?' Each one of his statements trailed upwards into a question.

'Yes,' she said. 'Better than the days when you fought on Hitler's side, wouldn't you agree?'

He raised a finger. 'What is that excellent English phrase? "Let bygones be bygones"?'

'Pretty recent bygones,' Nick said. 'You and Hitler were dividing up Poland between you just three years ago.'

Molochkov let it pass. 'Your husband, I believe, went to fight in Poland.'

She made her face a blank. 'Yes, and he did not come back.'

'I am sorry to hear it.'

'So am I,' she retorted, 'especially since you were attacking Poland from the east just as Hitler invaded from the west.'

'Was your husband Polish?'

'I don't know where you have learned about my husband.'

Molochkov smiled, at ease, and made a little wave of his hands as if to say, don't waste time becoming indignant.

'Your files should be more accurate. He was born in Chelm.'

'In what was once imperial Russia,' Molochkov countered.

'Before Lenin bartered it away to the Germans in 1918, at Brest-Litovsk. By that treaty, my husband's home town became part of republican Poland,' Asya said. 'So, naturally, Poland was close to his heart. Though he remained Russian.'

'An interesting history lesson,' Molochkov said.

'I was married to him for twenty years.'

'Indeed.'

She had the irritable feeling that he was simply playing out the line in order to reel her back in. His eyes did not leave her face. He was almost handsome, in a reptilian way.

'He maintained valuable business relations with my country until he went to Poland. You made no objection?'

She shook her head.

'Why not?'

She found this impudent. 'Because he was my husband.'

There was a long silence. They could both hear the drone of aircraft over the clatter of the train. Nick pulled back the blackout curtain and stared up into the sky. They were approaching a station, but he couldn't tell which one.

Molochkov smiled. 'It is a shame that not everyone in the émigré community is of your persuasion.'

Nick interjected. 'Look, Molochkov,' he said in Russian, 'none of us supports the White cretins who followed Hitler into "their homeland".'

Asya sat very still. The train was slowing down. There was an exhalation of steam, a grinding of brakes, a shudder transmitted from car to car. She said, 'Such people are misguided. They have been misled.'

Molochkov nodded equably.

Suddenly they were all thrown forward. The train shuddered, and the brake shoes screamed against the rails. She was sucked backwards into the pit of the seat by a violent deceleration, then thrown forward again with a lurch. She fell to the floor of the compartment, a hand pushed her head down, and the train stopped.

'Planes!' Nick shouted, and then threw himself on top of her. The air roared around her, glass splinters rained down, and Nick gripped her tight. On and on, seconds distended into minutes, hours, as the floor shook and the glass shattered and the mad suction of explosions tore at her clothes. Through tightly-closed eyes she could see flames, and she felt herself tumbling over and over, backwards in time to Mineralni Vodi station, sheltering under the buffet table, and then she was pitched forward into the screaming present, Nick on top of her, the explosions coming from every side.

Then it stopped. For a minute they lay there testing the silence, listening, hearing nothing but the crackle of flames, the air filling with the smell of burning paint. Nick relaxed his grip on her, and pulled himself up onto the seat. She looked up: the blackout curtain flapped in the shattered window. Nick's hair was festooned with glass splinters. Molochkov was staring straight ahead and blood was streaming from his right temple. The glass of the compartment door and the carriage windows sparkled all over his uniform.

Voices were crying out nearby. Nick tore the blackout curtain away, levered himself out of the shattered window and jumped down onto the track. Lapin followed and reached up to help Asya down. Nick pulled Molochkov over. He landed heavily, groaned, and Nick propelled him down the loose stone embankment. Lapin gave her a push and she slithered down the stones, until she lost her balance and pitched headlong through a split-cane fence.

She moved her hand around in the darkness. The earth was moist, freshly tilled: she felt rows of small plants, smelt compost somewhere close by. It was some kind of railway allotment. Nick and Lapin were nowhere to be seen. There was another explosion, a fireball of gasolene in the air, and she flattened out again.

When she lifted her head, she could see a body face-down on the grass ahead of her. She crawled forward, saw it was Molochkov, pulled him upright and propelled him forward by his collar. Glass crunched under her feet. There was a house ahead. The glass panel in its back door had blown out. She reached in and turned the handle.

They were in a kitchen: she saw a pump handle, a sink, rows of mugs on a rack, a dishrag on a table. She stepped through the kitchen into a dark corridor and followed floral wallpaper and a plush runner until she came to a door.

When she opened it, she saw three very white children's faces peering at her from under a brass bed and a woman in her nightgown on all fours, just getting to her feet. Asya lowered Molochkov onto a chair.

'I seem to have ruined your garden,' Asya said. Molochkov was examining his bloody hand. There was silence.

'Here,' the woman said warily, handing him a towel from the back of the chair nearest her. He wiped his face, looked at the blood, seemed puzzled.

The children's mouths were open. The woman stood watching them, listening to the sounds outside. There were shouts down the street in front, the roar of fire-engines, the ringing of a police-car bell.

On the mantelpiece above the coal fire a child's steel alarm clock was ticking. Asya listened to the clock, and suddenly felt herself begin to shake. She sat down against a deal dresser in the bay window.

The woman moved past her and went down the passage into the kitchen. The children came out from under the bed and stood in a little cluster opposite the two muddy and bleeding strangers. A kettle began to whistle. The woman returned and handed Molochkov and Asya cups of warm, sugary tea. She sipped one herself and handed each of her children a biscuit. She sat down and they crowded around her chair.

'Bert's at the station,' the woman said after a while.

'Where are we?' Asya asked.

'They're bombing the goods yard. Where Bert works.'

'Where?'

'Carlisle.'

The woman was wearing red puff slippers and a man's blue flannel dressing gown. Her hair was in curlers and she seemed to be about forty. She went into the kitchen and returned carrying an old shirt, a washcloth and a saucepan full of water.

'One of Bert's old ones,' she said, and then tore the shirt into strips. 'For him,' she said. She sat down and watched while Asya bathed Molochkov's head wound and picked the glass from his hair and ear. Molochkov tried to smile at the children, but it frightened the youngest one, who hid her face in her mother's lap.

'You're good at this,' Molochkov whispered in Russian.

'I used to be a nurse, or didn't your files tell you that?' she whispered back.

He had been cut and concussed, she thought, but nothing more serious than that. They watched as she wrapped the shirt strips round his head and tucked the ends in behind his ear.

'Where you from then?' the woman asked, looking at the red stars on Molochkov's uniform.

'We're from London,' Asya said. 'And he's on his way to Russia.'

'Oh,' said the woman, unsurprised.

'I must find my friends,' Asya said. 'Can I leave him with you?'

The woman nodded and they sat watching him while Asya got up and went out through the front door into the street. It was a row of narrow two-up two-downs, flush against the railway embankment. Bloemfontein Road, the sign said. Number 36. There were hoses underfoot and firemen running about her. The train was still on fire, and the glow lit up the chimneytops.

She wanted to call out Nick and Lapin's names but the sirens would have drowned out any cry. She walked in the direction of a building she thought might be the station. It was burning, and she walked towards the flames until she began to feel their heat on her face. Then she heard her name called, and she turned.

Nick said, 'You need help,' and Asya looked down and saw that her hands were red and her trenchcoat was damp with blood. 'Molochkov's, not mine,' she said, suddenly feeling absurdly well. They went back for him and found the three children watching over him as if he were an injured bird. Bert was there too, a small man in grimy overalls and a helmet, smoking a cigarette and keeping Molochkov under observation.

'Just popped back to see if everyone was all right.' His wife handed him a cup of tea.

'You had a scrape then, didn't you?' he said to Molochkov.

Molochkov said, 'I am a Russian man.'

'I don't mind,' said Bert.

Asya suddenly felt near to tears, standing in this children's bedroom, looking at their white feet on the linoleum, their clothes airing on the clothes-horse in front of the ash-grey coal fire. Their father had taken off his helmet: the little boy was holding it by its strap. The father ran his hand through his hair: a services' cut, short back and sides. There were carbon smudges on his forehead and cheeks. Everything about 36 Bloemfontein Road was neat: the clean lace curtains on the windows, the dresser, the football-player figurine on the mantelpiece. Asya bent down to the youngest one, the girl, and said, 'One day, you'll tell people you were asleep and you woke up and a train had caught fire and two Russians came through the door, covered in blood. And no one will believe you. But it will be true. Don't let anyone tell you it didn't happen.' And the little girl looked at her, and then hid behind the chair.

'Thank you,' said Asya to Bert, who nodded.

'That's all right,' said the woman, standing in the doorway, arms folded, watching them go.

By four in the morning they were on their way to Greenock by staff car. The headlights picked their way through the green tunnels of the country roads and the draught leaked in through the canvas top. Asya felt stiff and sore and cold. Molochkov sat in front with the driver, and the last thing she remembered, before her head slipped against the window and she fell asleep, was Molochkov's bandaged profile in the faint glow of the instrument lights.

When she awoke, the car's tyres were squealing along the steel tracks on the quay at Greenock. Giant cranes loomed overhead in the foggy dawn and she saw a tank hanging in the air, suspended above a ship's hold, as if in some absurd pause for thought. It was still dark, but the dockyard was alive with figures moving about among crates and bales, beckoning upwards to the big cranes overhead. She smelt the oily slick of the water on the frozen air and could see the mast lights of a dozen cargo ships. The car drew to a stop beside the stern gangway of one of the freighters. Molochkov stared at the *Frederick Johnson*, at the rust streaming from its rivets, at its salt-sullied portholes and bilge pumps flushing convulsively into the bay, and mockingly crossed himself three times. 'May the saints preserve us,' he said.

A crane had a net full of jerrycans poised above the decks and the crew were ringing the hatch to guide it down into the hold. 'Gasolene,' Lapin said to Molochkov, pointing to the craneload. Molochkov nodded. 'For Leningrad.'

Nick added, as he levered himself down through the hatch into the quarters below, 'One torpedo and you and me will be barbecued chicken.'

'What is barbecue?' Asya heard Molochkov say as he followed Nick below decks.

She knew she would feel suffocated and entombed in their quarters below, so she stayed above deck in the dawn air. She felt an extreme femaleness here, among these worried, busy men, rushing past her, carrying stores, checking the lashings of the lifeboats, oiling the flanges of the signal light by the bridge door. On the aft deck there was an anti-aircraft gun, and the gunner was in his seat, eyes turned skywards, swivelling rapidly through 360 degrees. It was a small gun, not much use against anything serious, and she could see from the way the deck railings had been cut loose to make way for it that it had just been bolted on.

It had all been so different at Novorrossisk. Not this calm, anxious bustle, but terror on every face. Not this rusted tramp, the *Frederick Johnson*, but the grand *Orient Star*. Not this light-smeared fog and aching chill, but the bright glare of the Black Sea coast. Not dawn but dusk. Not a beginning, but the ending of everything she had known.

Nick came up behind her. 'It's time for you to go.'

They were preparing to cast off the moorings.

'I was far away,' she said.

'Where?'

'In Novorrossisk, at the quay, just like this.'

'And somewhere down there, among the crowd, there is me, my father and my nanya.'

'Yes, you are down there too.'

'Which boat was it?'

'The *Orient Star*.'

'We didn't get on that one.'

'What was yours called?'

'The *Huanchaco*.'

'Goodbye,' said Nick, and kissed her three times.

'Goodbye,' she said, and ran her hand along his shoulder.

Lapin was with them and they stood silently for a while, not moving, waiting together as Russian families do whenever one of their number is about to embark on a journey, until Asya broke the spell and slipped down the gangplank, and walked away down the quay. Molochkov came out on deck at this moment, and he and Nick followed her with their eyes until she disappeared in the fog, Lapin following behind as she strode along, not looking back.

AFTER NICK LEFT, Asya plunged into 'the tunnel' — three straight weeks of night duty, ending with the news summary every morning at six. It was still dark outside in London, but across the continent the sun had risen on the besiegers and besieged at Leningrad and on the port of Murmansk. Her bulletins always beamed out the official message of hope: the German advance had been stopped, Leningrad was surviving the siege, Allied convoys were getting through, American guns and tanks were pouring ashore at Portsmouth and Southampton, the tide was turning. She read what they put in front of her, but she wondered how much of it was true. At the end of her shift the fatigue would hit her. She would walk through the corridors, by now teeming with the day shift, and she would think coldly and mechanically: In Russia, it is nine in the morning, and my son, my husband and my lover are on the other side of this continent. They may be alive, they may be dead, and I have no way of knowing. And she would suddenly be filled with hatred for the heartlessness of it all.

Gaby was also in 'the tunnel', so they met at the canteen most mornings, just after they came off-air, and ate their breakfast together. There was a new man in Gaby's life, and Asya worked on her for details.

'Name?'

'André Menard, from Toulouse, so we're from the same backyard. Well, almost.'

'Rank?'

'Captain in the Paras.'

'Age?'

'One of those you can never be sure: about thirty.'

Asya enjoyed the way Gaby appraised a man, estimated his stamina, his use to her. Her eyes narrowed, she tapped her cigarette on the ashtray and concentrated on the essentials. He sounded important. She was less derisive than usual. They had met at a Walton Street party and it had all happened very fast.

'And now he's gone.'

'Where?'

'Don't ask me. On a mission. Three of them: a saboteur for the railway lines, a radio man and him. He wouldn't tell me where.'

They walked together to the Underground in the early-morning drizzle, both feeling numb with fatigue. Gaby took the Piccadilly Line and Asya the Central, so they always waved goodbye at the giant, groaning escalators of Holborn station.

One morning Asya found herself compelled, by some malign desire to seek her own hurt, to ask the question that had always been there, that had remained suspended between them for as long as they had known each other.

'Did you sleep with him?'

'Who?'

'Seryozha.'

Gaby looked away, down the clanking escalator at the people sweeping by them into the grimy gallery below.

'Answer me!'

Gaby gave her a cold and amused look.

'What do you expect me to say? And in any case, it's not the point.'

'What is the point?' Asya said furiously, oblivious of the crowds pushing past.

'Wake up,' Gaby said. 'Do you know that Niki came to see me? "Tell me about my father. All I get from Mother is fantasy." So I told him.'

'What do you know?' Asya hissed.

'I know,' she said, and clattered away down the escalator.

It came to Asya, as clear and cold as could be, that Gaby had slept with both of them: father and son.

Storming through the streaked yellow-tiled tunnels, angrily pushing past the crowds, Asya knew they had not lacked for opportunities. Niki was mesmerized by Gaby, and Gaby never failed to notice attraction. When she sat down at table, she always

222

cast a sideways glance at him as he tenderly slipped her chair beneath her. Ah! Asya pounded her knee with her fist.

She had been such a simpleton! Inviting Gaby down to the Ourousoffs', leaving her and Niki all the time in the world to mount the cool dark stairs to the upstairs bedrooms. In Lapin's flat, she threw herself on her bed and lay face-down, hands clutching her temples, rigid with rage. Betrayed, betrayed! By that bitch! Her perfume, the way she held her cigarette, the sleek, blonde hair, firm upturned breasts so insultingly evident beneath her blouse, everything about her made Asya nauseous with spite. She lay there rigid and then fell asleep.

She woke face-down, the coverlet wet with her saliva, her mind cold and lucid. She looked at her watch: it was noon. She thought: And what if Gaby is right? What if Seryozha . . . and here she sat up and rubbed her face, felt the pattern of the coverlet on her cheek. She coldly weighed the composition of her anger. Was it only a screen to keep the truth at bay? No, it could not be true, it could not be true. She knew him better than she knew herself.

But Gaby was another story. With her, the betrayal was so obvious it made Asya pound her forehead with her fist to think she had not seen it coming. With bleak clarity she could see the upstairs bedroom at the Ourousoffs', and her child undressed under the eyes of her closest friend and initiated, at her hands, by the slanting light through the shutters, into the full fevers of his body. Asya sat down on her bed, as empty of feeling as a stone.

'I am losing my mind,' she said to herself, and went into the kitchen. There was nothing to eat in the cupboards except some dried oats, so she made herself porridge, and ate it with mechanical indifference.

Now she knew what Botynsky meant: 'Your moral charm will be your downfall.' Yes, he had been quite right. A certain kind of well-born person, he said, was invariably attached to an image of themselves as being 'above certain low intuitions', like rage or jealousy or envy. And so she had never allowed herself to feel jealous towards Gaby, or to allow her mind to travel along the route of probabilities in the case of Sergei. Oh, it was so much more attractive to think well of yourself, to think of yourself as generous to a fault, as 'above' such things.

I am sick of myself, Asya thought, and I am sick of that bitch. She rummaged through the drawers, found a cigarette of Lapin's and lit it from the burner on the stove. She paced furiously.

What people called her innocence, she could now see, was nothing more than an incapacity to think ill of others because she was incapable of thinking ill of herself. Her innocence had been an incorrigible variety of self-regard.

Immediately Asya felt her stiff, righteous anger begin to loosen and dissolve. For no reason at all, she found herself thinking of that night when Gaby took her to the strip show. How they had laughed! How soft her lips had been! How agonizingly close to the edge their caresses had taken them!

Yet, from pride, she checked her desire to be reconciled: she felt she must remain true to her anger, even though it was soon replaced with longing for Gaby's company. She worked 'in the tunnel' for another week, and when she was in the canteen she and Gaby did not speak. Asya watched her repaint her lipstick, close her compact with a smack and disappear down the corridor with a cool clicking of her heels.

One night in September when she was at work and Lapin was alone in the flat, the doorbell rang. Standing in the doorway, drawn and unshaven, was Nick.

'Nine hours on that bloody train, on top of seven days at sea. Is there a vodka by any chance, Alexander Vladimirovitch?'

Lapin kissed him on both cheeks, took the dufflebag off his back and pitched it onto the sofa.

'I will check my secret store.'

Nick crumpled into the easy chair by the fire. Everything was where it had been. Signs of the spare Galitzine style: through the kitchen door, the cooking spoons on their racks; to hand, the last week's copies of The Times folded in a pile. They were as neat as monks, the Galitzines. He was so glad to be back he could have kissed the carpet.

Lapin poured a measure of vodka into a shot glass, handed it to Nick, poured himself one and sat down on the chair opposite.

'Where's A?'

'On shift till six tomorrow morning.'

'Just as well,' Nick said, downing his vodka, smacking his lips, and then subsiding, just as suddenly, into a stupor of fatigue.

'Tell me,' Lapin said, but Nick just sat there, scratching the stubble on his face.

'You couldn't make me some scrambled eggs, could you?'

'I'll try the neighbours.' Lapin knocked next door. The severe-looking British major was already in his pyjamas, but he did have some powdered egg, and with that Lapin fried up an onion, the only vegetable in the flat.

Nick devoured it all, ran his finger around his plate, and asked for some tea. Lapin poured him a cup and waited.

'Was it terrible?'

'As bad as you can imagine. Threw up every meal for a week. Must have lost twenty pounds. Haven't had a square meal in three months.' Then he looked up at Lapin. 'Do you know what they're eating in Murmansk?'

Lapin shook his head.

'Seal. When they can get it.'

'And when they can't?'

'I saw men skinning and boiling rats.'

'And the convoy?'

'We lost one. Fell behind, a straggler. Couldn't circle back to pick up the survivors. Wouldn't have been any, anyway.'

He asked for more food. Lapin heated up a can of soup, and Nick wolfed it down. He talked in a low, obsessed murmur about the night the cargo shifted in a gale off the northern tip of Norway, how the waves pounded on the hatches above them as they worked to shift the cargo and how two crewmen, Scots boys from Greenock, had been crushed by a careening drum. They were heaved overboard. The conditions were so bad there wasn't time for a funeral service.

'You get people wrong,' Nick said. 'Molochkov, for example. When you're puking into the same bucket, you revise your opinions. He was OK.' One night, rolling in their bunks, just to keep sane in the infernal noise of the engines and the sea,

Molochkov had begun talking. He had fought at Perekop at nineteen as a gunner's mate. A veteran of the Civil War, fancy that. A true believer, not just a killer at a desk. And his parents were schoolteachers from Piatigorsk. In the Social Revolutionaries, he had whispered. Switched just in time to the Bolsheviks. Yes, he had been in the international bureau for twenty years – he had languages, you see, and yes, he had been in Vienna, in Spain. It was all true. And once when the ship had lurched so badly that the boilerplate above their heads had slipped its rivets and seawater cascaded into their bunks, Molochkov had said, 'Are we going to die, Nicolai Dimitrovitch?' And Nick had begun to laugh, because it was so insane to be lying in the steerage of this wretched merchantman, wallowing somewhere off the coast of Norway in a force 10 gale, in the arms of a Soviet secret policeman.

Having unburdened himself of all this, Nick fell asleep, right there at the table, head collapsing onto his arms. He awoke twenty minutes later, scratched his head and asked for some more tea. When they reached Murmansk, he said, they had been some days unloading the gasolene. They put the crew ashore into some British Nissens, completely covered with snow, like igloos, down by the docks, and they all slept and ate and huddled for warmth around the log stove. Molochkov disappeared, and Nick cooled his heels for a month cursing the Soviets.

'Could you hear the BBC signal?' Lapin wanted to know. 'Asya thought you might be able to hear her.'

Nick nodded, smiled. 'Yes. It was incredible. Through all the hiss and the static, that precise, deep voice. Wonderful. As if she were talking to me.' He seemed close to tears.

'Anyway, I spent a month in that damned Nissen hut. Molochkov kept saying, "Just wait, my superior is on his way. Be patient. Communication is difficult, the rail lines are down in many places, it will take him some time to get here." "From where?" I said. "Moscow. Be patient."'

Then, one night, a month later, the German bombers came and Molochkov led him down through a labyrinth of dark tunnels dug into the permafrost beneath the port. The tunnels were low and narrow and the frozen walls shook with the detonations above.

They crouched as they ran, and then suddenly they burst through a felt blast-curtain into a cavern, deep under the town, and there, seated at a desk, underneath a single white bulb, with a radio post at one side and a typist on the other, was the big boss.

'Did he ask for his presents?' Lapin said.

'Yes, like a tribal chief, underground in the permafrost, not giving a damn that the ground was shaking, daring me to admit how shit-scared I was. Then I said, "With the greatest respect, commander – "

'"Krivitsky," he says.

'"Are we here to do business?"

'And he said, "Of course we are." And so we did. A real shopping list. "I've already briefed our people: tanks, small arms, fuel, fuel, more fuel."

'I said, "You're going to clean us out."

'He said, "We're going to win the war for you."

'And I just couldn't resist. I mean, we had been cooped up in those damned Nissens and nobody would tell us anything, and so I just came out with: "Where were you in '39 when we needed you? We'd been in this thing for two years before you saw fit to join us."

'"I couldn't agree with you more, Captain," he says. "Not everyone in my country was in favour of the alliance we made." He actually said that. First Soviet I ever met who dared to question the official line. I thought: This guy *must* be senior. Then he says, very urbane, "Let's not talk politics, Captain."

'And I say, "All right."

'And then, when our business is done, he sends Molochkov away, and all the others, and it's just the two of us, across this little kerosene stove in this underground dugout. The ack-ack is still working up above our heads, and occasionally a bit of the dugout roof gives way above our heads and we have to take cover and I'm wondering whether I'll get out of this alive, and he stays quite calm and I begin to think the man is impressive.'

'They obviously sent the Moscow chief. But his name is new to me,' Lapin said.

Nick nodded. 'He had the whole file on me: father, mother, and he went over it just so I would know. He says, "I gather you were in Kislovodsk."

'"I was seven years old, commander."

'"Beautiful town."

'"There was a civil war on, so I don't remember whether it was beautiful or not."

'"It was," he says, "it was." Then he adds, "It is," and smiles at me.'

Lapin looked baffled.

'And then he shows me this . . .'

Nick, cigarette between his lips, burrowed around in his dufflebag and pulled out a waterproof pouch. Inside it was a tightly-wrapped sheet of paper. He unfurled it and handed it across to Lapin. There were columns and columns of names. Nick moved his thumb down the list, turned the page, and then stopped.

'There. Take a look at that.'

Lapin looked at the entry and said, 'Oh dear.'

Nick smoked a cigarette. 'This is the message. This is what I went all the way to Murmansk and back for.' He tossed the long list down on the table between them.

'I suppose you're right,' said Lapin bleakly.

And they sat and smoked and waited for Asya.

As soon as she came through the door, she put down her bag and, not waiting to take off her coat, rushed up to him and embraced him three times. 'You're alive!' She was clapping her hands. 'But so thin. God, what has happened to you?'

'I went on a diet.' And he looked at her.

'Let me make you something. An omelette, something.'

'Lapin already . . .'

Then she looked at Lapin and looked at Nick and said, 'What's wrong?'

Lapin sat her down and gave her a cup of tea, and Nick told her what had happened. She listened, hanging on every word, and then when he had finished he handed her the list.

There were pages and pages of names, ranks, serial numbers. It was a police document of some kind. 'State Security Bureau' on the top, 'Moscow', a date – February 1942. She glanced up at Nick, not knowing why she should be looking at this, and he said gently, 'Read,' and so she read. When she saw what it was, she moved her finger down the list, through page after page. When her finger reached the spot, she stopped and stared past them out of the window into the night.

In that single instant, she relived every moment: when he lay across her belly, his tiny blue fists clenched and smeared with blood; then staggering across the tile floor, arms outstretched towards her; then in the hammock at the Ourousoffs' staring up at the mulberry tree; disappearing down the dusty track with Seryozha; embracing Olga and Diinitri, standing on tiptoe to reach them; face to face with his father white-lipped with fury in the sitting room in the rue de Solferino. She felt his kiss upon her lips on the platform at the Gare de L'Est the night he returned from Germany; she saw him on the road to Smolensk in a half-track, white with dust, and she saw now the ultimate scene: the scavenging party going from body to body, ripping open tunics, snapping off dogtags, burrowing into inner pockets close to the warm parts of the body for the identification, for the papers, scattering letters and postcards about on the snow, finding at last the little Orthodox cross around the blood-smeared neck.

'So,' she said.

She moved her finger along from the name until she stopped by the words 'Sichevka, province of Smolensk'.

He would have volunteered to clear the place of snipers. He knew this place, he knew every stone of it, and he had led them in, she was sure of it, like a child in the dark, feeling his way along the walls, using her memories as his map of the precincts.

They had taken the gatehouse, they had cleared the stables on the left, they had moved from tree to tree up the long drive, and had vaulted the balustrade of the terrace and smashed through the big windows looking out on the lawns buried in snow. He had led them through the white corridors, the empty rooms, and some-where, she could not know where – underneath the stairs? In the big bullseye window under the eaves? – he had stepped into a stranger's gunsight. He would not have known it was coming, would not have known which direction to turn, might have felt nothing, only a millisecond's dissolution of everything. He had come home. He had fallen at Marino. And it was she who had led him there.

'Prince Nikita Galitzine, Translation Officer, 14th Panzer Division, Serial WN6435253. Identification marks: Orthodox cross, letters and documents in Russian. Killed by sniper fire.'

She ran her finger down the column under the word 'Date' and stopped at his name again. January 14, 1942. He had been dead eight months.

She rearranged the pages of the list, smoothed them on the sofa, handed them back to Nick and got up and went into her room. She closed the door and lay face-down on the bed.

THE V2S CAME in the winter of the following year, piping eerily through the air and then plunging soundlessly to earth. One fell on Holborn, five hundred yards from the studio where Asya was reading a bulletin. The building shook, the lights went out. A water glass in the studio fell over into her lap, and she sat shaking from head to toe.

Occasionally at night Lapin and Nick could hear her whimper in her sleep, but on waking she said nothing. She pulled on her clothes, put on her make-up in front of the mirror, drank her coffee and went to work. The troops fought their way ashore on the Normandy beaches. Nick, Asya and Lapin sat together by the wireless at night and listened to the correspondents' reports from Caen, Cherbourg, then the road to Paris. She broadcast the news at night. The Russians were in east Prussia.

One hot, airless night in August 1944, Nick took her out to dinner at Luigi's Grill in Jermyn Street. She wore a light print cotton dress and her legs were bare. Afterwards, she took his arm and they walked down Duke Street, weaving between knots of drunken soldiers, past crowds outside the pub in Crown Passage, and then across Pall Mall. They passed a cigarette back and forth.

In St James's Park, she took off her shoes and walked barefoot through the grass. He followed, watching her skirt swish to and fro. In the darkness he could make out a jumble of half-seen forms: overturned deckchairs, bodies, hiked skirts, a shoe, soldiers' caps. He heard the sound of laughter, bodies tumbling about on the grass. She crossed the bridge over the artificial lake and he came up beside her, and they looked down at two white swans gliding beneath them in the black water. She walked on. Under the big trees opposite Whitehall, she turned his face with her hand and kissed his lips. In the darkness he drew her down to the grass and made love to her.

Then they lay side by side and looked up at the night sky through the branches. Her dress lay around her hips. She put her hand between her legs and smeared his lips till they were wet.

Then she began to cry.

'My poor boy, my poor boy.'

Her eyes were shut and her head tossed from side to side. Nick moved to caress her face, but she pushed his hand away.

When they came home, she shut her door. Nick went to sleep on the sofa in the parlour.

His friend Rawlinson went off to the Rhine Army in September, and Nick borrowed the keys to his flat. He wanted to take Asya away to some place of refuge where she might get better. The first night, he stood by the door, the keys in his hand, and she walked from room to room, running her finger along the sideboard, examining the dust, and then disappeared into the bedroom. He closed the door and locked it and hung up his coat, and when he came into the bedroom she was standing naked in front of the bed.

Every Friday night he would wait for her when she came off shift and take her to Rawlinson's. She was avid, molten and silent. Of her son's death, not a word. There was only one thing she wanted from him: not his solace, not his comfort, not his words, but his body. She hungered for him. Her fingers dug into his back.

'More,' she whispered. More and more, until he was afraid.

'I will hurt you,' he whispered.

'You cannot hurt me,' she replied.

Afterwards she walked from room to room, smoking cigarettes. When he turned on the radio, she told him to turn it off. She lay in the bath by the hour, running her hands over her breasts in the water, while he sat on the edge of the bath and watched her. She stared down at her body, the delta of black hair, the water lapping her breasts.

'I can't seem to come back up,' she said.

'You need time.'

Once, when they were lying side by side in bed, he talked about Canada. He took out a photograph of a little boy in a snowsuit shading his eyes from the snow glare. He looked at it for a long time and then passed it to her. She was asleep. Her arm dangled

232

over the edge of the bed. He took the cigarette from her fingers and stubbed it out in the ashtray.

It was always the same at Rawlinson's: the gas-fire glow on their bodies, the empty cupboards, the trail of clothes on the floor, her silent hunger. Months passed, and that was when he took to calling her the Queen of Sleep.

One night early in winter he told her they were flying him into northern Holland, and from there he was to join the 2nd Canadian Division on the march across the north German plain. They needed a Russian speaker for the expected rendezvous with the Russians.

At the station she stood on tiptoes, cupped his cheeks in her hands and kissed his lips.

'You are crying.' She was surprised.

'I love you, for Christ's sake.'

'Don't be angry.'

As the train pulled out, she walked beside it, two thicknesses of glass away from him, her hands deep in her trenchcoat pockets, looking up only at the last moment as he slipped from sight.

She replied to only a few of his letters, and when he wrote to ask her why, she said that it was difficult to write to a man in the war zone. By the time his letters had told her what was happening, it would no longer be happening. So if she had written to acknowledge his letter about the children's bodies in the rubble, he would have moved on and would scarcely remember them. She knew what the war did to time, to memory, how it could pulverize everything inside a person.

At the end of April Nick cabled, begging her to join him in Paris. She wanted to refuse, but Lapin said she must be practical – the rue de Solferino might still be intact, and all her things were there. Through a friend of his at the Air Ministry Lapin arranged a place for her on a military flight.

Nick met her at Le Bourget. His face had new lines on it. They had promoted him. He held her tight and caressed her and she laid her head on his shoulder. On the bus into town he said he was going to quit.

'I was interrogating Russians freed from forced labour. In

Darmstadt transit camp. They were afraid to be sent home — secret-police squads would be waiting for them.'

'Why?'

'They kept repeating: "The Soviet soldier is never taken prisoner. They will shoot us for it." I believed them, but no one else did.'

He looked out at Paris, at the night.

He had to tell a whole hut full of men that they were being repatriated, and the next morning when he went to call them to muster and load them into the trains, he found two of them hanging from the crossbeams by their belts. At the station, another boy dived through the buffet window, gashed his neck and bled to death on the platform. At Nick's feet. Asya put her hand in his.

'You must go home, to Canada.'

'Don't talk about it.'

She lifted the blackout curtain and watched the city pass by. It was a raw evening in April. Everything was as it had always been: the slash of lipstick on the girl's face at the corner, the man with dirty hands selling newspapers at the entrance to the station, the streams of men and women with cigarettes hanging from their lips descending the stairs to the Metro.

'Why is it all the same?' she mused. 'I hate it. They all carry on as if nothing had happened. Look at them,' she said. 'Which of them informed for the Gestapo?' Her face was dark with bitterness.

When the bus passed the Madeleine, she whispered, 'The Café Weber.'

'Was that somewhere you went?'

She nodded. 'I had a dream about it once.'

In the forecourt of the Hôtel Scribe, near the Place de l'Opéra, GI drivers were lounging against their Jeeps. In the foyer a girl in a tall hat was arguing with an American, and when he grabbed her by the arm she slapped his face and strode out through the doors.

As they walked along the hall to Nick's room, she could hear a typewriter pecking away, a glass rolling across the floor and someone singing softly through a door.

'What is this? A brothel?' she asked.

'American Army Press Headquarters.'

'So why are you here?'

'It's the place to be.'

Music blared from a radio, and two girls danced in the doorways of their rooms as they passed.

'Used to be German Army Press Corps HQ.Telegraph, land lines, the best Siemens switchboard, it was all here. The Yanks just rerouted all the lines from Berlin to New York.'

There was a party going on in the room next to Nick's, and he pounded on the door: 'Shut up in there!'

He opened his room and she stood in the doorway, trying to take it all in: two cases of K rations stacked up against the wall, pieces of his uniform strewn about, a helmet, a small wooden Madonna and child propped against the mirror, a picture of her she couldn't remember giving him, a huge brass samovar, and a Luger on the dressing table.

The Madonna was from Lubeck, picked out from the timber and rubble where a church had been. The K rations, he said, were from the American PX in Frankfurt, and instead of eating them he used them as trade goods for barter. And the samovar came from an officers' mess in Darmstadt. He had found it beneath a portrait of Goering on the regimental sideboard. He turned it over and she read 'Solomon Brothers, Saint Petersburg'.

She nodded. 'We had one like it once.'

And the pistol?

'Off a Gestapo officer in Nijmegen. I've discovered there *are* people I don't mind killing.' He sat down on the bed.

She was still standing in the doorway. He beckoned.

'Take off your coat. Sit down. I haven't seen you for months.'

They sat side by side on the bed and drank some cognac he had found in a cellar in Mainz, and then they made love, in a hurry, with most of their clothes on.

She awoke next morning between the sheets. Her underwear was folded on the chair next to the bed, and he was sitting naked in the chair opposite, with a cognac glass in his hand, watching her come awake. There was grey light on his face through the lattices and he looked very tired. She said: 'I love you.'

She had never said it before. He raised his glass.

'To the Queen of Sleep.'

He pulled on his clothes, went down the hall and came back with two cups of *café national*. She wrinkled her nose.

'What is this stuff made of?'

'Chicory. My trade goods won't stretch to real coffee.'

He sat on the edge of the bath and watched her wash herself. She wrapped a turban of towel around her wet hair, and walked about the room, her breasts bare. Then she sat down at a table and dashed off a letter to the Ourousoffs in Saint Rémy. She ran her tongue around the envelope and then bunched her lips into a kiss for him. He never understood why her mood changed like this, why she suddenly surfaced from the depths, why she smiled at him as if the darkness had never been.

Because he could not bear to break that mood, he did not tell her about Torgau, about the day the Russian and American tank crews met in a field bisected by a stream in the middle of Germany and swapped insignia and pictures of girlfriends and sat in each other's gun turrets. He had been drafted in to translate, and he had met Krivitsky again, yes the same man as in Murmansk, mysteriously there, his opposite number from the Soviet side. Krivitsky and he had sat in a field together for a few hours, speaking Russian and English. No, he wouldn't tell her. She would be plunged back into it again. She would think of Niki, and he would lose her again, lose this opening of her heart.

The phone rang.

'Someone is waiting for us downstairs. A surprise.'

As they entered the lobby of the hotel, a woman with a hat slanting across her face, a tight black dress and very high heels got up and came towards them.

'Gaby!' Asya cried. 'Gaby!' They kissed each other on the lips. A big black American sergeant looked up from his newspaper in the lobby and gave an approving whistle, and everybody laughed. Asya held onto Gaby, and Nick could see that she needed Gaby so much she would forgive her anything.

'What are you doing here? I can't believe it!'

'You don't expect me to miss the liberation of Paris, do you? Absolutely impossible. I've been here since last August.'

Gaby took them to a bistro she knew around the corner. Her captain had been located on the lists and they were flying him home in a week. Asya kissed her and Nick said they should celebrate with a bottle of champagne.

'Let's not, Nick,' Gaby said. She patted her lips with the napkin, and looked at the mark the lipstick made on the linen.

'He was in Buchenwald. I've seen them brought in to the Lutetia, to the repatriation centre. They can't walk, can't talk. Some of them weigh thirty kilos.' They sat together, still among the chatter from the other tables, and then Gaby said she had better get home. They walked her to the Metro at the Place de l'Opéra.

'Tomorrow, at the Lutetia,' Asya said.

Gaby shook her head. 'You mustn't look for Sergei. You will make yourself miserable.'

'I have to.'

'You are hopeless,' Gaby said.

Asya took Nick's arm and they walked down to the river. They passed a building gutted by fire, its walls pockmarked with bulletholes. At one corner was a pile of mouldering wreaths where a street fighter had fallen. The streets were sinister. Everyone was wearing long dark coats and seemed to be hurrying to shelter from the rawness of the night. Their eyes were averted. Gazes went unreturned.

At number 8, rue de Solferino, Asya leaned on the porte-cochère and ushered Nick in. The lace stirred in the concierge's window.

'Madame! It can't be! I thought you were dead!'

'I was in London.' She shook Madame Conte's hand. 'I've come for the keys.'

'Ah, madame, no. You mustn't. The Germans . . .'

'Which ones?'

'Very polite ones. Yes, monsieur, and they requisitioned all the empty apartments. There was nothing I could do.' The concierge held the doors of the lift open.

'But I saved monsieur's suits and your clothes, madame. I carried you down in the lift, with Monsieur Razumkin.'

'I don't remember.'

The lift shuddered its way up into the dark, inside the unfolding coil of the stairway, and light played through the lift cage onto the stairwell walls. A child had once taken her lipstick and run it in a bright red smear along these walls. She had slapped his hands to make him stop.

'You left in a terrible hurry. Everything was a mess. I didn't know what to do.'

Madame Conte looked at Nick, at his uniform. 'They said I was a collaborator because there were Germans in my building. The tobacconist on the corner denounced me. I told the police: "I am a concierge. They were in my building. What do I know about collaborating?" And one of the policemen said to me: "All concierges are collaborators." Can you imagine?'

Nick took the key from her hand and opened the apartment. The shutters were closed, the windows sealed. It was cold, musty and damp. In the light from the bare bulb overhead, the dust hung suspended in the air. Asya walked slowly into the hall, past the marble table where they used to throw their keys. There had been a hatstand there once. The parquet creaked beneath her feet. There had been a Turkish carpet there which Sergei had brought back from Ankara, rolled up in red cotton bands that they had untied together on the night of his return. She pushed open the door of the sitting room and turned on a light. She sank onto a chair by the door.

She counted the bare patches on the walls, the edges charcoaled with dust from the draughts. Where had the pictures gone? The sofas were covered in dust-sheets. The floors were strewn with glass and plaster. When she looked up, she saw a jagged hole in the ceiling where the chandelier had been. Nick followed her into the library. Some of the books had been looted, but a few were still on the shelves. She pulled one down and flipped through the pages. She seemed to be debating with herself whether to take it with her. Then she laid it down on the table. Nick picked it up: Gide's *Retour de l'U.R.S.S.*, published in 1936, pencilled with derisive annotations. She went over to the desk and opened the drawers. They were empty. She picked up the phone. The line was dead.

They let her go through all the rooms, slowly, in a trance. She opened the linen cupboard, which was bare, as were the kitchen cupboards, and she looked at herself in the hallway mirror. She stood in Niki's room looking at the single bed in the corner, the gooseneck lamp on the table, the blotter and the empty shelf where his books had been. She stood and took it all in. Her face was empty.

Nick followed her into the bedroom, hers and Sergei's. The cupboards along one wall were open and empty except for some hangers. She ran her finger around a circular watermark on the dresser and then turned and stood for a long time looking at the large double bed. The mattress was bare. There was a darkened smudge against the pink wallpaper where a head had rested, and in the middle of the mattress a dark stain of blood and semen. She · went into the bathroom and shut the door. He heard her being sick.

When she came out, she walked past Nick and the concierge out into the hall.

'I did my best, madame,' the concierge said as they went down in the lift. Asya stared out at the shadows of the lift-cage on the dark stairwell.

'What are you going to do now, madame?'

'I am going to sell it.' Asya turned and stepped into the street.

'And your clothes, madame? And monsieur's?'

Asya did not reply. She strode across the bridge, across the Tuileries gardens, through the place Vendôme, echoing and dark, and up the rue de la Paix towards the hotel. Nick ran after her. Her body was bent, her shadow was racing ahead of her.

Next morning she went to the Hôtel Lutetia alone. It was raining when she came up out of the Metro at Sèvres-Babylone and crossed the boulevard Raspail to the Lutetia side. She remembered the bar, how she and Gaby used to sit on the high stools in the fashionable half-light, sipping cocktails, and waiting for Sergei to join them for dinner. But she knew that that life had now been erased as if it had never been. When the Germans took over the hotel in '40, Nick had told her, they used the upstairs rooms as a brothel, and the basements as a torture chamber.

A military truck pulled up outside the front door, and the drivers jumped out and unfastened the tailgate. Nurses rushed out through the doors of the hotel and helped the orderlies to lower the men on stretchers down to the street. Asya caught a glimpse of a young man on a stretcher, unshaven, his complexion grey, his eyes tired beyond imagining. Women were pressing up close to see. They ran their hands over the stretcher, over the boy's body. They called out the names of their sons and fathers, uncles and brothers, and their regiments. The men looked stunned, shocked, happy. They listened, as if from far away.

Two women were waving photos and shouting, 'Buisson from Valence, 14th Mortar. You were in Leipzig, did you see him?'

'Arthur Dupont from Lyon, 2nd Parachute Regiment. My son.'

The men shook their heads.

Held upright by orderlies, the men who could walk slowly climbed the stairs past the women and disappeared through the doors of the hotel.

When the lorry was empty, the drivers got in and drove off. A stout, plain-looking woman in a faded winter coat put her son's photo back in her bag and said, to no one in particular, 'I've been here every day for three weeks. They told me this, they told me that. Now I meet every shipment.' She unrolled a string bag and went off to join the queue at the bakery on the corner.

Asya mounted the steps to the hotel. There, in the lobby, every pillar, every inch of wall, every one of the bulletin boards was jammed with pictures and notes on scraps of paper. Round and round the room went the shuffling crowd, searching every note, studying every picture. Asya filed slowly by with the rest. The pictures were all of young men, smiling, unsmiling, hair slicked down, hair tousled by the wind, in the square brown photo of their *carte d'identité*, or in the torn half of a marriage portrait, or as part of a soccer team, their face ringed in ink. Some held dogs in their hands, some had their arms around girls. Some were in uniform, some in bathing suits, some in business suits, some in berets. Beneath the pictures were handwritten messages in a thousand different scripts, all asking the same question: Have you seen him?

from Blois, from Apt, from Lille, from Carcassonne, from everywhere, from every regiment, a whole generation was tramping its way past the corpses, through the fields, down the endless country roads, trying to get home.

Those who had made it back left messages to those who had waited for them and missed them:

'Arrived. Gone to Bayonne, to Lucie.'

'Safe and sound, Poste Restante, Bordeaux.'

Others who had made it had left messages about the comrades they had left behind:

'Louis Menand, Jean Legrand and Jo D'ambois from Bleuvac are in Dusseldorf hospital. I saw them with my own eyes. Fantin, Jerome, gone to Bleuvac, April 2, 1945.'

And the mothers and sisters, brothers and fathers, cousins and uncles and friends shuffled slowly by, peering into the photographs, deciphering the messages. Once in a while, a hand would rip a message from the wall, a woman would press a photo to her lips and begin to cry.

There were queues of people lined up in front of tables at the end of the lobby. Each table was marked with particular letters of the alphabet and behind each sat a woman with boxes full of file cards, listing names of men missing, found, in hospital, confirmed as dead, reported as having been seen alive.

Asya joined a queue. There was a chair in front of each table and when it was her turn she sat down and waited till the woman raised her eyes from the file.

'Name? Regiment? Date taken prisoner?'

The woman's nails were painted red and they were poised on top of the dog-eared cards.

'Gourevitch, Sergei. September 1939.'

'September '39?' The woman looked up over the top of a pair of bifocals. Her hair was immaculate and she was wearing earrings. This was charity work.

Asya forced herself on. 'He went to fight in Poland.'

'We wouldn't have anything to do with him here, madame.'

'But he was a French citizen.'

'You should have said so.'

Asya watched the red fingernails flicking through the cards. They stopped, plucked a card out. She took her time.

'Ah, no. I'm sorry, madame.' The woman had taken off her bifocals. Her eyes were neutral and intelligent.

Asya stumbled on: 'I had thought he might have turned up with the others, as the Russians reach the camps in the eastern sector. I thought someone might have seen him . . .'

'I'm sorry, madame.'

'Are there more shipments due?'

'From where, madame?'

'From Poland, east Prussia.'

'You will have to do like the others, madame. You will have to wait.'

When Gaby found Asya, she was sitting on the paper-strewn marble floor in a corner of the lobby, wrapped in her coat, staring at her feet. Gaby stooped down.

'I told you so.'

Gaby took her upstairs. Along the hallways were rooms made into wards for the men waiting to be debriefed. Lying on the beds were emaciated men in striped pyjamas, talking in low voices to women with notecards. They were gazing into space, trying to remember. This was a memory factory, a place where a name, a fact, a date were to be extracted, like shell fragments from flesh.

Next day Asya came to the Lutetia and spent the day at the bedside of a small man from the Vaucluse. His voice was very low, and he had lost so many teeth from malnutrition that his face had caved in. The pupils of his eyes were fiercely black and he stared at her as he talked. From his capture in May '40 until February '45 he had done forced labour in the fields of north Pomerania for a German potato farmer. He slept under potato-sacks in bare sheds with his comrade, Jacques, and every winter they nearly froze to death. The best thing that had happened was the baker's wife in the hamlet across the fields. For three months she left the back door unlocked for him when the baker went out to work at dawn.

'First time I slept in a feather bed, till now,' he said.

The only meat he had eaten in the last two years had been a rabbit.

'Jacques and me saw him just peeking over the furrow, and I got him by the foot and we thumped him and took him back to the barn, and madame, we skinned him and ate him raw, we were that hungry.'

He remembered the boys in the muleteer company he had joined in '40. He remembered them all, how the mules had all been cut to pieces in the artillery attack on the quarry where they had been tethered, how Fernand had fallen by the road near Amiens when they marched back into Germany as prisoners, how Patrice had been shot trying to pick up an onion by the side of the road, how Jacques – the one he spent his captivity with – had died.

'The Russians were firing incendiaries. They were ten kilometres away. One of them landed on the farmhouse roof and set it alight. We were in the farmyard lying on our faces. And the farmer says to Jacques, "Get up there on the thatch and put the fire out." And Jacques looks at him and says the war is over. And the next minute, another bomb hits and when I look up, Jacques was spread all over the farmyard. There wasn't any more of him left than you could put in a matchbox. Nor the farmer.'

His black eyes stared up at the ceiling. She listened and then read from the printed muster of his company, dated March 15, 1940.

'Oh, he was dead by May . . . and he was run over by a half-track on the march back into Germany . . . and he got left behind, too weak to move, when we bivouacked in the onion field.'

The names, the names. Old Joe. Francis, the kid from Apt or some other bloody place. Sometimes he couldn't remember the names, but Asya could tell from his eyes that he did not forget their faces.

Nick waited for her and took her home to the Hôtel Scribe and cooked her dinner. It was like Kislovodsk all over again, she said, when the boys had talked to her at night in the black shadowed tents.

'I am their confessor.'

The men were returning from points further and further east, from the Russian borderlands. If Sergei was anywhere, he would be coming from there, from the border marches of Poland and Russia, on the roads, like them, living on onions and raw turnips, on milk and eggs stolen from ruined farmyards, hitching rides on half-tracks, sleeping in lofts, trudging west, feet bound in rags to make them hurt less, a cap tied onto his head to keep his ears from freezing, wearing clothes picked off corpses.

He was among them, she became sure of it. But every day the shipments were getting fewer. The reservoir was drying up. Nick tried to get her to face facts.

'Facts?' she was furious. 'All right, here is a fact. He returned to me once before. He came home from prison. Thousands of miles. Against all the odds. If he is alive, he will come back. So I will wait.' She turned and stood at the window of the hotel room, motionless, implacable.

As if to prove that faithfulness would have its reward, Gaby's Captain André was brought home on a hospital train from Buchenwald. The orderlies brought him out on the stretcher and they all walked beside him to the ambulance. He was wrapped in a blanket. He weighed forty kilos.

Gaby took him home to an apartment on the rue St Jacques. Asya came once a day with the shopping and helped Gaby to turn him in bed and to lift him. He cried out every time they lifted him onto the slop bucket, and she feared that when she gripped his withered forearms she would tear the papery skin from his bones. His Buchenwald number was tattooed on his skin, a seven-digit figure in denim blue.

The first time Gaby and Asya sponge-bathed his body, Gaby burst into tears. Captain André whispered, 'Why are you crying?' Asya had never seen Gaby like that, all the veneer cracked, her hands shaking, tears streaming down her face.

Asya took her outside to the landing, to smoke a cigarette, to calm down.

'I want to run away. It is not a body, it is a corpse. I can't stand it.' Gaby shook all over. 'I want to kill the people who did this to him. To kill them. And I want to run away.'

They heard a groan. André wanted water.

'Coming,' Asya said, and in she went, leaving Gaby propped against the radiator in the landing, smoking and trying to stop her hands from shaking.

But Gaby returned to herself. Two days later, when Asya came with the shopping, the room no longer smelled of André and his stained, wet sheets. Gaby was wearing perfume again.

By then André could sit up and take soup. A week later, he was able to walk to the toilet, if Asya and Gaby held his arm to steady him. He had gained five kilos by then and was able to talk a little too. Always about what there was to eat. Never about Buchenwald. At night, Gaby said, he cried out in his sleep: as if the hurt could only drain away when he was unconscious.

One day Gaby told Asya that she and André were going to get married. Gaby lit a cigarette, smiled. 'Don't look so bleak. You will marry again yourself. Don't worry.' Asya leaned her head on Gaby's shoulder. They passed the cigarette back and forward, until Asya said quietly, 'Congratulations, dearest,' and caressed Gaby's cheek.

The next day Asya was putting the shopping away in Gaby's kitchen when someone came up behind her and said, 'Remember me, madame?'

'Josette! You are the same, the same!' She kissed Josette's cheeks and held her sharp, angular shoulders.

'Not at all, Madame Asya. I am older, and my husband is dead.'

'Oh, Josette.'

'And you are not the same either.' Josette looked at her with dispassionate eyes.

'You saved my life.'

'You were not wise to travel with that man, madame.'

'I haven't been wise about anything, but here I am. And so are you. It is wonderful.'

'It is a surprise.' Josette's upper lip, dusted with its little moustache, her face thinner, pert and prim, now edged towards a smile. 'I did not think you would make it over the mountains. He was a very bad man, you know. I think he was the one who turned in my husband.'

'The trainman at Cerbère? The one I thought was your brother? Razumkin turned him in?'

Josette nodded.

'Oh, Josette, what can I say?'

'It was not your fault.'

'I am sorry, Josette.'

'You were innocent, I knew that.'

'Not innocent, *an* innocent. It's different. I'm ashamed.'

Josette filled the kettle and put it on the stove. 'André needs some tea.'

'They are getting married.'

'Yes,' Josette said, 'the war is over. It is really over.'

On VE night, Asya and Nick joined the crowds and were swept along the boulevards. Everyone was singing and the searchlight beams danced across the rooftops of the city like a huge illuminated clown on stilts. Up in the distance on the balcony of the Hôtel de Ville figures were waving and the crowd around Asya roared. The boulevards were so crowded that she had to hold on to Nick to keep her balance. It seemed hours before they could move sideways through the eddying waves of people and escape into a sidestreet. Back at the hotel, everybody in the bar was singing, and when they went into the kitchen to get some food the waiters were throwing plates against the pantry wall. Nick picked one up, and Asya did too, and a crowd gathered and soon there was smashed crockery all over the downstairs lobby. In the salon people were dancing. A Glenn Miller record was stuck in a groove and everyone was too drunk to do anything about it. An American leaned on her shoulder and said he was from St Paul, Minnesota, and would she like to dance? 'I would like to go to bed,' she said, and Nick picked her up and carried her upstairs. He stripped off her dress with a great sweeping gesture of one hand that made her laugh, but they didn't make it to the bed.

She awoke several hours later, lying naked in a puddle on the bathroom floor. He was asleep next to her, breathing in her ear, a strand of her hair between his lips and his hand cupped around her breast. She slipped loose, covered him in a towel and jumped into bed. Sirens were wailing in the night, in the world beyond the closed shutters; once in a while there was a burst of gunfire, someone firing from the rooftops in celebration, and Jeep horns were klaxoning everywhere. There were clothes all over the room, and Nick's feet were sticking out through the bathroom door. She thought: I am forty-five years old.

Next morning a letter arrived from Olga Ourousoff.

Dearest Asenka,

It is a miracle that you are alive! I am rejoicing. If only our Dimitri were here to see you. Will tell you of our tribulations when I see you. I long for news of all your dear ones. Come immediately.

I embrace you
Olga

When they stepped down on the Avignon station platform the next evening amid a tide of demobilized soldiers, Olga was waiting for them, a small, walnut-coloured woman in full skirts, a kerchief around her head, older, more bent, yet the same, heroically the same.

Nick stood apart as the two women wept and kissed each other.

When Asya introduced Nick, Olga exclaimed, 'The one we used to call old man Isvolsky?'

'My father.' And Olga kissed him three times, and squeezed his elbows and wrinkled up her Siberian eyes into two slits of pleasure and amazement.

The old Citroën was standing in the station forecourt.

'Do you drive now, Olga?'

Olga had lit a cigarette and was starting up the car, already hunched over the wheel, tiny and frail.

'He died in '42, dearest. I've had to learn a lot of things since then,' she said, reversing with a roar.

They were soon on the straight road through the cane-breaks, and the house came into view exactly as Asya expected. It was the same as ever, as if none of their losses had ever occurred, tucked up in the shadow of the Alpilles, among the heavy plane trees, the dark-green shutters closed against the heat of the morning, the stone sand-coloured and splashed with shadow and light.

'One morning, I woke up and I heard a sound, so I opened the shutters and there at the end of the drive, just there, is this Jeep, with a white star on the bonnet. Two American boys, guns slung over their backs, jumped out.'

Olga carried their bag from the car and shooed Nick away with one hand when he tried to take it from her.

'Just there, by the gate.' She opened the door with a long key on a string tied to her belt.

'So I threw a shawl over my nightgown and I rushed down. And what do I see? This boy – he couldn't be more than eighteen – is buttoning his flies. He has been relieving himself on my azaleas. He was terribly embarrassed when I embraced him.'

'That was the liberation?'

'Exactly. Now some coffee. Some *real* coffee. Saved for this moment.'

She scuttled around the low, dark kitchen with the heavy black beams. The icons in the corner flickered faintly before their spirit lamps. Asya sank into her usual chair by the big stove. When the coffee was ready, they drank it in a sacramental silence.

'Ahhh!' Olga said. 'The war is over. From this moment. From this cup of coffee.'

Then Olga settled Nick in the hammock under the mulberry tree and the two women set off for a long walk up the hill. He watched them go, arm in arm, heads close together, framed between the cane on either side, stopping, bending over to pick a wildflower on the verge, slowly disappearing from sight in the heat-haze.

Olga learned what had happened to her Niki, and Asya learned that Dimitri had died of a heart attack in the men's barracks of the Marseilles internment camp, after the first night of questioning in December 1942. They walked all the way to the walled cemetery in the shadow of the bare hills, and through the tightly-packed rows of memorial stones, some dating back to the turn of the century, of the shepherds and farmers, wine merchants and postal clerks, widows and wives who had returned to this hard, baked earth. On nearly every monument there was a photograph of the deceased.

'It is wrong, these photographs. A trick. They are dead. It is all wrong. Illusions.'

'Yes, dearest,' Olga said, and they stood together for a long time in front of the only tombstone without a photograph, with only a name and a date and two Russian words which Olga had managed to get the stonemason to chip into the stone: Eternal Memory.

'It is better for him. He was spared everything,' Olga said as she knelt and filled the jar of wildflowers with water from the cemetery spigot. 'It was better.'

'What was he spared?'

Olga shook her head. 'Let's not . . .'

Nick was still in the hammock when they returned, dry-eyed and silent, the hems of their skirts blanched with white dust, each with a bunch of sun-wilted wildflowers in their hands.

'The fools took us for Jews. Can you imagine such a thing? And he hadn't taken out his citizenship, so all he had was his Nansen passport.'

They were on the second of the two bottles left in the cellar and Olga was washing potatoes furiously, squeezing her eyes shut, a cigarette between her lips.

'If it hadn't been for Razumkin, I wouldn't even have been able to bring the body home. The bastards!'

Asya started violently. 'Razumkin?'

'Our very own collaborator. Working as doctor for the Marseilles police. Naturally, he found out we were in the camp.'

'Maybe he put you there.'

'You think so?'

'Razumkin is capable of anything.'

'So,' Olga continued, 'I have my Dimitri in my arms and they are saying he is to be thrown into some public burial pit for common criminals, when Razumkin appears and whispers in the ear of the chief cop, and they let me at least bury him properly.'

'Yes, he is that kind of bastard. The tender-hearted kind.'

'How do you mean?' Nick handed her a cigarette.

'Because he saved me, didn't he?' Asya said bitterly. 'Got me safely to the border. And betrayed me at the same time.'

'A complicated kind of bastard,' Olga agreed. She was popping about the kitchen, slamming plates down on the table, checking the potatoes roasting in the oven, smoking furiously and wiping the tears from her eyes with her sleeve.

Asya said, 'I was a fool.'

Nick rubbed her shoulders, and she let his hands knead her neck.

'The last time I saw Razumkin, he was holding his two front teeth in a handkerchief in the gendarmerie in Cerbère.'

'So they told him, "Work for us or you'll lose more than your teeth,"' Olga said. 'I know how it goes.'

'Exactly.'

'But what did they have on him?' Olga wondered.

Asya did not have the heart to discuss it, so she kept silent.

'A wretched man,' Olga said, and emptied her glass.

After dinner, Asya and Nick went up to bed in the room with the prints of the Chinese market in Moscow and the view from the window over the mulberry tree. The window was open and vineleaves rustled against the shutters. They could hear Olga pottering about below them, banging pots together, putting things into the sink to soak.

Asya stared up at the shadows of the leaves on the ceiling.

'I slept in this bed with my husband. And my son slept next door.'

Nick rubbed his face with his hands. She stroked his arm.

'You poor thing. There isn't a single place you can escape my past, is there?'

'Nowhere at all. But it's all right.' He nestled her head against his shoulder and watched the shadows on the wall till he fell asleep.

At the station the next morning, Olga clung to Asya.

'Just think, we were going to leave everything to Niki.'

'We were foolish to count on anything,' Asya said, stroking Olga's hair.

'And Seryozha?'

'Least of all.'

'Will he come back?'

'He is dead.'

'Do you believe that?'

'It is what I say,' Asya murmured, holding little Olga in her arms, feeling how slim, how tiny she was, how the odour of cigarettes filled her thick grey hair, tied at the back like a girl's.

'Come back, please,' said Olga.

'Always.'

On the train to Paris, in the dining car somewhere past Dijon, when they were having their coffee and looking out at the golden fields in the late afternoon sunlight, the cutlery trembling on the white linen, Nick took Asya's hand and asked her to marry him.

'You and I, we are encumbered,' she said softly.

'I am going back in a week. To get a divorce. To get free.'

'From your child, too?'

'Asya — ' he gripped her hand.

'You're hurting me,' and she pulled her hand away.

When the time came, she went with him all the way to Cherbourg where his boat was waiting. The port was still rubble-strewn, the town flattened, and a dusty wind blew along the dark quays. They walked arm in arm to the lighthouse and back while the ship was loading. He told her that he would sell up, that he would come back to London and set up as a journalist. If his wife took the boy there was nothing he could do. But he would start again.

'When?'

'Christmas.'

She felt his hip next to hers, his arm around her waist, the woodsmoke and hay smell about him that she loved. She held back nothing: he was all there was, and when he went up the gangplank for the last time and waved from the top deck, as they slipped the hawsers loose and the dark stain of water grew between them, she felt all her numbness gone, all the shell grown since Niki's death fall away from her, and nothing protecting her now from the pure pain of his departure. All the way back to Paris in the train she pressed her cheek against the cold, rainstreaked window and wept.

She went to the Hôtel Lutetia one last time. There were no crowds of women outside the doors now, for the shipments had stopped, and inside there were no queues in front of the women with the card files. But messages still hung from the bulletin boards, beneath the photographs, and here and there was a woman searching the faces, or a man in his new civvies searching for news of his wife. Some harpies in sharp suits hovered around offering to find loved ones for a fee.

She took a photo and a message from her handbag. It was the photo of them together in London in the spring of '39, the one she liked best because it had caught him unawares, uncomposed, his eyes locked in hers in an instant of happiness she would give anything to live over again.

As she pinned the photograph and the slip of paper with her London address to the bulletin board she was sure he would find them, just as he had found his way to her door at the Square des Batignolles. But when she stood back a pace and looked at it, smaller now, among the hundreds of crumpled photographs and abraded messages in a thousand different hands, she felt weak and tired. All the vacant faces staring back at her from the bulletin board made her think of the cemetery in Saint Rémy where Dimitri was buried, where photographs of the deceased lay on every tombstone. As she stared at the photo, she had no idea whether she still hoped to find him or whether she was finally saying goodbye.

She was to leave for London the next day, but she needed something to wear for Gaby and André's wedding that evening. She let her feet guide her back to the rue de Solferino. Madame Conte led her down to the basement, to the caged space where the trunks had been stored.

'I put naphthalene in all of them, madame.'

The concierge unlocked the trunks and swung back the lids. Yes, everything was neatly packed and folded away, and the moths and damp had not touched them. Someone had taken great care. A life she had once lived lay under her fingers, embalmed.

'I will leave you, madame.'

Asya crouched in the cellar darkness, under the glare of a bare bulb, and ran her hands over the dresses. So many of them, the blouses, the silks and crêpe de Chine slipping through her fingers. They had been rich then: she knew she would never be so wealthy again. Race meetings came back to her, and evenings dancing at the Bataclan in the tight full-length gown she held between her fingers. But she did not want this pathos. She had business to do, a particular dress to find. It was there, near the bottom, and it would do for the wedding. Gaby would be wearing the new look, but it was pointless to compete with Gaby. This one, simple and black, would do. She slipped out of her clothes and tried it on. The naphthalene smell was disagreeable, but it would ebb away in the street. She felt better: the dress fitted. She was still the same. She thought: This is my past, this dress, this is all I will take with me. Madame Conte can sell the rest.

The photograph albums, perhaps she should take them. But where were they? There were two trunks of her things, but the albums were not in them. She looked in a third. At the top was a pair of tennis shoes, dusted in red from the courts, and a shirt she remembered. Niki's things. She slammed the lid shut.

She rubbed her face and looked at her hands. They were black with dirt, and now her face would be smudged. She must stop. She must get out of here. But where were those pictures?

She opened a fourth trunk. Sergei's suits lay on top of each other, separated by layers of tissue paper. In the corners of the trunk, his shoes in their shoe-trees from Lobb of St James's. A pair of fawn gloves. His singlets. His white underwear. Everything clean, in its place, creaseless, smelling of naphthalene. How small he was, she realized. How small his feet were, how neat and compact his body. Like a cat. She knelt before the open trunk and felt she was gazing into his casket.

There was a sound on the stairs behind her. She turned.

'Madame Conte?'

Someone was coming down the stairs. She was motionless in the pool of light, searching the blackness of the cage.

'Who is it?'

The feet made no sound on the cellar floor and the figure was standing in the light before she could rise to her feet.

He bent down to lift her up, but she rose and pushed him away.

'Go away! Away!' she shouted and pushed him again. His head hit the light bulb and set it guying back and forward between them.

'Please listen,' Razumkin said.

He reached up to steady the bulb, and his features ceased to flash before her eyes. Sweating, fat, frightened, with that look of supplication that made her want to scratch his eyes out.

'You have no shame.'

'I packed these trunks. I looked after all your things.'

'You disgust me! Get out! Leave me alone!'

Madame Conte called from the top of the stairs: 'Are you all right, madame?'

'Keep out of this. You shouldn't have told him. It was none of your business.'

'Asya, I came to tell you.'

'Nothing. I will hear nothing. You betrayed me. You turned in Josette's husband and Uncle Dimitri. And Botynsky. You are disgusting.'

'Never, I swear. I never did.' His back was against the cellar cage. His face was sallow and wet with perspiration.

'I have a message. About Sergei. You must listen.'

'I believe nothing you say.'

'You must believe me. I want to spare you suffering. I saw you pin the photograph on the wall in the Lutetia. I could not bear to see you still thinking he was alive. I want you to start again with the Canadian officer. You must believe me.' He reached into his pocket and handed her the photograph she had pinned to the noticeboard at the Lutetia. She snatched it from him.

'You filthy spy!' she shouted.

'Listen to me,' he said, backing away from her. 'Just listen. Sergei helped the Russians. Yes, you suspected it. He went back in '39, but he was killed in '41 in the Leningrad siege. The embassy told me. You must believe me. He wanted me to save you, to protect you no matter what happened, to help you escape. And I did, didn't I? I did save you.'

She hit him across the face. Then she hit him again, harder, and then again. She thought: I have never done this before. This is new, this is not me, this is someone else. But this is good, she thought. This is very good. Again. Again. Her hands swept back and forward across his face. Blood from his nose began splashing onto his collar. He did not stop her. He let his punishment come.

She hit him until her hands hurt, until her tears came, until the blood on her hands disgusted her. She pushed her way out of the cage and climbed the stairs into the street. It was dark, and she walked on blindly until she saw people staring at her, at the black cellar-dust and the blood on her hands, and her face smeared with tears. 'Stop looking at me!' she muttered. 'Go away! Leave me alone!' She strode through the night streets, drunk with loathing for these disgusting people in their stained clothing, with cigarettes hanging from their lips, these tarty women and their clicking heels, the spit on all the pavements, the taste of blood in her mouth, the vileness, the irredeemable vileness of everything.

She stopped at a café to clean her face. The liar! The liar! The filthy liar! She beat her fists against the sink. A waiter was watching her over the top of the door.

'What are you looking at?'

'You're mad,' he said.

'Leave me alone!' she cried, enraged, exalted, far beyond reach.

They were waiting for her at the mairie – Gaby with her arm around André, shrunken inside his uniform, and Josette in a dark dress, holding some violets.

'Are you all right?' Josette whispered.

'Perfectly,' Asya said.

She listened as the formulas were intoned, she saw André kiss Gaby, she heard them pronounced man and wife, and when they came towards her to embrace her, she stared at them like a ghost.

PART FIVE

IT WAS A catastrophe to have lived so long. They were all gone now: Olga, Dimitri, Niki, Sergei, Botynsky, all her loved ones, even Majiec and Gaby. It was senseless to have outlived all her reasons for living, and yet life went on and on, and she sat there waiting for the end to come. But it didn't.

All her strongest emotions were bleaching away like bright coloured scarves that had been left out in the sun: even love, even regret were fading now, and she took this as a sign that her hold on life was weakening, that she was preparing her own departure. All passion spent? Well, not quite... She had only to think of Razumkin and a fierce, vivifying jet of fury coursed through her veins. It even amused her, in a grim sort of way, to know that of all the human feelings which gave her a continued sensation of being alive, this hatred of Razumkin was by far the strongest. It was an irony Razumkin himself would have savoured: Asya the good kept alive by the bright flame of hatred.

She could still say she loved life. It came to her rescue every day, effortless and unbidden. But each morning when she awoke, she would think: Oh dear me, not this again. She had long since ceased to see the point of it: everything was tinged with a melancholy absurdity, even the rising of the sun, the brightness of the day, the fading of the afternoon. When she was little she had been convinced that she was immortal, and that having been born with the century, she was destined to live out its course. Well, beware of what you wish, she told everyone who came to visit her, because you will get it. Look at me, she said: condemned to immortality.

And now there was this man who had come all the way from Canada to see her in London. Why? His letters said that she could help him, but how? It had all been so long ago. But what could she do? If she said she could not help him, he would think she had something to hide. And she had nothing to hide. She would tell him everything, but it wouldn't do him any good. Since when had the truth done anyone any good?

She was seated by the fire at the end of the sitting room looking out at the dusk settling over Eaton Square. There was a tea service for two set in front of her. Close by was a large TV set which cast its bluish radiation over her aged face.

Her dark grey hair, held in place with a fine black hairnet, was pushed up from the nape of her neck into an Edwardian-style chignon and topped with a startling red bow. Age had laid bare the sharp ridges of her cheeks, and the thin curve of her nose lay outlined beneath the papery translucence of ancient skin. She wore a white blouse with a high ruff which set off her long thin neck, and a pair of black linen trousers with razor creases. On her feet were a pair of bright patent-leather pumps.

The housekeeper poked her head around the door.

'Peter Isvolsky to see you.'

She held out a delicate, liver-spotted hand which he pressed to his lips.

'Let me look at you,' Asya said.

Her voice was deep, smoky, slightly hoarse. Her eyebrows were etched with a coquettish liner and egg-blue eyeshadow highlighted her lids. She was ninety years old.

'You are hiding behind that moustache of yours. I cannot form any impression of your mouth.'

'Do I look like him?'

'Something in the eyes, maybe.'

Clear, grey eyes: wide open, Canadian, innocent. Big shoulders, sandy hair, raw, untutored decency of manner.

'I was ten when he died,' Peter said as he sat down.

'So you hardly knew your father at all,' she said.

'No, hardly at all.'

He looked away so he would not have to watch the tea's uncertain spattering into his cup.

'You take milk?'

He nodded.

'How did he die?'

'Fitting snow-chains on a car by the side of the road.'

'But what was it, heart attack?'

He looked down at his teacup. 'How did you find out?'

'Lapin is very methodical. When the annual Christmas card did not arrive as usual, he wrote to your mother.'

There was a long silence. She put her teacup down.

'So we are sitting here, wondering what to do with each other. You are thinking: Why have I flown all the way from Toronto to see this old wreck? And I am thinking: So this is his son.'

She smiled, and her face suddenly became as bright as a girl's. 'Everyone I ever knew is dead. I wake up every morning and I look at my legs, like two sticks, and I think: God has forgotten me.'

'Forgotten?'

'Must have. Otherwise why does this ghastly business go on and on? Too terrible.' She laughed and reached for a cigarette.

'I have something for you,' he said, and pulled the notebooks out of his briefcase and laid them on the table. There were four of them, one on top of the other, black-bound, with white lettering on the spines: 1942, 1943, 1944, 1945.

She opened one with a long, vermilion fingernail, glanced at the writing, then shut it. She fitted a cigarette into an ebony holder. When he reached over with his lighter, she touched his hand briefly. She held the cigarette-holder in the old way, underneath, between thumb and forefinger.

'They're all about you.'

'All lies, of course.' She blew smoke high into the air.

'Of course.'

'When did you find them?' she asked. He told her he had found them in a trunk right at the back of the cellar when they were clearing out the place after his mother's funeral. Opening it, Peter said, had felt like lifting the lid off a coffin. Inside was Dad's uniform, the medals on a purple cushion wrapped in plastic, a file of his old cuttings from the *Montreal Gazette* and the *Kingston Whig Standard* and the *Toronto Globe and Mail*, his dress shirts, a tuxedo with a cummerbund; all preserved with funeral-parlour correctness. At the bottom were the notebooks.

'What do you remember of your father?' she asked, and was touched when he said that the clearest thing in his mind was not a memory at all, but eight minutes of home movie his mother had shown just once, one afternoon after Sunday lunch when he was about sixteen. There they all were, flickering across the bedroom wall, in the rinsed-out colour of another life: his mother waving away the black flies and tending the fire; his brother and him, naked as worms, running along the flat rocks; Nick looking out over Seven Mile Bay, shielding his eyes from the sun.

'You see, after the accident, Mother never talked about him, ever. That's why I came to see you. I thought you might be able to help.'

She appeared not to have heard what he said.

'I was in North America after the war,' she began.

'Where?'

'A man wanted to marry me, an American from Detroit. Rather a good man. He was a military lawyer on his way back from Berlin. Anyway, that's not the point. He said, "Come with me now. The plane is leaving tomorrow." I thought, Why not, what am I leaving behind? Nothing. So I went. Grosse Point, Michigan. Do you know it?'

'A classy surburb of Detroit. Where the auto executives live.'

'Yes. A paradise for automobiles.'

She lit another cigarette. 'I must stop. The doctor says I am killing myself. At my age, who cares . . . Where was I?'

'Grosse Point, Michigan.'

'Yes. The conversation in Grosse Point was very curious. A woman came up to me at a party and asked me why I was wearing black. I said I was in mourning for my husband, and she asked when did he die, and I said at the end of the war. "Well," she said, "I'm a widow too. My analyst says mourning is inappropriate if it goes on longer than eight weeks." That is America for you.'

'I'm a Canadian.'

'Have you been analysed?'

'Not exactly. Some therapy.'

'Ah,' she said. 'So you think we can be repaired?'

'No, I don't think we can be repaired.' And they smiled at each other.

'In any event, I endured Grosse Point, Michigan for two months, and already when the arrangements were far advanced for our wedding, I said to my friend, "I think I should go home. I do not belong here." Naturally, he was disappointed. He took it badly. Married another woman.'

'What did happen between you and Dad?'

'Some more tea?' He shook his head and was about to repeat the question when she looked up at the TV, reached down into the recesses of her chair, pulled out her channel-changer and pointed it at the screen. Up came the sound.

The network had gone live to the outside of the embassy. The situation had been unfolding all week. The marksmen were taking up position. The reporter was crouched behind a wall whispering commentary. Then two second-storey windows exploded and the attack squad abseiled from the roof and leaped into the building. Through the smoke came a sharp, crackling sound.

'Small arms,' Peter said.

'What do you do?' she asked, not taking her eyes from the screen.

'I'm a journalist,' he said, watching the smoke billowing from the windows.

'I *am* gaga,' Asya said. 'So you told me in your letter.'

The muffled crepitation of handguns continued through the smoke in the building.

'Amazing,' Peter said. 'This is in real time.'

A hostage had emerged from the building, looking white and shaky. Behind him a member of the attack squad, revolver drawn, face masked.

'What is real time?'

'Unedited. As it happens.'

Ambulances were screaming into place, taking the hostages away, and reporters were standing up now, doing their pieces to camera amid the sirens and the smoke. The attack squad was inside, laying out the corpses.

'I wonder,' she mused, 'was my life in real time?'

'Anything else is for the movies.'

She laughed.

'Real time,' she said. 'Such a fantastic phrase. If this is real time,' she said, pointing to the screen, 'what is unreal time?'

'Edited time,' he said.

'But what about memory? Look what it does to time. I cannot remember any real time, you know, when you just float and nothing happens. My memory has edited away all the real time. There are nothing but photographs, frozen, one after another, meaningless. And voices.'

'I don't follow.'

'I seem to have lost all the real time. It has been swallowed up. That is what is so terrible.' She looked out into the darkening square.

'Tell me what happened between you and Father.'

She returned her eyes to the television. The room was dark now, and the blue phosphorescence of the TV screen played over her face, making her look still more ancient, like a pharaoh. She spoke in a flat, distant voice.

'Toronto. Nice little place. I was there once. On my way home from Grosse Point, Michigan. In 1947. There were wooden houses on your street, with porches and green shingle roofs, and men raking the leaves out the front. I remember. And a park at the end of the street, and a bench where I sat and watched.'

He said nothing.

'Your house was on the corner, and there was a car outside, and first your father came out and started it. He sat in the car while the engine was running, just staring straight ahead. He didn't see me. I was just across the street on the bench. He kept staring at nothing.'

She looked over at Peter.

'And then you and your brother came down the steps. You must have been about six, and he was hardly more than a baby. You were wearing identical jerseys with Toronto Maple Leafs written on the back. I remember that. And you jumped in the back seat. And then your mother came and sat in the front seat. And then your father drove off. And do you know something?'

Peter said nothing.

'You looked straight at me, as the car turned the corner. Right into my eyes, this lady in a black hat and a green coat sitting alone on the bench in the park at the corner of your street. Right into my eyes, as you are doing now.'

They were silent then, just looking at each other. The housekeeper came in, removed the teaset, drew the curtains and lit the lamps hanging over the hunting prints on the walls.

Eventually he said, 'Why didn't you ring the doorbell?'

'I did love your father. It was rather a surprise to discover it. I realized only afterwards, when he had left, and I thought: Don't let this chance go by, don't resign yourself to being alone. You understand. You are married?'

'I was. It went wrong.'

'How wrong?'

He laughed. 'Very.'

'You look as if you are still hurt.'

'How can you tell?'

'I can. I know the signs.' His eyes had a dark, bruised quality that made him handsome.

'The Royal York Hotel, does it still exist?'

He nodded.

'Yes. It was a nice room. High up. After I had gone to find your father and sat in the park and watched him, I went back to this pleasant room. In your Royal York Hotel, I looked out at the railway trains and that flat grey lake of yours and I thought, Well, that's over.'

'You should have rung the bell,' he said in a husky voice that made her understand why he had come.

She was fierce: 'You would have lost your father. I would not have stayed in Toronto. One Sunday there was quite enough. I would have taken him away. No, no, when I saw the look on his face, I knew I would never ring the bell.'

'What look?'

She considered the possibilities.

'Defeat.'

He let the sound of the word die in the room.

'You sacrificed yourself,' he said after a time.

'Dear boy, it had nothing to do with sacrifice. If you had seen his face. He was beyond rescuing. The light had gone out.'

265

'You should have rung the bell.'

'Why?'

'Just read the diaries.'

'Dear boy, I have no intention of doing so.'

He got up and went to the window. She knew he did not want her to see his face, see him struggling for control.

'He wasn't putting snow-chains on the tyres. That was Mother's version, but it wasn't like that at all. My brother and I went to the archives after she died. We dug out the OPP files.'

'OPP?' She wasn't following.

'Ontario Provincial Police. There wasn't any snowstorm on Highway 9. It was mid-October. There was nothing in the accident report about blizzard conditions, like she said.'

He turned and stood opposite her. 'Asya, my father was hit in the middle of the road. Facing the oncoming traffic. Not on the side, by the car, like Mother always said. Right in the middle of the road. The driver of the logging truck said Father just stepped out from the side of the road and held his hands out, like this.'

With tears in his eyes, Peter opened his arms, palms outstretched, in a gesture of welcome, like a man going to greet his deliverance.

Asya leaned back in her chair and covered her face with her hands.

'That's why I came. Can't you see? Fathers are where we all start from, where we get our reason for going on, for living. Do you understand what I'm saying?'

She nodded. 'My father died when I was eighteen. I know.'

'But he died.'

'Yes, in my arms.'

'But he died. That's the point. Mine didn't want to live. And I feel him behind me, draining everything out of me, draining the point of everything, emptying me out. Do you know what I mean?'

She let him talk: so like his father, so earnest, so lost.

'And so when I found the diaries and found what you meant to him, I thought you could tell me what he was like, you could help me . . .'

266

'With what, child, with what?'

'To find out what he was like before he was . . . what you said. Defeated. Before he was defeated. When he was with you, and everything was all right.'

'Was everything all right then?'

'Read the diaries. You'll see.'

'My dear boy, I don't want to read them at all.'

'Why not?'

'You are like all young people, like I was when I was your age. Selfish. You think of nothing but yourself. Imagine what it is like for me. It is painful. Your father . . . is a painful subject.'

'I see.'

She stared into the fire, as if he wasn't there. 'I am very tired. It has suddenly gone. My energy has deserted me. I cannot do any more.'

'Can I come again?'

'Whenever. What else does an old woman do, but sit here?'

'Tomorrow?'

'Tomorrow.'

She held out her hand. He kissed it and left her running her finger over her lip, looking out into the darkened gardens.

The next day she was waiting for him in a bright room on the second floor. There were vases of cornflowers in front of the windows. She snapped her book shut when he came in and made as if to get up.

'Peter, dear, pass me that stick. My legs are on strike today.'

It was an elegant black cane with an ivory handle, and she levered herself up with it while he took her elbow. She was much too thin.

'Let us pay a visit.'

He would have kept his hand cupped under her elbow to steady her, but with a tug she disengaged herself and tapped her way down the hall to a door at the back of the house.

She knocked, listened and went in.

An old man with white hair and bright blue eyes was sitting in a wicker chair in front of an open window that gave out onto the communal gardens below. He was wearing pyjamas, and the brittle bones of his chest were visible. His feet were bare and the nails were yellow and gnarled.

'Peter Isvolsky has come all the way from Canada to see us,' she said in Russian, and kissed Lapin's forehead.

'You do speak Russian?' she asked, motioning to Peter to sit on the bed.

'Yes, but you wouldn't like it.' He gestured to his ears and said to Lapin, 'Tapes.'

'He only understands Russian now.' She took Lapin's hand and held it. He smiled at her, from a long way away.

'Lapin took me in after Olga died.'

'Olga?'

'She will be in the diaries somewhere. Your father knew her. My aunt. After I retired from the BBC, I lived with her in the house at Saint Rémy till she died. Then, when I had buried her next to my Uncle Dimitri, I came back to the house, looked around at her dried mushrooms hanging from the beams in the kitchen, and thought: No, this is over. So I sold everything and came here.' She gestured about her. 'This is Lapin's house, you know. We are the last of the line, living together like two old crows, these twenty years.'

It was Lapin who sent the Christmas cards year after year from 36 Eaton Square, with a Russian greeting to 'dearest Nick', and when there was no more Nick, the cards kept coming every year, 'To Nancy and the children' with 'Fond regards, Alexander Galitzine'.

'Thank you for your Christmas cards, Uncle Lapin,' Peter said in Russian.

'God, what a noise you make in Russian!' Asya said.

Lapin said nothing.

'He was very faithful to your father,' she said. 'More faithful than I was.' Lapin's blue stare was unblinkingly focused on Peter. His mouth was open. His teeth were yellow. He looked as if he might speak, but he didn't.

'Maybe that's what Dad would look like now,' Peter said.

They sat in silence for a while.

'Lift me up, darling.'

Peter pulled her to her feet and felt her, once again, disengage her elbow. She kissed Lapin on each cheek and smoothed down the hair on the back of his head.

'This young man is going to accompany me on my walk, and then I shall come back and read to you.'

Peter touched Lapin's hand.

Lapin looked away at the garden.

She stumped vigorously along the gravel path that wound its way between the azaleas and the jasmine, the dwarf pines and the rockeries of the communal garden behind Eaton Square. When Peter looked up, Lapin was still at the window, staring out at the day.

'My brother is such a curious creature. He made a quite extraordinary amount of money for his bank, you know. He is not at all what he seems.'

'What do you mean?'

'Oh, you know, a kindly old Chekhovian figure. The English are so condescending about us old Russian types. Lapin was tougher than anyone ever suspected. His secret.'

'Yours, too.'

'Clever boy.'

'It's Alzheimer's, right?'

She stopped on the path, exasperated.

'Darling, please.'

'Asya, he's gone.'

She sat down on a bench and patted the space beside her.

'You are just like your father. There are plenty of things you will never understand. Lapin married the wrong woman and endured her patiently until she died, thank goodness. His children are perfectly nice boring boys with whom he has nothing in common. He worked with unstinting devotion at making money for his bank, an activity in which he had not the slightest interest. He is tired. No one understands him but me.'

'But . . .'

'But nothing. Darling, when I read *Eugene Onegin* to him and we are side by side, just the two of us, I hear him anticipate, very softly so only I can hear, Pushkin's very next line. So please . . . '

269

She sat for a moment and inhaled the winter jasmine that framed the bench on either side.

'It is paradise, this garden. I sit here for hours and float. I do not think of a single thing. This is happiness. As you say, real time. Everything turned out very well in the end. Now, once again, lift me, please.'

He cantilevered her up and they walked back to the house, still under Lapin's unblinking blue gaze at the upper window.

'I am going to Moscow at the end of the week,' Peter said.

'You told me in your letter. I am not as senile as you think. You are going to be the bureau chief of your network. My congratulations.'

'I'm not sure I should be congratulated. I was there once before in the Brezhnev days. You cannot imagine what lying went on.'

'I can indeed. It is a Soviet speciality. Or it was. Perhaps this new man is different.'

'Perhaps.'

'And perhaps you are going for the sake of your roots. I was very attached to your grandfather, dear old Isvolsky.'

'My grandfather is buried in Montreal, and my father in Toronto.' Peter paused, as if working up the courage to say it. 'Asya, all my roots are here, with you.'

'Dear boy, what a thing to say!' But she was pleased.

'You are as old as the century. You were there. You saw it all.'

'I did indeed, child, I did indeed.'

Next morning, he phoned her and asked whether he could take her out to lunch at the restaurant of her choice.

'Wilton's, at one,' she said and hung up. She made herself ready and felt a certain sly gaiety come over her. She had a new admirer. At ninety years of age. Fancy that!

No sooner had he sat down opposite her than she returned the menus to the maître d'hôtel and said briskly, 'We have arranged your fate. It is either sole, lobster or turbot. I'm having sole.'

'Turbot.'

'And the usual,' she said, taking off her glasses and putting them back in her bag.

'Yes, madame.'

The usual turned out to be a bottle of white burgundy, and as Peter poured it, he said, 'You're not what I expected'. He laughed. 'You're not a nice old lady at all.' She liked that, and smiled, eyeing him with a shrewd squint.

'Wounded. In the diaries, you seemed wounded. That's what Dad wrote once.'

'The wounds healed.' She was brisk.

'Tell me.'

'I decided that my husband was dead.'

'Did you ever find out for sure?'

'For sure.'

When the fish came, she dissected it expertly, lifting the skeleton onto her side plate, her hands as steady as a surgeon's.

'I *was* wounded. And then I gave up Seryozha. I said, He is gone. After that things began slowly to improve. My love life especially.'

'Tell me.'

'I will tell you nothing.'

And then she relented.

'He was very hard to get over, my husband. He was not like your father. He was not – what is the word? – amenable. He imposed himself. I was very young when I met him, and he moulded me into his image. After he disappeared, it took me a long time to find my shape again. I felt lost. It was very hard for your father. I was in mourning, forever. To your health.' She raised her glass and smiled at him.

'What happened with Dad?'

'In a minute. Everything in its proper place.'

She told him about going back to work for the BBC, how she rose from being an announcer to the head of the service.

'You were the boss?'

'Don't look so surprised!'

'Did I look surprised?'

'Men's faces are absurdly transparent.'

'To you.'

'To me, yes.' She raised a forkful of fish to her lips.

'I loved my profession. Splicing tape, listening to playbacks, the red light going on, the phone ringing, hiring people, dismissing

271

them too, sometimes. There was no time for our terrible Russian melancholy.'

'But you said in the garden you liked floating best.'

'There was no time for floating at the BBC. Now I am an old woman, I float. I sit in the garden with my jasmine. I take care of Lapin.'

'You've changed.'

'How would you know, dear boy?'

'You weren't so tough then.'

'You think so? It is possible. Yes, I have changed. I love being tough!' She looked delighted and took a vigorous sip of her wine. 'Our dreadful Russian milieu. I see them in church, such mild, well-brought-up creatures, so innocent and vulnerable. I do not want to be innocent.'

'Or vulnerable.'

'Or vulnerable. When I was young, I paid such a terrible price for my vulnerability. And now, at my age, if you are vulnerable, you are finished. It does not get easier, you know. Gaby used to say old age is not for the young at heart. Gaby said you must have iron, here,' and she tapped her chest.

'Gaby, who married the man from Buchenwald?' Peter asked.

'Yes,' Asya said, and looked away. Her voice was soft and gentle. 'Did you ever see a film called *The Wages of Fear*?'

Peter nodded. 'With Yves Montand?'

'It was like that. You deliver the dangerous cargo safely after horrible adventures. You survive everything. And on the way home, you get yourself killed in some stupid accident. After Buchenwald, after all my nursing, after all the love, after everything, they were both killed in a car accident in 1956. What is it all for?'

But she was not going to let this draw her back. She was not going to be claimed by her losses today. He made her feel young. As the waiter cleared their plates, she looked over and caught the eye of an old man with white hair, eating alone across the restaurant, too far away to talk to, but within waving range. So she waved gaily, an old-fashioned wave, just the fingers.

When the old man had turned back tremulously to his fish, she whispered, 'A tremendous philanderer in his day, tremendous. Really, the most promiscuous man I ever knew. Look at him.'

Peter looked. The old boy was taking a long time lifting the bones from his fish onto his side plate.

'He even proposed to me once.' She leaned over with her cigarette in her holder. Peter lit it and she blew smoke ceilingwards.

'Men can get very difficult if you don't take them seriously. But in this case it was too ridiculous. So I said to him, "Where do you think you are? In the music hall? At our age? In any case," I said, "you sleep with anything in a skirt. Stop being ridiculous."' She laughed. 'I have had a great deal to drink. This is good.'

'How old were you then?'

'When? With him? What an impertinent question! I was seventy.'

She smiled at him. 'You are thinking: How disgusting! A woman of her age carrying on like that.'

'What are you talking about?'

'There, you are blushing! I was right! The young are so very arrogant: they believe that they know everything there is to know. I was the same at your age. But let me tell you, life is extremely long, and I have never wanted to give up anything. Not smoking. Not drinking. And not that either. Until it became too ridiculous.'

'Why won't you tell me about Father?'

'You're very persistent.'

'I'm a reporter.'

'But this is not a "story".'

'You're just playing for time.'

'What time have I got?' and she looked out at the street.

'My visa has come through. I'm leaving Friday.'

'For Moscow?'

He nodded. 'Why don't you come?'

'It would break my heart.'

'What do you remember?'

'Nonsensical things. The *isvoschiks* – the taxi drivers – ah, but I keep forgetting you speak Russian – the *isvoschiks* doffing their shapkas and standing in front of the icon at the Kremlin's Troitsky Gate.'

'What else?'

'More than I could ever tell you. The railway stations. The servants refilling the kettles at the big samovar in the station buffet and then carrying them back and passing them through the carriage windows. All the steam. I see it very clearly.'

'Do you miss it?'

'Dear boy, what a question! No. It is forbidden to me. It is the farther shore. I shall never cross. Too late.'

A silver salver was slipped onto the table beside his place, but before he could reach for his credit card she had slipped a little wad of twenty-pound notes onto the salver. 'Lapin says I am very extravagant,' she said.

She took his arm and they walked through the restaurant together. She bowed again to the old man in the corner, who gave her a doddery wave and went back to fussing with his cheese.

They walked arm in arm down Duke Street, because she said she wanted to look in the windows of the galleries. For a long time she gazed at an eighteenth-century painting – sub Fragonard – of a blue-veined nymph with pert pink breasts lying on a couch in a froth of tulle. She smiled faintly: 'I love kitsch.'

She turned away from the window, pivoting on her stick.

'I used to walk here with your father.'

'I know.'

'What else do you know?'

He paused and looked embarrassed, and she said, 'That we strolled down this street one night in 1944 and walked into St James's Park and made love under the trees?'

'Yes, I know that.'

'I wish you didn't know.'

'I'm sorry.'

'But there is a lot you do not know. Not everything is in the diaries.'

'You said you weren't going to read them.'

'I changed my mind.'

'Why?'

'At my age, I do what I want.'

'What made you change your mind?'

'I thought: Don't be childish, it was a long time ago. And

besides, I thought, I must find out what this young man knows.'
She smiled and gave him a poke in the chest with a painted
fingernail.

'So what do I know?'

'You do not know everything.'

'Such as?'

'You do not know that he proposed marriage.'

She was right. He did not know.

'A curious omission. Very characteristic of your father, really.'
She took his arm and sauntered for a while. 'I thought that I should
spare you, but you seem very interested in the truth. So.'

She stopped and pivoted again.

'He was weak, your father, very weak. He asked me to marry
him, said he would return at Christmas, and . . . ' She resumed
walking, pegging steadily down the street, saying over her
shoulder, 'And never did.'

She peered into an art bookshop on the corner. 'He sent me a
very curious letter, saying that he couldn't come back after all.
How he couldn't leave because of his son. Because of you. I
thought it was very cowardly at the time.'

'Asya, he killed himself.'

'Yes, that took courage,' she said flatly.

'He killed himself over you.'

She looked him over.

'I have taken enough responsibility in my life. I am not taking
responsibility for your father. Get me a taxi.'

Next night, Peter was at Brown's Hotel packing for Moscow
when she rang.

'It's me.'

'Look, I'm sorry about yesterday.'

'Sorry for what? You asked, I told you. It is finished. But I am
ringing for another reason. When are you leaving?'

'Tomorrow morning.'

'How early?'

'Early.'

'Then you must come tonight.'

'Asya, it's nearly midnight.'

'I know very well what time it is. You must come now. It is very urgent.'

'Asya, what's going on?'

'Just come. Right away. Forget what you are doing.'

The housekeeper was in her nightgown when she came to the door at Eaton Square. As they went upstairs, she said severely, as if it were his fault, 'She is very upset, you know, very. I've never seen her like this.'

Asya was standing looking into the fire, leaning on her stick, shadows cast by the flames flickering over her face. Her hair was down about her shoulders, giving her a wild and ravaged air. He was hardly in the room when she began.

'Your father should have told me. It was absurd. He has missed out the most important thing. If I had known that, it would have made all the difference. Why didn't he tell me? Why?'

'What are you talking about?'

She picked up two volumes of the diaries from the mantelpiece and held them out to him.

'Read.'

'I have already.'

'Read.'

The places were marked with sheets of her notepaper.

Peter looked up at her.

'I'm sorry. I should have realized it would hurt to read all about Niki again.'

She looked scornful and impatient.

'Naturally, but that is not the point.'

'What is it, Asya? Tell me.'

She grabbed the book from him and moved her hand down the page until she found the passage.

'Now read.'

March 3, 1942, cont.

Then we came to the trade goods. Krivitsky asked if I had fulfilled the order to the letter. To the letter, I said. I undid the knapsack and unrolled the oilskin pouch on his table. It was so strange to see the complete shaving kit with the lettering of Geo. Trumper, Jermyn

Street, on the badger-bristle and on the lemon-lime shaving cream, in the middle of this Soviet bunker, beneath the permafrost in Murmansk. I began laughing. And he rubbed his stubble and laughed too.

'This is how to build fraternity with the Soviet ally,' he said.

'And get a close shave,' I said.

Peter looked up.

'I don't follow.'

Asya seized the book from his hands. 'You are like your father. It was staring him in the face and he did not see it. And when he told me the story of meeting this man in Murmansk, he did not think it worth mentioning. A detail, not important.'

'What are you talking about?'

'The shaving cream, you fool! The shaving cream! From George Trumper of Jermyn Street! How could he have failed to tell me that?' She sank down in the sofa opposite him, breathing heavily, drained by her fury. When she spoke, she looked out at the sliver of night between the curtains.

'It was my husband your father met in Murmansk.'

Peter was still several steps behind her.

'You know this from the shaving cream?'

'Seryozha never used anything else.'

'Can you be sure?'

Her mind was made up. She spoke from a long way away.

'I knew he had gone back. Somewhere in my mind I always knew it. Razumkin told me at the end of the war, but Razumkin lied, as he did in everything. Seryozha did not die in the Leningrad siege in 1941. He was in Murmansk in March 1942.'

'Talking to my father.'

She looked at him with real contempt.

'Only your father did not see fit to tell me.'

'How could he have known?'

'Every detail was important. He should not have missed out the shaving soap. How typical of a man. A woman would never miss out the details.'

'And so when this Krivitsky –'

'My Seryozha.'

' – hands my father the list with Niki's name on it – '

'He was sending me the news. He wanted me to know our son had been killed.' She sat and looked out at the darkened square and did not wipe away the tears that ran down her cheeks.

'You see, don't you? My Sergei was sending me a message. Everyone believed him to be a traitor. But he sent me the message. He did not forget me.'

After a while, he said, 'I'm sorry.'

She said drily, 'Don't be ridiculous. It is not your fault. You did very well, bringing me these diaries.'

She turned and looked at him with glistening eyes. 'Because these diaries prove he survived the war.'

'Torgau?'

'Exactly.'

He read the entry again.

April 25, 1945.
We sat together on a hedge overlooking the mustard field, churned up by the armour. Krivitsky had aged. More grey in his hair, and he looked bone-weary. He said he had been riding all night. There was no business to transact, no shipments to agree upon, so we just sat together, watching the Soviet female sharpshooters making time with the gunners on the Sherman tanks ranged around the field. He asked me, once, about Asya, and I said it was none of his business. A man only says that when he's happy, he replied.

I offered him a pack of Luckys and he gave me a bottle of vodka, and we drank some shots out of his canteen. I said I was sorry: no lemon-lime shaving refill, and he replied, 'I'm cured of longing for bourgeois comforts.'

We sat there for maybe three hours. I told him about the Darmstadt transit camp, how the Soviets hanged themselves from the roofbeams. 'I'm not surprised,' he said, and I could tell he knew exactly what was going to happen to them when they got home.

Then, when we were looking out at the Americans and Russians exchanging photographs of their girlfriends, and the Russians smoking Luckys and admiring their new American watches, Krivitsky said, 'This won't last.'

'Why not?'

'We are going to be enemies. We're going to hate each other. It's already begun. We'll look back on this and we won't believe it ever happened.'

It was time to go, and the armoured were saddling up. So we embraced, like good Russians, in the middle of the mustard field, and he drove east and I drove west. As I left I couldn't help feeling that he wanted to stay behind, to prolong our time together in the field as long as he could.

'Why didn't your father tell me about Torgau?'

'I don't know. Maybe it was better he didn't.'

'What do you mean, better? Never!'

'This is going to make you unhappy. You thought you knew the truth. Now you don't. You will have to live with this.'

'You understand nothing. When I thought Sergei was dead, I had to kill what I felt for him. I had to kill part of myself.' She beat her ribbed chest with a bony fist, her eyes gleaming with fervent, exalted light.

'Now he might be alive. You cannot imagine!'

'Asya, the chances are against it.'

'Young man, the chances were against me. And here I am. He would be ninety-three years old. Anything is possible.'

'Asya, do you know what it was like in the Soviet Union after 1945? Do you have any idea?'

'I am not senile. Zhdanov purge. Doctors' Plot purge. Everyone purged. Especially in the intelligence services. I have had time to think of everything.'

'What makes him so special? Why does he survive when everybody else gets killed? Asya, he betrayed you.'

She would not be deflected. 'He came back once before. In 1924. I did not give up then. I waited, and he came back. I will find him again.'

'How?'

She looked at him radiantly.

'I am coming to Moscow with you.'

Boris met them in the dimly-lit chaos of Sheremetievo airport arrivals and guided them to the car. Boris had been driving for the office on Peter's last tour. He wore big wide ties, double-breasted suits, elevator heels and had dirty blond hair down to his collar. He drove the office Zhil, a vast black-finned creature with the reptilian good looks of a '58 Chevrolet on the outside and faded green leather upholstery on the inside. No Mazda or Volvo could tempt Boris away from what he called the Politburo machine.

'Who's the VIP, chief?' asked Boris.

'Princesse Anastasia Galitzine,' Peter said, and Boris made a little bow. Asya smiled and let him lift her from the wheelchair and lower her gently into the back seat.

'Sheremetievo,' she mused, as she looked out at the taxi touts brawling for custom on the airport arrivals ramp. 'How strange, I used to know Daisy Sheremetieff in Paris, in the twenties. Completely lost, the poor thing.'

Boris drove into Moscow right down the median strip, as he always did, as if he were driving some Party bigshot, hunched over the wheel, holding it as if he were about to rip it off the steering column. He swore as he passed a lorry full of rocks, belching exhaust. The highway was choked with trucks and buses, bumping in and out of the potholes. Asya stared out at row upon row of Khruschev apartments and desolate waste-ground.

'Mother Russia,' she said, and smiled at Peter. 'I have arrived. We must start immediately.'

'What?'

'To find Seryozha.'

'I'm going to call Deep Throat,' Peter said.

'Who?'

'His name is Petyunkin. An old contact. If anyone can track down Sergei, it is Deep Throat.'

'You do your work, I will do mine.'

'But you don't know anybody here.'

She smiled. 'Sir Roger Maitland. Do you know him?'

She was incorrigible. Of course he knew Maitland: Minister Counsellor at the British embassy, a white-haired old bachelor as thin as a stick and as uncommunicative as a turtle.

Asya lapsed into silence and gazed out at the stream of traffic as it thickened on the way into the city. A rat was struggling across four lanes of traffic on Kalinin Prospekt. She watched it shivering on the median strip while the Zhils and Moscvitches roared past. Boris swerved around it. 'This is not typical, your highness.'

'Is the Kazan railway station still standing?'

'I will take you everywhere,' Boris said.

'I am not a tourist.'

When they came around the Manege, with the golden cupolas rising above the brick fortress of the Kremlin on the right, she suddenly straightened up.

'*Okhotniy Ryad*. The hunter's street.'

'I wouldn't know, your highness.'

'Yes, yes,' she said impatiently, pointing to the yellow- and white-columned eighteenth-century buildings. 'The university. My street is right here.'

Boris screeched to a halt in the middle of the expanse of Manege Square and turned up what was now Herzen Street.

'You mean you lived here?'

'Opposite the university. I could hear the bells of the Kremlin at night from my room.'

'Where?'

She was peering out of the window. The narrow pavements were packed with people going home. The car passed a university research institute in blackened sixties concrete and the Tass building, and beyond that the round, white church where Pushkin had been married. She smiled when she saw the church, and then frowned.

'Yes the church. So it was back there, somewhere.'

'Your highness, I turn round.'

She shook her head. 'Demolished.'

'Home, Boris.'

'Yes, chief.'

She sat back in the seat and blinked.

'This is going to be very hard,' she said.

It took several days to get the apartment in order. Peter made over his bedroom to her and laid out covers for himself on the sitting-room sofa. While he phoned and ordered in food from Stockmans and took calls from the Toronto office, she spent most of the day sitting by the window, gazing out at the city ten floors below. He pointed out the Stalin Towers, the Lenin Hills and the Kremlin. The view was the only good thing about the apartment.

'There used to be so many spires, so many bells. Thundering . . .'

She turned down a glass of vodka.

'Have you made enquiries with your Deep Throat?'

'Petyunkin is on the case.'

The first night, Peter switched on the news and they watched Gorbachev touring a dairy farm near Bryansk. He was wearing a white coat and rubber boots, and he was talking to the dairy workers, his head cocked to one side, a shrewd, hard smile on his face.

She said, 'His Russian is very southern. From the villages. It is good.'

'Did you ever think you'd come home?'

'This is not home. Let us not be sentimental. Of course not, darling.'

'Did you ever think you would live to see this?'

'Of course not. It is quite absurd. I saw Nicholas the Tsar in the Kremlin church when I was fourteen, and I am seeing Gorbachev at a dairy farm, wearing those ridiculous rubber boots. I have lived far too long for my own good.' She watched some more and said, 'Perhaps Sergei is watching this.'

The thought that somewhere in Moscow, or in the vast Soviet Union, there was a small old man, perhaps in carpet slippers and a cardigan, watching the same broadcast in his Party flat and

282

smoking foreign cigarettes from a silver case made her suddenly look very young.

'Why don't you hate him?'

'What a question, darling,' and she went back to studying Gorbachev stalking through the farmyard. A swarm of sound-booms and tape recorders held by outstretched hands hovered around his face.

'I have had time to hate him. But not now.'

'But he deserted you. And Niki.'

She nodded and kept watching the screen.

'I just want to see him.'

'Why?'

She looked wide-eyed, hopeful.

'To say to him, "I am alive, you are alive. After everything. After all the things we have been through, we are still alive."'

After the news she said she wanted to go to bed, and while he lay on the sofa and took a call from the Toronto desk about tomorrow's files from the Party plenum, she went into the bedroom.

He had just put down the phone when she appeared in the doorway, returning slowly from the toilet at the end of the hall, steadying herself with her hands against the walls. She was wearing a nightdress buttoned to the neck, and he could make out the curve of her hips, the shrunken, bent shoulders, the exposed, swollen ankles. She looked down at her bare feet.

'I have forgotten my slippers.'

'Borrow a pair of my socks.' She shook her head shyly and Peter looked away, stricken by her age, her thin, skeletal desolation.

'I am an affliction to you,' she said with a little smile, as if she understood everything he felt, including that shiver of revulsion that had gone through him. 'I know that. But everything will be all right.'

'Do you need any help?'

'Of course not. Goodnight.'

She was soon asleep. He lay on the sofa and listened to her through the open door. Her breathing made a faint whistle in her throat. Then she began muttering Russian syllables from out of the depths of some dream. He got up and went to the bedroom door.

Her skirt and blouse were neatly folded, her shift and under-clothes were laid out on a chair, her small suitcase was open by the bed. She lay on her back, with her hands folded across her chest, her hair combed out against the pillows. She seemed like the wife of some pharaoh mounted on a bier, ready for entombment. But life still coursed through her. Her chest rose and fell, the breath whistled faintly in and out of her open mouth, and as he came closer, he could see that the ancient, drooping lids of her eyes fluttered occasionally. A dream was making its transit through her mind. Of the jumble of words that she whispered, Peter could make out only one: *Lyod*. The Russian word for ice.

He tiptoed to her side. There on her night table, beside the Russian Bible, was a photograph in an oval silver frame. They were arm in arm, their eyes meeting, their shoes a fraction above the pavement and about to touch down in tandem. The hem of her dress and the cuff of his suit were moving to the identical rhythm of their stride. He was wearing a dark fedora and a double-breasted suit, she a cloche hat and a bright print dress. She was carrying a package done up in ribbon. They had been shopping. They were on their way somewhere, on a street in Europe before the war.

Sergei was smaller, more compact than Peter had imagined, with precise, sharp features beneath his hat brim, and the arc of his beardline as clear as a scar. His body had a tensed, athletic quality, and you could imagine a Biretta in his hip-pocket. Father would have been a head taller, bigger in the shoulder, but he could never have worn suits like that or carried himself with the same conviction.

Asya stirred, and her lips formed blurred syllables from her dream. Peter put the photograph back on the table. She became still again, and her breathing resumed its deep rhythm. He stood there a long time at her bedside in the dark, looking at her then, looking at her now. He wanted to kiss her, to take that terrible, diminished bundle of bones into his arms.

Next morning, she came into the kitchen, embarrassed.

'Dear boy, will you zip me up?'

She turned and stood with her back to him at the breakfast

table. He could see her old lace slip and the exposed vertebrae of her bare, bent back. The black crêpe dress hooked at the top. It had been a long time since he had hooked a woman's dress.

'It is comical. We are like an old married couple,' she said as she sat down. 'My God!' she exclaimed, looking at the plate.

'Maria Ivanovna has cooked you kasha and serniki.'

Maria Ivanovna went with the apartment. She had been there on Peter's last tour. Now she appeared in the doorway, wiping her hands on her apron. She was small and plump, and when she smiled her eyes narrowed into Asiatic slits of amusement.

'You have to eat.'

Asya ate like a bird, nibbling tiny portions. Maria Ivanovna observed her with fascination.

'Could you reach Sir Roger for me?' Asya asked Peter.

'Done. You are expected for lunch.'

'Excellent boy.'

As Maria Ivanovna picked up Asya's plate, she managed a tiny, just perceptible curtsey. What was going on? Silent, stolid Maria Ivanovna had fallen under Asya's spell. As Peter gathered up his tape-recorder and his laptop computer and struggled out of the door, he could hear Asya talking softly in the kitchen and Maria Ivanovna clicking her false teeth and saying, 'Yes, ma'am, yes . . . '

When Boris picked Peter up at the end of the day, the summer crowds were spilling over the pavements on Gorky Street. The middle lanes were busy: militia in light-blue summer tunics with red batons were waving the big Zhils through the stop-lights, and more than once Boris had to grind to a halt while a cavalcade with whirling lights and outriders slid past, carrying some Politburo chief to the next meeting. Boris tensed up like a hunting dog as one of the big limos went by, and watched it cross his field of vision.

'The KGB chief,' he grunted, and moved off when the militia waved the traffic on. 'Coming from the Lubyanka,' he added, nodding wearily.

'Bet you wish you were driving for him.'

Boris smiled and treated Peter to a display of his steel-grey false teeth.

'What about Asya?'

'I wore my hat all day.' Boris kept the chauffeur's hat on the seat beside him and never put it on except inside the Kremlin or when dropping Peter at the Central Committee.

'Where did you take her?'

'After the British embassy, I thought: She is unhappy. So we drove around. She looks out the window. Sad. She says: "I remember nothing." At last, at the Kazan station, she gets out and stands there a long time, leaning on her stick. "What's the deal, madame?" She says: "I left Moscow for the last time at this station." "When, your highness?" "Summer of 1917." "Did you see our Lenin?" She laughed. "No, Boris, not your Lenin, but I did see the Tsar." She is amazing, chief. Like going to a museum or something. She was there.'

'She was there,' Peter repeated.

Boris glanced into the rearview mirror. 'And then she asks: "Does the restaurant called Slavyansky Bazar still exist?" I say: "No problem, your highness." Anyway, Sladko is on the door. I slip him a five-dollar bill – you will forgive such expenses, chief – and we are in. She looks at the portraits of Dostoyevsky and all the bigshots who used to eat there a hundred years ago. And then she says: "I will buy you a drink." Sladko puts us in one of the booths in the big dining hall with the domed roof and he brings us some nice Georgian wine and she asks me about the family. I say: "Thank God, there isn't any, just like the boss," and she says: "Does the boss have a girlfriend?"'

'And you told her?'

'Chief, please. Then she is looking up above us, in the dining hall, at the walkway that leads to the private rooms, where the brass have the parties, and she says to me: "Shall we hire some gypsy musicians and book one of the private rooms for the afternoon?" I say: "Your highness, you have had experience of this?" and she says: "I have had experience of everything." Your relative, chief, she is top class.' Boris drew up in front of the militia man guarding the journalists' compound where Peter had the network apartment.

Boris looked in the rearview mirror. 'She looks at every old man in the street, staring at them, like she is supposed to recognize them, like she is trying to find someone.'

'And she hasn't a hope, Boris.'

When he got upstairs, Asya had laid the table for supper. Maria Ivanovna had made boeuf stroganoff and Asya had managed to get it into the oven and heated up. She was watching the conference news on the big TV in the living room.

'Real time,' she said.

He shook his head. 'Tape.'

She watched attentively as the camera swept the hall, the row upon row of the empire's faces; the flaxen-haired Balts, the sparrow-eyed Asians, the Armenians with grey hair coiled like springs, the men with big hands, the bemedalled veterans, the generals, the women with decades of life marked on their faces. As the camera moved across the gigantic auditorium, up and up past the raked balconies and boxes, Asya looked away. 'I saw Rodzianko once in his carriage. Such a big man. Such a coward.'

'Who?'

'President of the Fourth Duma. 1916.'

'That's what it's like, they all say. 1990 is like 1916 all over again. Everything is just unravelling.'

'If it is,' she said, 'you won't be sure until it's too late. We didn't know anything. One morning there were banners in the streets and the bread went mouldy. That was the Revolution.' She levered herself up and pegged over to the stove.

'You don't need to do this,' he said, coming to her assistance.

'I tell you, darling, we are like an old married couple,' and she stubbed her cigarette out briskly and sat down opposite him in the candlelight.

'And your beau at the British embassy?' he said as he served her.

'The perfection of boredom.'

'MI6?'

'Doubtless. I almost married him.'

'He must be twenty-five years younger than you.'

'That was the chief – the only – attraction.'

'Any news?'

'I am not sure. Perhaps.'

Maitland had been stationed in Moscow in '61, early in his career. There had been, he said, one chap who might have fitted the bill. 'But he wasn't called Krivitsky. Definitely not. Something else. But, my dear, you will forgive me, it was such a long time ago. He was the head of the European desk at the Central Committee. Not like the others, dear, that's the point.'

'What do you mean, not like the others?'

'Well, he wouldn't have been out of place at White's or Boodle's,' Maitland said. 'His suits, of course, were terrible – standard issue – but his manners were very polished and his French was fluent.'

'How old?'

'Hard to say, dear. Older than me, in any case. Early sixties. White-haired, smallish sort of fellow. And in any case, very much the top man. So I asked him: "Where did you get such excellent French?" and he looked at me and said: "You imagine we are all thugs and carry revolvers?" I remember that. Irony was not the style then.'

She took the oval photo out of her purse. 'And then I showed him this.'

'And?'

'Old Maitland said it was a terrible shame the hat brim was so low, you couldn't get a very good impression of the eyes.'

'But Asya, my dear,' he continued, 'you look simply splendid. When was this taken? Before my time, I can see.'

'Not the point, Roger.'

'Quite,' he agreed, and then he studied the face. 'The picture was taken in '39, in London, you say? Well, dear,' he said, handing it back with a rueful gesture, 'I can't be sure.'

'Oh Roger, isn't there any more?'

'Afraid not, dear.'

'But weren't you a spy or something? Don't you have files on these people?'

'I'm not sure I'm happy with the term spy, Asya dear, and in any case, we couldn't let you see the file, now could we?'

There in his huge office at the British embassy, looking at his long, pink features, with that permanent schoolboy air that some Foreign Office types retain right to the end, she had kept her discouragement to herself. But in Peter's apartment, she banged her stick on the floor. 'Damn!'

'Was it a sighting?'

She shrugged, levered herself up, stumped around the room, smoking irritably.

'Asya, your husband was a Soviet spy.'

She stared out of the window at the Moscow skyline.

'Don't pretend you didn't know.'

Her back was turned, her head back. She might have been staring into the sky. She might have had her eyes shut. He couldn't see.

She said nothing.

'If what Krivitsky said at Torgau means anything, it means he wanted you to marry my father and forget him.'

She turned around very quickly and said, 'But I didn't, did I?' She went to her room and shut the door.

He opened the fridge and rolled the chilled vodka bottle over his face. Then he poured himself a shot and lay down on the sofa. He could hear her rustling about in the bedroom and then slamming the cupboard door. He lay there, listening to the traffic thundering down Kutuzovsky Prospekt ten floors below. It was still too hot to sleep. He decided to phone Deep Throat. There was music on the other end of the line, Mozart, or perhaps Schubert. Petyunkin was full of surprises. No one knew who he worked for: he seemed to be at home in the artists' studios, the cocktail circuit, the press centre. A classic late-Brezhnev era fixer, still doing business in Gorbachev times. He did people favours, traded in gossip, knew everyone, was trusted by no one. Peter was always being warned about Petyunkin.

The voice on the other end was slightly slurred. Petyunkin was drinking.

'Peter Nicolaevitch, the name you gave me was wrong. No Krivitsky anywhere. But I did find a contact. The one you want was a big fish. Very. The old boys' association has great respect for him.'

'Name?'

'Let us forget names, Peter Nicolaevitch.'

Just like the good old days, Peter thought.

'You must come alone. Leave the old woman behind.'

'Why?'

'You are in the Soviet Union. Please do as you are told.'

'Where?'

'Novodevichy.'

'When?'

'Tuesday at six. Visiting hours. He will be at the gate.'

'What do I owe you, Petyunkin?'

'I do you this favour out of the goodness of my heart.'

'Do you expect me to believe that?' Peter said, laughing.

'As you wish,' replied Petyunkin, and hung up.

Next morning, the door to Asya's room remained closed. Peter sent Maria Ivanovna in with a cup of tea. She came out with a disapproving look on her face.

'Your relative does not wish to be disturbed.'

He went off to the Party conference for the day and filed two reports, one for the six o'clock news, one for the nine o'clock, on Gorbachev's report on food shortages.

He heard her coughing when he came through the door, and found her in bed, wrapped in a shawl.

'*Grippe*,' she said. 'One of those excellent French words frozen in our Russian language like flies in amber.'

'*Garderobe, lift, étage, parterre*,' he contributed.

'*Carandash* – for pencil,' she added and coughed. 'All the ancien régime is still there, in the language.'

'*Temperatura*?'

She shrugged. He felt her temple. Yes, she was feverish.

'I was rough on you last night,' Peter said. 'I'm sorry.'

She raised an eyebrow. 'I am ill and you are overcome with remorse. How very like a man.' She took a sip of water and gave a little wave of her hand. 'I understand. You are thinking: When she lived with Sergei, either she was naive, or she was wicked.'

He loosened his tie and went over to the fridge. The vodka plummeted down his throat.

'So which was it? Were you naive or were you wicked?'

'Neither. I was in love.'

He heated up the bouillon Maria Ivanovna had left on the stove and brought her a tray. She sipped a few spoonfuls, made a little face and shook her head. 'Enough.'

But it was not enough. She was much too thin. She smiled and made a mocking face. 'It is too late. I'm never hungry now. Were you ever in love?'

He nodded.

'And what happened?'

'She left me.'

'And then?'

'I tried to kill myself.'

She took his hand, just like that, as if it was the most natural thing in the world to do.

'How stupid. Just like your father.' She laughed softly, an ancient, wise, throaty laugh that surprised him more than anything she had ever done. It surprised him so much he began laughing too. Yes, how stupid it had been. How stupid. He sat down beside her and laughed until he cried.

'Better now,' she said, and ran her thin, papery, liver-spotted hand over his. The nails on her hands were sharp, clawlike, vermilion-coloured.

'Better now.' He wiped his eyes and went to the window. The clouds were surging past the moon. 'He wrote about you till the last night of his life,' Peter said after a while. 'Did you know that?' She did not reply. 'There are six versions of the night he met you in Walton Street, on the stairs at Gaby's party. He never did get it right. The last version just trailed off in mid-sentence.'

She looked at him tenderly.

'He was trying to live it all over again,' Peter said.

She smiled. 'You can't get your life back at a typewriter,' she said.

'No, you can't,' Peter said.

She spread one of his maps out on her lap. He came away from the window and sat down on the bed beside her, feeling her gaunt hip against his.

Her bright red fingernail moved along a river to the west of Moscow.

'The Vasousa. Marino was on the Vasousa, darling. Tomorrow is Saturday. Boris is picking us up at nine o'clock.'

'Boris?'

'I took the liberty of phoning him at the office. I hope you don't mind. I have agreed to pay him overtime.'

Peter shook his head in weary disbelief.

'You're too ill to travel.'

'Nonsense. Besides, Maria Ivanovna and I have even prepared the picnic.'

He took another drink, and glowered at her. She looked amused.

'I know, darling. It is difficult to live with me. They have all said the same.'

An hour and a half after leaving the apartment the next morning, they were off the Moscow–Smolensk highway and careening down a dirt road rutted as a washboard, Maria Ivanovna in the front seat crossing herself, Asya staring intently out of the window, gripping Peter's hand, and a cloud of dust billowing out behind them. They came to a village, and Boris slammed on the brakes, leapt out and strode down the track between the houses in his best East German jeans, shooing the chickens out of his path and looking for some sign of life.

The roofs of the village were of beaten tin painted grey-green, faded like washing in the sun. The old porches sagged, the picket fences were gap-toothed, and holes in the old clapboard walls of the houses were jammed with painted rags. Out in a back garden, an old woman in a cheap print dress and a headscarf was hoeing tomatoes in her bare feet. The gardens were small and dense, the vegetation lunging forward in summer growth. The beans rose up in a six-foot wall of thick, tangled runners, and the little irrigation channels at their base were a rich, moist black. A man sat on a porch in his undershirt and bare feet, listening to a football match on the radio. There was a cow in a halter gnawing at the grass beneath a beech tree by the edge of the road. Swallows were nesting under the curled wooden eaves. Here and there an old faded curtain stirred behind a window. Asya sat and looked at the village through the window of the car. The morning air was full of the smell of barley, of midsummer, hay and chickens.

'Has it changed?' Peter asked.

She shook her head and smiled. 'The same. Still the same.' She looked intensely happy, restored to her childhood self.

Boris returned and made a bow. 'I have found the river.' Then they were off, the great Zhil thundering down a rocky track bordered on either side by the dense confusion of Russian kitchen gardens. At the end the road gave out, and there was the Vasousa, stretched before them like a large, slick snake. A dusty Moscvitch was parked by the river's edge and a family was spread out on the banks. A boy in shorts was picking up old tin cans and throwing them into the turbid water, and the mother – who had taken off her blouse and was sitting in her slip and an industrial-strength bra – was cutting pickles into slices and feeding them to her husband who lay on a blanket in shorts and a singlet reading *Sovietski Sport*. They turned and stared at the old lady in black trousers leaning on a walking-stick being helped past them by a foreigner, followed by a maid and a chauffeur carrying blankets, a picnic basket and four folding chairs.

'So. My river,' said Asya, from her lawn chair, as she sipped a glass of wine and looked across at the tanning plant, and the rusting steel girders of an abandoned factory, and a row of concrete apartment blocks.

'Somebody's been pissing in it,' said Boris, looking down at the dirty brown water and knotting his handkerchief to make a sun hat.

'Indeed they have,' Asya said.

Maria Ivanovna cut the sausage and cracked open the beer, and Boris and Peter lay back on the rug and drank while Asya watched the river, sipping her glass of wine.

Was it all forests then, Maria Ivanovna wanted to know. Yes, all forests, and willows down to the banks, frothing and coffee-coloured in spring when it burst its banks and flooded the English garden, oozing brown and turbid in mid-summer, with fish idling in the shallows under the willow branches. Lapin sat by the hour, as patient as a cat, fishing for carp from one of the branches, staring down into the water.

'It's so small. I thought it was as wide as the Mississippi when I was a child.'

A boat came into view, men bare-chested rowing hard, the women sitting in the back nattering to each other, wearing bicycling hats, their blouses rolled down to expose their shoulders. Asya followed them with her eyes.

'Boris, you must find a boat and row me past my Marino. Like a galley slave.'

But Boris was asleep, flat on his back on the blanket, with the knotted handkerchief on his head and the remains of a sandwich in his outstretched hand.

Maria Ivanovna fussed about, trying to get Asya to eat a pickle. Well, if not a pickle, at least some rye bread, or if not rye bread, then some good bouillon. A few sips, no more.

Asya dozed in her chair and then woke and smiled to be where she was.

'I crossed this river once.' she said.

'In a boat?' Peter asked.

She shook her head and laughed. 'I walked on water.' She sat still and watched the river flow until the sun had left their bank and the chill came on. Then she poked Boris with her stick. 'Up! Get up!' Boris grunted and roused himself and Maria Ivanovna gathered up the remains of the picnic, munching all the while on the end of a sausage round.

'Now we find Marino,' said Asya.

For an hour the Zhil criss-crossed the thin, stuttering lines of the country roads. Boris stopped every twenty minutes or so to quizz the people working in their vegetable gardens. Some pointed one way, some the other. A woman who was pickling cucumbers on her porch came out, wiping her hands on her apron, and said there was a place that had been burned down in the war; a man roused from a hammock at the bottom of his dacha garden said that it had been turned into the administrative offices of the tannery; everybody else just shrugged their shoulders.

At about six in the evening they came to a small cluster of grey- and green-painted wooden cottages. Boris stopped the engine and went down the lane between the houses looking for some old people to question. He came back after twenty minutes with an old woman in a kerchief. She was seventy-five. She didn't know anything about a Marino, but she did know there was a big house up the road. She pointed the way: left at the oak, then across the main road, then down over the railway tracks.

'What was it like here in the war?' Asya asked.

The old woman leaned on the open window of the car.

'The Germans came in the winter of '41–'42 and searched the village for partisans. There was only one teenage boy in the village then, and he was a bit half-witted. All the rest had fled or joined the partisans. So they dragged Fedka out by the hair and the interpreters were shouting at him and he just shook his head and whimpered when the soldiers hit him. Everyone watched from their windows. An interpreter was down on his knees beside Fedka, and a German was standing over him holding his hair and they kept asking him over and over where the firing had come from. But how could Fedka know? He didn't know anything. And then there was an argument and the interpreter said they should forget it, but the one holding him by the hair said no. And he pulled his pistol out of his holster, looked around so he was sure we were watching, and put a bullet in the back of his head.'

The woman turned and pointed to a place in the middle of the lane from which she had just come. 'Right there.' That was where they had left Fedka, splayed out in the snow with a round hole in the back of his head.

'Those Germans were billeted at the big house,' she said.

The old woman pulled her kerchief back over her hair, bowed to Asya and walked slowly back down the track, between the picket fences.

'Dear God,' Asya whispered, and bit her lip. Maria Ivanovna felt Asya's head and began rubbing her arms with a handkerchief dipped in mineral water.

'She's burning up. We must go home.'

Asya shook her head. 'We must go on.'

Houses, barns, dachas, old picket fences, flew past her window. All around, buried deep beneath the furrows, there would be helmets, spent cartridges, lead impacted in bits of bone, scraps of flag, skulls, the untended and unremembered graves of centuries of war. Peter watched the dappled light of evening playing across Asya's face. She lay back against the headrest and shut her eyes.

It was dusk when Boris drew up and stopped. 'This must be the place.'

'Smolensk Regional Agricultural College' said the sign on the lawn.

Asya opened her eyes and peered through the window.

'You've made a mistake.'

Boris shook his head.

Maria Ivanovna held her arm and Peter pulled her out of the car. They gave her her stick and got her upright. It was Saturday, dusk, nobody about. The gravel of the driveway crunched underfoot. She pivoted slowly around, walked a few paces towards the building, then turned, shook her head and looked back at the trees that grew right up to the edge of the lawn. The sun had gone. It was green and dark around them.

'Is this it, Asya?'

The chapel was gone, the greenhouses were gone, the stables were gone, the English garden was buried beneath the trees, the stone lions had gone, the balustraded porch that used to girdle the whole building had been ripped off, and the wings that held the children's theatre and the library had been destroyed. But yes, this was the place.

She turned and walked towards the building. It was on three storeys, with a classical porch over the entrance supported by Corinthian pillars and painted a faint peach colour.

Boris had found a caretaker.

'Chief, we need some lubrication.'

Peter slipped Boris a ten-dollar bill and Boris palmed it into the caretaker's hand.

'Make it quick,' the caretaker said, and stubbed out his cigarette as he unlocked the large doors. Asya stood in the hallway and stared down at the black-and-white marble tiles, then up at the two pillars that framed the double stairway that led up past Father's study on the left, Mother's Japanese day room on the right. Where was everything? Her father's boots, the stand for sticks, the *dvornik*'s chair, his blue uniform with gold buttons? Where were the floor-to-ceiling Dutch stoves? Into what darkness had all these objects vanished? And into what silence had all the sounds gone: the train of her mother's dress sweeping over the tiles, the keys on the ribbon, lightly chinking at her waist?

Asya's stick tapped across the tiles. She gripped the balustrade of the double stairway and ascended the worn red carpet. There was Maroussia, climbing the stairs beside her, with the washing under her arm; there was the smell of cranberries being boiled in tureens, wafting up from the kitchen. Ahead of her were the upstairs maids on ladders polishing the brass wall-brackets, where the portrait of Lenin now hung; and there at the back, where the formica table with the typewriter stood, had been Mother's writing desk, overlooking the English garden. No Dutch stoves now, no watered Japanese silk on the walls, no plants in étagères in front of the window, no battery jars full of tendrils and viscous green mould, no Khivan carpets, no smell of rosewater and lavender from the bowls left on the tables. But time and forgetting could not efface the unique distribution of light in these rooms, the way the tall, narrow windows framed the green lozenges of garden lawn. The bare administrative drabness of every object could not shield Asya from the full force of recognition: the present was only a thin gauze screen, through which there streamed, with all its unbearable brightness and clarity, the ivory light of her past. There was a red plastic chair in front of the director's desk. She sank into it and they stood around her.

'My mother died in this room,' she said in a loud, angry voice. 'The bed was right here.'

Maria Ivanovna wiped her eyes, and Boris looked down at the floor.

'We go home now.' She did not want to see the room under the eaves with the bullseye window. She did not want to look down the parquet hall to Lapin's room. She did not want to imagine where the body might have fallen, where her son's blood might have flowed. She fixed herself in the saving present. She saw only classroom doors, chipped paint, the faded carpet, the smeared light from the naked bulbs, the walls scraped by the passage of book-trolleys, the blackboards in each room she passed, with their blurred white signals in chalk.

A leafy darkness was descending as they left the house and drove home through the forest again.

Her eyes were shut. She lay back against the headrest, clutching a handkerchief in her hand. They drove home to Moscow without speaking. From time to time Maria Ivanovna bathed Asya's head and hands with a damp cloth.

Boris and Maria Ivanovna carried her upstairs. Asya kept saying, 'You mustn't,' and Maria Ivanovna was whispering, 'Hush, you are sick.' The embassy doctor came and put her on antibiotics. Maria Ivanovna stayed to feed her borscht with a spoon and to bathe her forehead. In the morning, Peter found his cook asleep in the chair by Asya's bed.

Boris and Peter were heading for the door on the Tuesday when Asya called from her bed.

'Where are you sneaking off to?'

'I have a lead.'

'Where?'

'You stay in bed.'

'Where?'

'Don't move.'

She sank back against the pillows and Maria Ivanovna resumed her manicure.

At the red-brick gatehouse of Novodevichy, Peter told Boris to return to the flat in case the women needed anything and to pick him up again in an hour and a half.

It was visiting day and a small queue had already formed at the gatehouse flowershop. Next to the Kremlin Wall itself, Novodevichy was the most prestigious cemetery in the empire, the resting-place for generals, scientists, senior Party officials, Artists of the Soviet Union. There had been no equality in Soviet life; so there would be none in death either. Yet death's survivors did not look like the grand of the earth. The patina of power had rubbed off them: they seemed tired and abandoned, with string bags over their arms, old medals on frayed suit jackets, and that special Soviet disillusion on their faces. One florid lady in a red print dress and violent dyed hair eased off her shoe and stood on one foot, massaging her bunions.

The guard knew most of them, and at the stroke of six he swung back the gate, and the crowd – of about thirty people – scurried off into the dark leafy lanes of the cemetery to their graves. Peter waited at the gate. The gatekeeper's wife was rearranging the plastic flowers in her vases on the tiled floor. The gatekeeper was chatting to a gravedigger with dark soil on his hands.

Looking over the low brick wall, Peter could see the old kerchiefed women at work, sweeping the walkways with brooms, weeding tombs or chivvying away at the ivy on the graves, removing the dead flowers, rearranging the bouquets. From time to time they would stop work and gather in one of the dark walkways, to lean against the old tombs and gossip. It was a warm, sunny evening in June. There were moments when he loved Moscow. This was one of them: the delicate, white-bordered brick towers of the monastery rose above the trees, the gravestones were canopied with shade, and he could feel the equable passage of time in the sunbeams' passage across the dirt at his feet.

Since the night Asya had taken his hand, since that moment she had laughed, deep and long, he had felt something healing inside. Don't be afraid, she had seemed to say. The world is full of your sort of shame, brimming with it. Somehow she seemed to know about everything, to know about all that desperation in him, in Dad. She seemed to be saying, Break the chain, child, that binds you to him. He is not you. You are not him. His death does not prepare your own. Break the chain. Don't be afraid.

He suddenly knew exactly why he had come to her at that moment in his life, why he had fallen so completely under her spell. Get close to her, Father seemed to whisper. Attend to that. It is the source of what you could be. She is not just a character, not just a personality, but a noble being, faithful and undaunted.

Hadn't he written: 'She was the only person I ever met who was not afraid of life'? Get there quickly, Father seemed to whisper. Get there before the flame gutters out. Cup your hands around it.

The sun laid a mantle of dappled shadow on his coat. The graves disappeared into the warm darkness beneath the trees all around him. He thought of Asya, of this love of hers that had risen above all betrayal.

Peter felt a presence behind him and turned. A man of about his own age in a suit, short and compact, with a Party badge in his lapel and a crisp haircut was standing in front of him, looking at him with surprisingly clear grey-green eyes.

'Let us go for a little stroll.' His English was from one of the best Party schools.

The graveyard walls were high, the canopy of leaves was dense overhead and the alleyways were narrow and twisted. Everywhere there were tombs, some cracked and heaved up by frost, others clawed under by the vines and roots. Some of the dates on the headstones went back to the nineteenth century. It was a convent yard that had become the burial ground for the best of late-nineteenth-century Moscow society. Peter saw photographs on some of the tombs, old faces from before the Revolution, with handlebar moustaches or crinolines buttoned to the neck, couples united in death. In the twentieth century, the cemetery had been confiscated for the Party, and it was now the necropolis of a dying system of power.

'I am an admirer of your television programmes. I watched your reports, *en poste* at the embassy in Ottawa. An enjoyable town.'

'When?'

'The seventies.'

The man stopped and bent down to remove the ivy from a tomb. A photograph of a desolate woman's face stared up at them both.

'Vosnesenskaya. The poet's mother.'

Peter looked at the deep circles under the eyes, the mourning in her gaze. It was the face of the thirties, of arrest and disappearance and loss.

'What's your connection to Krivitsky?'

'He had many names.'

'His wife knew him as Gourevitch.'

The man in the suit was running his hands over a model tank, in bronze, that a general had had cemented onto his tomb. Next to it was an air-force general's monument, topped by a model of a fighter plane.

'We hear she has come for a visit.'

'From Petyunkin?'

'Our mutual friend is always the soul of discretion. No, we knew before that.'

'So, you've been into the visa computer?' The man shrugged and continued walking. His face was neat, trim, intelligent and entirely controlled. His tie was crisply knotted. His trousers just grazed the tops of his loafers. He said, 'I am consoled by this place. All our history is here, and it is all one, from pre-Revolutionary days to our own, from Rimsky-Korsakov to this cosmonaut.'

The man paused over the burnished model spaceship spiralling above the grave of a pilot killed in an explosion at the Baikonor space centre. 'The only one like our Russian cemeteries is Père Lachaise in Paris, don't you agree? I always feel at home in Père Lachaise.'

'She has to know.'

'I understand.'

There were crosses among the gravestones, old and rusted among the modern concrete and marble slabs, the funerary urns, the trees pushing up on either side of the tombstones. Some graves were fenced off with rusting nineteenth-century ironwork and the plots inside were tangled with vegetation. At the foot of most tombs were wan and wilted flowers in rusted tin cans. And on benches in the leafy seclusion, an old man or woman could be seen pouring themselves coffee from a flask, or replacing the water in a milkbottle of flowers, or just sitting there, surveying a father's resting place, a mother's tomb.

'So I will tell you,' and the man sat down on a bench beneath a birch tree. His hands were delicate and smooth. He wore no rings. He rubbed his fingers as he talked, and he switched from English into Russian.

'I am a child of the siege.'

'Leningrad?'

He nodded. 'Yes. My mother died there.'

'I'm sorry.'

'Our graveyards are very dear to me. They are the best places in our country, the most honest.' They sat together for a while on the plank bench between the graves.

'The man you call Krivitsky was one of our longest-serving officers.'

'But he fought for the Whites,' Nick said.

'He crossed over. He was trained and sent on active service.'

'When? Was he on active duty from the beginning, from 1924?'

'Possibly.'

'In Paris?'

The man nodded. 'His work was of fundamental importance to our government.'

'She didn't have any idea.'

'Are you so sure?'

No, Peter was not sure. He would never know what she willed herself to believe, what she allowed herself to ignore, what she suspected and then drove from her heart.

'He used her as an accomplice,' Peter said. 'No one suspected him because no one suspected her. He used her. Doesn't that bother you?'

The man looked down at a little column of ants, filing from one crack in a tombstone to another. He put a soft leather loafer down in their path.

'Why should it bother me? It is not my story.'

'It bothers *me*,' Peter said.

The man's voice was brisk and contemptuous. 'Since you have started to moralize, you should realize there are two moralities at stake here. The man you call Krivitsky was a Soviet patriot. Without his intelligence material on German and French military preparations, without his shipments, our country would have been even more unprepared than it was in 1941.'

'What shipments?'

'Come, now. Small things, but of great interest to our military authorities.'

'"The man you call Krivitsky." So what's his real name?'

The man waved the question away.

'If he was so useful in the West,' Peter persisted, 'why didn't they leave him there?'

'The war was coming. It was time for him to come home. His usefulness was over. There were other assignments in store for him.'

'And it doesn't bother you that he left a wife and child behind?'

'Don't create a picture of a monster in your mind. We are dealing here with a human being. And don't forget something else,' and here he took out a curved silver cigarette case and flicked it open. 'His son was a traitor. That is very important. A fascist.'

'Why does that matter?'

'The father was betrayed by the son.'

'That has a nice sanctimonious ring. Come on. Niki wanted to come home, so he went back with the German army. His father wanted to come home, so he crossed back into the Soviet Union with help from the Gestapo. What's the difference? Or have you forgotten about the Hitler–Stalin pact?'

The man looked about him at the graves, the leaves, the bees picking away at a vase of roses.

'Krivitsky was ordered back. He was on active service. He obeyed his orders.'

'Sure,' said Peter, and they smoked in silence. It was cool and quiet in the graveyard.

'My father met him twice. Murmansk and Torgau.'

'Of course.'

'How do you know that?'

'I know.'

'Tell me your name.'

'It is not necessary.'

'Why? I thought everything had changed here. I thought we no longer played these games with each other.'

'Some things do not change here at all.'

They agreed about that, at least.

'She knew him as Gourevitch. In Murmansk and Torgau, my father knew him as Krivitsky. What is he now?'

'Now?' He looked up at the leaves of the birch tree overhead, plucked one and began slowly dismembering it between his fingers. 'Now?' he repeated. 'No, I am not going to tell you.'

'Why not?'

'It is better for her.'

'Why is it better?'

'Trust me to know this.'

'Why should I trust you?'

'You have no choice.'

This was true. If he could keep it going, keep this contact, there might be a chance of more. If he pushed too hard on the first meeting, the quarry might bolt, might run for cover. So Peter nodded.

'And after the war?'

'Berlin with our military commission. Then Warsaw in 1948. Budapest in 1956.'

'All the hot-spots of counter-revolution, I see.'

'He was one of our most distinguished officers. His range of experience was unique.'

'The European desk of your Central Committee too?'

Now it was the other's turn to be surprised.

'How do you know this?'

'We had a sighting.'

So it was true. Maitland had met him. Still alive in the 1960s. How could she bear to know this?

'Then Washington and Bonn.'

'By then he would already have been in his seventies.'

'I told you, his experience was unique in our service.'

'And he never saw fit to let her know, even when he was abroad, even when he could have slipped her a message?'

'But he did send her messages.' Here the man smiled and glanced directly at Peter. 'Your father was the messenger.'

Then he said, quietly and emphatically, 'He was not a monster. He did not want her to suffer.'

They sat together for a while and smoked, watching the bees pulling at the flowers in front of the little grave. The air smelt sickly sweet from the blossoms and the bees were in a frenzy, making the blooms bob and bend under the weight of their attack.

The man looked at his smooth white hands, then stubbed out his cigarette.

'It is easy to condemn. You should realize he was not indifferent to her situation. He thought it better to be dead to her. That way she would suffer less.'

'How do you know?' Peter rose to his feet. 'How can you be so bloody sure?'

The man sat on the bench between the graves, calmly smoking, not looking up.

'Because I am his son.'

Suddenly shouts came from the gatehouse. Peter could hear gravel churned under feet, voices clamouring. Through the trees he caught a glimpse of Boris, Maria Ivanovna and Asya in her wheelchair. He ran towards them, and then stopped and turned around. He heard footsteps on gravel, thought he saw a flash of grey between two trees. He called out, but heard nothing in return. The contact had vanished.

Boris was wheeling Asya up the main alleyway towards the fresh graves, and the guard officer was pursuing them. 'Only next of kin are allowed! Where are your papers?' the guard was repeating, red in the face.

'She *is* next of kin, blockhead!' Maria Ivanovna was indignant. Meek, stolid Maria Ivanovna had been transformed. Asya had done this.

When she caught sight of Peter, Asya said, 'He is here. I know it. He is here! Who did you meet? Tell me!'

Like all the men she had ever known, Peter had reached the moment of truth with her, and like all the men before him, he failed her. All he could think of was that, if he told her the truth, it would kill her.

'A former colleague. Asya, you were right. He did come back.'

She was hardly listening.

'He is here! I am telling you, here! That is why you have been brought here!'

'Asya, he changed his name. There is no Krivitsky here. He became someone else.'

'We will find him.'

Maria Ivanovna was in tears. 'She is ill. We must stop this.'

'Why did you let her out of the apartment?'

Boris looked sheepish. 'She insisted. She said she would never forgive us.'

Asya shook her head. 'Forward!' she said in a hoarse, angry whisper.

There would be no Krivitsky, no Gourevitch, just possibly 'Sergei Apollonovitch' and some dates from which identification could be made. Yet even Peter was now caught up in Asya's quest. Even he now thought that the truth might be found in this darkening cemetery.

Up the tight, cramped alleyways in the flickering light, the wheelchair ground its way between the tombstones. Boris heaved and levered Asya past headstones that had fallen onto the path, while Maria Ivanovna scurried on ahead, pulling away the ivy that obscured a name, a sprouting of grass that hid a date or a photograph. Peter was soon on his knees beside her, digging away, clawing at the roots that had grown over old graves. They dug deep in the archive of death, until their fingernails were black with the soil. Sweat poured from Maria's face and Boris panted with exhaustion. Deeper and deeper into the cemetery they went. The flock of women who tended the graves began to follow behind, then understood and went before them, sweeping and tearing, cutting and cleaning, to lay the graves bare to their sight. On and on they went, the wheelchair knocking over bottles of flowers, sticking between headstone and gravelway, Asya's head darting left and right, shouting hoarsely at every headstone, 'What does it say? What does it say?'

All around them the dead had left their trophies behind: swords, tanks, guns, an oceanographer's bathysphere, a coral hunter's coral, a botanist's rare flora, a clown's Pierrot costume preserved in bronze or marble or black stone, atop headstone after headstone; authors with their books, scientists with their slide rules, commanders with their tanks, past presidents, past members of the Central Committee, Artists of the Soviet Union in the flushed and florid photographs of the 1950s and '60s, bemedalled gymnasts and chess players, crowded between the high brick walls, clamouring in vain for the memory of the living.

She could not be stopped now. All the other visitors had left, and she had waved away the custodian's pleas and entreaties. The little cortège made its way up to the most recent graves. Asya was flushed, exhausted. Peter said they must stop, get some rest, return the next day.

Asya shook her head. She gripped his hand. 'No. We go on.' Here, in this cemetery, she was going to bring her life full circle.

The earth under their feet was brown, recently turned. The new graves were heaped with earth, piled with flowers: Central Committee men, President Podgorny, the names carved deep into the stone. Asya scrutinized every one. Ambassadors, ministers of transport, chiefs of police. Some of them listed their professions, their achievements, even a quotation from Pushkin to light them on their path downwards.

The light was fading now. The grave women were cutting the undergrowth and scrubbing the tombs like court attendants clearing a path for a ravaged queen. They fanned out over the remaining rows, calling to each other, searching for the names. The custodian ordered them to stop and they refused. He said he would call the police. They waved him away. He went off down the path to get the militia. Asya was looking to the left and the right, beyond fatigue, in a state of exaltation. They had come as far as they could now. The great north wall of the cemetery loomed above their heads. The last row had been reached.

Peter found the tombstone at the very back of the cemetery, under the ancient brick wall. The earth was fresh, the flowers placed recently, perhaps that very afternoon. The black basalt glowed and glistened as if alight from within. When Asya saw it, they all stopped. She rose from the wheelchair, Maria Ivanovna took her arm and she went forward. The sky above her head was a cobalt dome, a canopy of darkening light stretching from horizon to horizon above the cemetery wall. She knelt down and ran her hand across the black basalt surface, felt the fresh earth, arranged the flowers. They stood around her, Boris with his hands on the back of the wheelchair, Maria Ivanovna crossing herself, and Peter leaning against the wall. He could hear the militia running up the path, but their footsteps seemed far away, in some other zone of time. Asya sat by the basalt slab and caressed its surface. She ran her hands over and over it, a gentle, soft gesture, at rest. Her own face was reflected in its hard gleam. Tears ran unchecked down her cheeks. Looking down at her, so small, so diminished, Peter could not say whether she believed she had come to her journey's end or whether she had been defeated at last. For there was no inscription on the tomb. The smooth black basalt was absolutely bare.

Then, from behind the circle around her came the chatter of walkie-talkies, and they were surrounded by angry policemen demanding to know what they were doing. Boris pushed one back with his fingers against his chest, and muttered, 'You keep out of this. This is a graveyard.'

Maria Ivanovna cried out and they turned. Asya had fallen against the tomb. Peter bent down and scooped her up, a bundle of bones and clothes prostrate beside a nameless grave.

She was so light as he bore her away, as the militia men stood back and Boris and Maria Ivanovna followed behind, and they walked down the white gravel path at the centre of the grave-yard now glowing in the June sunset. As he carried her through the cemetery, he knew that his love for her and his father's love for her had joined, had become one. She was close to the edge, her breath faint against his sleeve, her voice whispering name-less syllables. The great trees cast their blackest shadows over them, and the bowed and bent graves seemed in the gathering darkness like a crowd of mourners. He wondered whether he would ever tell her what he had found out, whether the grave had been his tomb or whether, somewhere in the darkness of the city, an old man at a lighted window was still watching in the night.

She was like a child in his arms, her head crooked in his shoulder, her eyes shut, her mouth open. Maria Ivanovna, Boris and the grave ladies with their brooms had formed a procession, and even the militia men now followed silently behind. They were at the iron gates of the cemetery entrance when the fullness of night came at last. And then she spoke. Peter bent to catch her words. She said, very distinctly, angrily, as if in dialogue with a voice in her past, 'I saw the skater. The great skater. On the ice.' But no one in the circle accompanying her on her journey had been alive long enough to know what she meant.